Charlie Houston has lived a long life of continuing adv[enture?]
Yet he has never sought praise, recognition, or cred[it?]
the action and accomplishment, not in adulation or app[reciation?]
he remains one of the most remarkable men I have ever met—and one of the
least celebrated. This book is a necessary corrective, an important contribution to preserving the legacy of a great life, and a ripping good story.

Here is a man who became one of the world's foremost authorities on
high altitude medicine, who helped defeat Japanese imperialism and Hitler's
Luftwaffe by showing American pilots how to fly where no man had ventured. Here is a pioneer in our understanding of the heart, who led the
Peace Corps into India, and who still never fails to fill the bird feeder at his
home overlooking Lake Champlain.

Through it all, as Charlie climbed higher and higher on mountain after
mountain; he went deeper and deeper into the experience of life. What he
calls the Brotherhood of the Rope—a philosophy earned the hard way, on
steep slopes and rocky ridges, with death shivering next to you—goes to the
crux of what America needs the most right now: a sense that we are all in
this together and we need one another.

— Bill Moyers

Charlie Houston achieved fame as both a physician and a mountain climber.
His contributions to the medical profession and his expeditions to K2 and
Nanda Devi are the outstanding highlights of his career. I know him as a person who radiates curiosity, joie de vivre and compassion, that characteristic
described by His Holiness the Dalai Lama as "the foundation of our unity."

Charlie Houston is an extraordinary human being, whose life story will
inspire all who read it.

— Reinhold Messner; first man to climb all fourteen 8000-meter
peaks and author of more than three dozen titles

Charlie Houston is an authentic American hero, and in Brotherhood of the
Rope, Bernadette McDonald has pulled off a tour de force of biography,
probing deep into the soul and life of a complex, troubled, brilliant man and
mountaineer."

— David Roberts, author of several titles including *Sandstone Spine,*
Moments of Doubt and *On the Ridge Between Life and Death:*
A Climbing Life Reexamined

A remarkable man and a remarkable life. The breadth of his experiences is
matched only by his incredible personality. I wish everyone could know him
as well as I do.

— Page McConnell, musician

BROTHERHOOD
of the ROPE

For Maurice Isserman

BROTHERHOOD
of the ROPE

all good wishes

— *The Biography of* —
CHARLES HOUSTON

Chuck

BERNADETTE McDONALD

LEGENDS AND LORE SERIES

Charles S Houston

THE MOUNTAINEERS BOOKS

THE MOUNTAINEERS BOOKS
is the nonprofit publishing arm of The Mountaineers Club, an organization founded in 1906 and dedicated to the exploration, preservation, and enjoyment of outdoor and wilderness areas.

1001 SW Klickitat Way, Suite 201, Seattle, WA 98134

First edition, 2007

Manufactured in the United States of America

Copy Editor: Uma Kukathas
Cover Design: Karen Schober
All photos courtesy of the Charles Houston Collection unless otherwise noted.
Cover illustration: © Dee Molenaar
Back cover photo: *Dr. Charles Houston at K2 base camp in 1953*
Frontispiece: *Dr. Charles Houston*

Library of Congress Cataloging-in-Publication Data
McDonald, Bernadette, 1951-
  Brotherhood of the rope : the biography of Charles Houston / Bernadette McDonald. — 1st ed.
      p. cm.
  Includes bibliographical references and index.
  ISBN-13: 978-1-59485-067-7
  ISBN-10: 1-59485-067-4
  ISBN-13: 978-0-89886-942-2
  ISBN-10: 0-89886-942-0
  1. Houston, Charles S. 2. Mountaineers—United States—Biography.
3. Mountaineering—Pakistan—K2 (Mountain) I. Title.
GV199.92.H85M33 2007
796.52'2092—dc22
[B]
                                            2006039248

♻ Printed on recycled paper

CONTENTS

CONTENTS

ACKNOWLEDGMENTS

I am indebted to all who assisted me on this project. To Helen Cherullo of The Mountaineers Books, I am grateful for your personal interest and commitment to the important stories that our most esteemed mountaineers have to tell, and am immensely proud that you have chosen this book to launch your new series, *Legends and Lore*. Your ongoing support is very gratifying. Paula Rondina, once again, spent hours transcribing the many long audiotapes I had the privilege of recording with Charlie Houston. I know she enjoyed reliving those conversations, but it was hard work all the same. Dr. Robin Houston helped enormously with the medical terminology and Bill Buxton generously gave me access to his formidable mountain library, as well as many words of encouragement. Jim Wickwire provided private papers and correspondence, as did Helen and Doug Canning, whose son, Steven, penned words that inspired Charlie profoundly.

A sincere thanks to all who wracked their memories to share Charlie stories with me: Tom Hornbein, Page McConnell, Robin Houston, Stephanie Zehler, Rob Roach, Bradford and Barbara Washburn, Bob Bates, Nick Clinch, Peter Steele, Dee Molenaar, Mell Schoening, Bob Craig, Gail Neale, Tenki Tenduf-La, Anne-Marie Littenberg, Bob Maynard, Bob Oden, Bill Luginbuhl, Bill Graham, Reinhold Messner, Rick Ridgeway, Jim Moss, Jim Curran, and Jon Beal.

A special thanks to Tom Hornbein for his thoughtful introduction and his unflagging support. Norbert Meier's translation was very much appreciated. Thanks to Mell Schoening, not only for the interview but for gifting me Pete Schoening's magnificent book, a superb source of information and beautiful to look at. Thanks to those who gave generously of their time to read early versions of this manuscript: Bill Buxton, Robin Houston, David Roberts, and my mother. Kudos to Stephanie, who was such a good sport when I came out to Burlington to monopolize Charlie's time for days.

Once again, I was privileged to have the research and editing expertise of Anne Ryall. My deepest appreciation goes to Leslie Miller who, although we've never met, has become a friend through the process of editing this book. We've had many lively email discussions (and negotiations), and I truly value her work. Thanks to Uma Kukathas for her meticulous copy edit, and to the entire Mountaineers Books team for being the wonderful group that they are. My husband deserves a huge thank you for his encouragement over the past eighteen months while I immersed myself in the life of Charlie Houston.

Finally, thank you Charlie, for being so wholeheartedly cooperative and supportive of the project from the first moment that I suggested it in my office; for being open beyond my highest expectations; for an exceptional sense of humor; for allowing me to root around for days in your photographic archives, for giving me access to your most personal papers, and for "never letting the truth get in the way of a good story." It was a distinct privilege to get to know you, your remarkable family, and your devoted friends.

INTRODUCTION

Charles Houston is a bouillabaisse—visionary mountaineer and scientist, caring doc, educator, catalyst and curmudgeon, opinionated critic, and so much more. As you journey through Bernadette McDonald's insightful exploration of this uncommon man's life, you will see how curiosity, creativity and courage melded to touch and enrich (and at times frustrate) the lives of so many of us.

I began this introduction sitting uncomfortably on a small rug covering a piece of the damp dirt floor in a mud-brick schoolhouse in Kurimbeg, a small village 14,000 feet up in the mountains of Ladakh, India. Outside, big wet flakes fell from an opaque sky that concealed the stark, steep world around us. Water poured through the roof, some collecting in buckets, the rest transforming the floor to a less friendly consistency. The deepening dusk made my barely legible handwriting yet more problematic. My thoughts bounced between chilled hands and the man half a world away who is the subject of this book.

Charlie, just turned 93, would soon be awakening, groping down stairs, fixing a cup of coffee, then heading to his chair before the big window in his living room with his golden retriever, Pooh Bear, following to sprawl on the rug beside him. With the mug warming his gnarled hands, Charlie would be gazing out at a wintry scene he can see clearly only in his mind's eye; he is now legally blind. I imagine myself sitting in the chair across from him, sharing this early hour of meditation. We savor the silence together, looking out across the lake to distant hills. Then it's time to talk. This experience, I would add, is one many who have visited the Houston home have tasted.

I fell under the mountain sorcerer's spell when I was thirteen; my parents sent me to a camp in Colorado where I discovered that cliffs and mountains had it all over the trees and houses I was wont to climb growing up in Missouri. Though I did not know it at the time, the direction of my life was to be forever changed by this meeting with mountains. When each of those halcyon summers ended and I returned to the flatlands, I passed the time by escaping into a fantasy world of mountaineering literature. James Ramsey Ullman's history, *High Conquest,* was my bible. Here is where I first met Charles Houston. Ullman described incredible strivings on the world's greatest mountains—including Houston's expeditions to Nanda Devi in 1936 (for nearly two decades the highest mountain ever climbed) and K2 two years later. Long before our paths intersected, Charlie Houston was a mythic, heroic figure to me.

Back then, Everest had yet to be climbed. Nor had Houston's second attempt on K2 taken place. Both of these landmark events unfolded almost concurrently in 1953 at opposite ends of the Himalaya. On May 29, Hillary and Tenzing brought an end to the question whether humans could climb to and survive at 29,000 feet (which actually was no surprise to Charlie, who in 1946 gradually acclimatized Navy "volunteers" to the equivalent of Everest's summit in an altitude chamber). Only a few weeks later, Charlie and Bob Bates' second expedition to the world's penultimate summit played out in the ennobling drama with which this book begins. Like Shackleton's grand attempt to cross Antarctica in 1914–15, the 1953 American K2 Expedition is above all a story of human bonding and heroic courage. Indeed, it is among the foremost examples in the annals of mountaineering of how sometimes, inspired by what Charlie calls "the brotherhood of the rope," individuals find themselves putting their own lives on the line to try to save the life of one of their team.

Charlie and I finally met in person a decade after this epic on K2. At the time, he was in India directing Sargent Shriver's fledgling Peace Corps program there. The setting was poolside at the home of the American ambassador in New Delhi, John Kenneth Galbraith. Our 1963 Everest team, homeward bound, had been invited to a reception that evening hosted by India's prime minister, Jawaharlal Nehru. As Dr. Houston and I sat on the grass together chatting and sweating, I shared with him the tale of our climb of Everest's West Ridge. His clear pleasure with our accomplishment was seasoned with a wistful speculation about whether it could have been done without the use of supplemental oxygen. I tasted firsthand Charlie's philosophy that mountains should be approached with simplicity and reverence. It was a lesson in humility that has stayed with me ever since.

Two decades were to pass before we reconnected. The venue was one more of Charlie's many visionary creations, the biennial Hypoxia Symposium that brought together researchers and physicians from many disciplines and many countries. Charlie was trying to drum up interest in Operation Everest II, a multifaceted research program to study adaptation of lowlanders to extreme altitude. My project examined whether the extremely low oxygen pressure at the summit of Everest might result in residual brain damage. Charlie figured that as the principal investigator of OEII he should be a co-author on each and every publication. He did not shirk his responsibility as an author, playing a vigorous and critical role in the preparation of each manuscript. Examining our study's results and feeling that they did not justify our interpretations, he threatened to remove his name from authorship. After some invigorating exchanges, the paper was eventually published in the *New England Journal of Medicine* with C.S. Houston listed among its authors. This skirmish between our two stubborn wills proved precious to the bond that would grow between us over the years.

I never climbed a mountain with Charlie; the rope that connects us is metaphorical. As the years ticked by, transporting us both into the land of elders, our times together have grown to be more talk, less walk. Virtually anything was fair game. Charlie's irrepressible curiosity and relentless questioning challenged me constantly. Inevitably we found ourselves dipping, cautiously at first, into our personal lives and feelings and values.

Charlie's restless mind still needs challenges, even as his aging body makes accepting them a growing challenge in itself. He cannot cease to meddle, still hoping to make this world a better place. Can you imagine this blind nonagenarian atop his soapbox in downtown Burlington, railing against a political system that he feels has lost its moral compass?

Not long ago, I showed up in Burlington, Vermont just in time for Charlie's weekly meeting with two teenagers from the King Street Youth Center. We four explored a topic dear to us both, the premise that risk is an essential dietary constituent for a life fully lived. The perfect proof for our analysis, of course, was the life recounted in this biography.

Charlie is a piece of work, more accurately a *magnum opus*—generous, brilliant, loyal, at times heroic. He can sometimes drive you up the wall with the intensity of his convictions and need to make sure things are done to fulfill his definition of right. As I reflect on this story about the life of an explorer of life, I see, among other things, an ancient alchemist turning dreams to gold. This magic has made itself felt in many realms, from mountaineering to medicine to research, and most of all in the lives he has inspired and the love he has shared. Charlie looks back, I think, at all this with reluctantly admitted pleasure and perhaps maybe even a little pride. Yet none of this seems to mollify his abiding conviction that he has not done enough.

So, now, turn the page and savor the journey, with Bernadette McDonald as your guide, through the life and times of a super *mensch*.

—Tom Hornbein
November 6, 2006

EARLY YEARS

Something hidden——Go and find it! Go and look behind the ranges.
——Rudyard Kipling

That night, the wind began to howl, dampening whatever dawn might have broken. It roared all night, pummeling and contorting the tents so badly that the climbers were unable to light their stoves. Snow sifted through the seams. One of the tents split, forcing its two occupants to crowd in with the others. Their breath condensed on the ceiling, only to fall on their faces as rain. The wind would sometimes quite suddenly stop, only to resume with even greater ferocity. It became impossible to talk. Snow seeped in, covering everything. Without functioning stoves, the climbers could neither cook nor melt snow for water. They grew weaker. As the storm continued to pin them down day after day, their thoughts of the summit faded; survival became their priority.

After weeks of grueling effort, Charlie and his team were poised on a vertiginous outcropping 25,000 feet high on the relentlessly steep flank of K2. Their tents were pitifully small under the majestic pyramid of ice and rock that loomed 3,000 feet above them. From this high camp they had planned for a final push to the summit of the unclimbed peak.

Then disaster struck. Art Gilkey, twenty-seven years old and superbly fit, crawled out of his tent and fainted. When Charlie got him back in the tent and examined him, he found evidence of blood clots in his leg—thrombophlebitis—a problem that Charlie, a trained physician, had seen only in a hospital setting before. "It was probably a few hours before the truth sank into my mind: Art could not climb down the mountain and probably would not be able to do so for many days, if ever." It was Charlie alone who comprehended the seriousness of the situation, realizing they were now fighting for their own lives, as well as Gilkey's.

When Charlie told the team, they were aghast. He explained that not only could Gilkey not walk down, there was real danger of the clots traveling to his lungs. If that happened it would almost certainly kill him. During a slight lull in the storm, the seven remaining climbers sprang into action. Wrapping their companion snugly in his sleeping bag and a tent, they made him as warm and comfortable as they could. Placing a rope under his head, they decided to drag and pull him straight down the steep snow slope they had climbed just a few days before.

As they prepared for their retreat, Charlie went back to throw the tents and their accumulated trash over the cliff. He had been brought up to always leave a clean camp. The others shouted at him to stop and to get moving. Had he persisted, they would all most certainly have died. Almost immediately after beginning their descent, they discovered that the snow slope was ready to avalanche, so they laboriously hauled Gilkey back up to the campsite. By noon they were back in bed, exhausted. The storm howled anew.

Over the roar of the screaming wind, they reviewed their options. If five or six climbers could get down to the next lowest camp, they would at least save on food and fuel. Charlie and perhaps one other person would stay with Gilkey until the storm broke or—but none of them said this aloud—until he died. Leaving Gilkey was never an option. Meanwhile, their liaison officer, Colonel Ata-Ullah, was lower down on the mountain with his Hunza support team, relaying the grim weather reports; more bad weather lay ahead. Ata-Ullah could only pray.

Astonishingly, during a brief lull in the storm, two members of the team, Bob Craig and Pete Schoening, initiated what can only be described as an act of defiance: they left their tents and headed up the mountain toward the summit. Their futile attempt took them only a few hundred feet above the camp.

Then a clot appeared in Gilkey's other leg and the situation worsened: "Art was coughing, and my examination confirmed that pieces of the clots had gone to his lungs. This was almost certainly the end, but how soon we could not tell. The weather the morning of August 10th looked a bit better. We decided to go for it." Charlie radioed down to Ata-Ullah and told him they were going to start the rescue descent and would call in again at 3:00 PM. Ata-Ullah gathered the Hunzas together to begin their vigil. He fully understood the impossibility of the situation and yet he marveled at the men. "We were witnessing an epic of endurance and devotion, and no stage could have been worthier in its loftiness and grandeur. The actors were all children of the West. We who watched it with concentrated souls were all from the East. Under the shadow of this grim mountain, East and West had not only met, but had been fused into one."[1] And so they began their long wait for that 3 o'clock call. It was fifty hours before they heard Charlie's voice again.

These children of the West were about to undertake one of the landmark rescue operations in the history of Himalayan climbing. Their sense of teamwork would get them all—save one—safely down the mountain. Their behavior high on K2 provoked wide speculation and divergent opinions in later years. Some felt their strategy was seriously flawed; they shouldn't have risked the entire team's safety for one life. Others referred to the expedition as seminal, an inspiring example for generations of climbers to follow. Reinhold Messner simply said: "They failed in the most beautiful way you can imagine." It was a defining moment for each member of the close-knit team, their desperate actions high on K2 branding each of them for the rest of their lives. For Charlie Houston, physician and leader of the expedition, his response to the crisis was the natural one—and the only one that was appropriate for him. His entire life had prepared him for this moment, and the choice he made was the culmination of the values instilled in him by his family, his traditions, his friends, and his experiences. Time and again, throughout his life, Charlie would make his most important decisions based on these core values. Some believed that these decisions resulted in failure; others regarded them as amazing achievements. Who was this man whose legacy would be to fail in the most beautiful way imaginable?

Charles Snead Houston was born in New York City on August 24, 1913, on a fire escape, according to family lore. At the time, the Houston's neighborhood, Morningside Heights, was almost rural in nature. This proximity to nature was important for the family, who often took short bicycle excursions into the country for picnics. His parents spent their honeymoon canoe camping in Algonquin Park in Ontario, and one of Charlie's earliest holiday memories was of tenting in the Adirondacks.

Charlie's father was born in Logan, Ohio, in 1883 and lived eighty-three years. Oscar Rempel Houston, descended of a distinguished northern Civil War family, was an only child who lived a somewhat solitary childhood. His best and only close young friend was an African-American boy—an unusual situation since segregation still prevailed in the late nineteenth century. Oscar attended Columbia Law School, where he graduated Phi Beta Kappa. He was afflicted with very poor eyesight, and perhaps to compensate, developed a phenomenal memory. Despite his poor eyes and thick glasses, he thrived as a lawyer, specializing in Admiralty Law. Oscar worked hard at his demanding profession, determined to use his fine mind in the pursuit of meaningful work and to provide a good life for his family. He eventually became president of the Admiralty Law Association and the International Bar Association.

Charlie's mother came from a much larger family; she had four brothers. Christened Angel Bunny Snead MacDonald, she was a fifth-generation MacDonald of Glengarry—a powerful clan best known for its adventurous ways and black moods. Her immediate family was Southern, cultivated, and proud—but poor. Angel Bunny, named for a Broadway character, grew up in Louisville, Kentucky, where she lived with her family on the third floor of a large building owned by two maiden aunts. There, they relied on the charity of the rest of the family. Her father had abandoned them early on and gone off to California; whether it was to find a job or to be with another woman was never clear. Despite this humiliating situation, the family rallied together, proud and determined to rise above their trials.

In an unusual and independent move for a Southern belle, Angel Bunny headed north to New York City to study interior decorating. Before she left, she received some charmingly pointed advice from her mother: "Nell, I want you to treat those Yankees as if they were just as good as you are." Nell evidently took her mother's advice to heart, for while she was in New York she met Oscar, then a law student at Columbia University. They married in 1912.

Angel Bunny was creative, outgoing, and charismatic, with a lilting Southern accent that became more pronounced when she was trying to impress, and a truly dazzling smile. She clung to many Southern traditions that Charlie eventually embraced as well. Though he grew up in the Northeast, he would always consider himself "Southern."

Oscar began working as a junior attorney in a well-known law firm in

New York. Like many other New York professionals at the time, he moved his family to the "country," the village of Great Neck on Long Island. They lived in a comfortable home on three quarters of an acre of land at the end of a dirt road called Wooley's Lane. This relocation left Oscar with a tiresome hour's train commute each way to his city office, but provided a veritable paradise for the family. Six days a week Angel Bunny would deliver her husband to the railroad station in the morning and dutifully pick him up again at seven that evening.

Despite Oscar's hard work and thriving career, the Long Island move was costly. Money was sometimes scarce, which resulted in occasional serious deliberations about the family's financial commitments. As a young boy, Charlie overheard his parents discussing something called a "mortgage." He remembered the word was spoken with a trace of awe, as was "foreclosure." Although he didn't understand the expressions, he knew enough that they made him anxious. Notwithstanding the financial concerns, Great Neck was nirvana for Charlie, with fields and woods, and a brook that ran down through the valley from the back of their garden. Surrounded by nature, Charlie made his first forays into the world of biology, venturing off to catch frogs, snakes, and tadpoles in a nearby swamp.

About half a dozen children of similar age lived nearby; they walked or biked to school, played, explored, fought, and learned together. Charlie and a grubby pack of boys and girls trekked the two-mile distance to school en masse, fearful of the parochial school kids who walked in the opposite direction on the other side of the road and who constantly threatened to beat them up. Eventually he began to prefer reading to playing with his friends, a reclusiveness that remained with him throughout his life.

When Charlie was still a toddler, his grandmother, Fanny Snead Mac-Donald, moved in with them. For five years she doted on Charlie, taught him to read, and awoke in him a passion for books that never diminished. Even as a child his tastes were eclectic: Jules Verne, *The Rover Boys*, Howard Pyle's *Book of Pirates*, as well as a twenty-two-volume set of American history called *The Real America*. The series, given to Charlie when he was twelve years old, traced the lives of three American families through several generations, from when they arrived in the United States in the eighteenth century until the end of World War I. Lavishly illustrated with photographs and paintings, they completely captured his youthful imagination.

These were Charlie's halcyon days at the end of Wooley's Lane, perched on the very edge of the Atlantic Ocean. Across the sea the world was ripping itself apart, yet Charlie's only memory of World War I was of standing on the deck waving at a plane flying high overhead as his mother observed, "That could be your Uncle Francis going to war." His father's poor eyesight, and their relatively solid financial position in the community, provided them a comfortable isolation from the grim reality of trenches, guns, and death.

The wild beauty of Charlie's idyllic neighborhood led to his growing interest in the natural world, in biology, and, inevitably, in the wonders of his own changing body. During these pre-teen years, Charlie was secretly in love; he was desperately infatuated with a pair of identical twins, Lois and Helen Lions, but felt too shy to actually approach them, afraid of rebuff. In his diary, he made terse mention of his sly stalking of the pair, writing "NLDNS—No Luck, Did Not See" when he was unsuccessful in catching a glimpse of them. In stark contrast to this skulking around was Charlie's instruction by his next-door neighbor, a precocious young girl named Dollo Andrews, who took great pleasure in sharing her more highly developed knowledge of sex with him. They played physical games together, and despite Charlie's attraction to her (they were eleven years old), he didn't understand what was happening when his body responded, and was frightfully embarrassed. Despite poring over anatomy books, he simply had no clue.

Meanwhile, a doctor friend of his parents, William Bradshaw, heard of Charlie's fascination with biology and began to take a special interest in him. A hemophiliac, Bradshaw had chosen not to have children, leaving him the time and energy to mentor Charlie. When Charlie was eleven years old, Bradshaw gave him his first microscope, plunging him into a new world. Charlie raced around, madly exploring the cellular world around him, from studying tiny living organisms in pond water to finding paramecia in "hay infusions" (hay immersed in water) that he proceeded to "feed" milk so that they grew larger and visible to the naked eye. He examined sediments and crystals in evaporating urine and solutions of salt and sugar. Because of his growing fascination with all living things, Bradshaw gave him Paul de Kruif's *Microbe Hunters*, and Charlie devoured it.

The microscope and books drew Charlie increasingly away from his friends as he spent more time in his "laboratory" in the basement. One afternoon Angel Bunny was hosting the local bridge club with about a dozen lady friends. She decided to introduce her young, curly-haired chemist to her guests, and she sent down for him to come upstairs. Charlie didn't want to. After a couple of requests, he became sulky and angry. The young scientist added some iron pyrites and sulfuric acid to a flask, put a stopper in it, and then inserted a rubber hose, which he ran up through the radiator pipes that led into the living room where his mother's bridge club sat. The putrid smell of rotten eggs oozed mysteriously into the room, causing an abrupt end to the party. His mother was furious at his petulant behavior. But she brought a traditional approach to parenting that indulged the firstborn, particularly if the child was a boy, and so Charlie was forgiven. Charlie enjoyed this special treatment, but along with privilege came pressure: pressure to be special and pressure to achieve. To relieve that pressure, Charlie increasingly retreated into privacy.

In his pursuit of solitude, Charlie began experimenting with nitrogen iodine. By taking iodine crystals and soaking them in ammonia, he found he could create crystals that were perfectly innocuous as long as they were wet, but when dried became volatile on contact. So he mixed up a batch and scattered the wet crystals on the stairs leading upstairs to his room. After they had dried, any and all who attempted to come up to his room were startled when they were surrounded by mysterious loud explosions as the invisible crystals exploded. As Charlie used his newfound scientific knowledge to defend his private time, he began to develop a "solitary researcher" persona that would remain with him, and sometimes haunt him, throughout his life.

He acquired a small aquarium, into which he placed all sorts of creatures he had collected from the surrounding creeks and ponds. If they died, he simply dissected them. He never grew tired of staring at the algae, frog's eggs, moss, slime, and myriad microscopic beasts that darted and swirled beneath his lens. It was during this time of youthful discovery that Charlie determined to become a doctor. Brazenly, he wrote to the American Cancer Society asking for cancer samples so that he could study them. Proud of her son's growing interest in science and medicine, despite his sometimes malodorous experiments, Angel Bunny never forgave their lack of response.

Meanwhile, the Houston family was growing. The first of Charlie's two younger sisters, Barbara MacDonald Houston, was born in 1916. She was a chubby, pleasant, but not terribly outgoing little girl. In contrast, her younger sister by three years, Janet Scott Houston, was blond, pretty, vivacious, and the life of the party. Charlie would never grow close to either of them. As the spoiled eldest child, he became somewhat aggressive with his sisters, and he was often moody and difficult to get along with. He teased Barbara and Janet constantly, forced them to eat worms, even painted them green on one occasion, and generally brought terror to their poor, young lives.

※

When Charlie was fifteen, the family moved to Kings Point and a new, much larger home with a splendid view of Long Island Sound. It was here that Charlie spent his teen years, and it was here that "the clouds of adolescence" formed. He was now isolated and miles away from his former friends. The Houstons' new neighbors were rather wealthy, at least until the stock market crash in 1928. Although the crash didn't affect the Houstons greatly—Oscar's law practice grew steadily during these years—it was Charlie's first lesson in economics as he watched several neighbors lose their entire fortunes overnight. Fortunately for him, he was shielded from the searing poverty that much of the country endured during that catastrophic economic downturn. For many, it was no work, no shelter, no food, and, ultimately, no self-respect.

The Kings Point property was spacious, offering new opportunities for the increasingly affluent Houstons: house decorating for Angel Bunny, and a splendid garden in which Oscar could cultivate wildflowers and indulge his passion for his cocker spaniels, Bitter and Jitters. Although Oscar was not athletic, he was active and he dearly loved to walk. His dogs provided him the perfect excuse, and he exercised them daily for miles along the empty Long Island beaches. Angel Bunny had her own flower garden as well as a grape arbor, and there was a vegetable garden that was tended by their newly hired help.

The house itself was large and tastefully furnished, thanks to Angel Bunny's training in interior design. Charlie once made the caustic comment that the house looked as if it belonged in the pages of *House Beautiful,* deeply offending his mother. In truth, he admired his tasteful home and enjoyed the upscale living, but he felt uncomfortable bringing home his school friends who didn't live in such formal and opulent style. As his family had moved up the social ladder, Charlie felt compelled to perform at a higher level. A well-brought-up Southern girl who was very aware of New York society, Angel Bunny worked hard to have the family registered. This opened up a vast array of social opportunities for them, few of which Charlie enjoyed. His relationship with wealth and all its trappings was one of ambivalence, something that carried through to adulthood.

Like many Long Island families of the day, the Houstons acquired domestic help when they moved to Kings Point. They hired a French couple whom his father had met while traveling in France. Flora, the cook, was rotund and affectionate, and Joseph, who performed duties as butler, major domo, and disciplinarian, was a wounded and decorated veteran of the Great War. Thanks to them, the children quickly became bilingual.

Each spring, the entire family embarked on an annual search for fragrant bouquets of arbutus. Packing an ample picnic, they would drive twenty miles to the Motor Parkway, where they deposited their 25 cents in order to drive on a well-banked and graveled toll road, allowing them to roll along at the breathtaking speed of forty miles an hour. After a day of sun and food and arbutus-gathering, they arrived home sandy, sunburned, exhausted, and perfumed. Long summer days found the family on the great south shore beaches of Long Island, which at that time were virtually empty. Charlie's uncle Angus MacDonald taught the children how to swim safely in the ocean and how to play in the immense, pounding surf.

Soon the focus of the family summers changed. Oscar learned from his highly placed New York clients about an exclusive private club on Honnedaga Lake in the Adirondacks. The 360,000 acres of land were owned by a group of people whose interest in the area was a combination of recreational retreat and environmental protection. Various prominent New York families invited the Houstons up for a visit, and Oscar soon became determined to invest. The neighbors included former presidents, vice-presidents, and major corporate players. It was a unique—and privileged—wilderness enclave.

Reaching Honnedaga each summer with his mother, two younger sisters, Flora, and Joseph, was a pleasant ritual for Charlie. After boarding the night train in Grand Central Station, with its spotlessly clean cars and heavy green curtains shielding each bunk, Charlie would fall asleep immediately, waking up occasionally to the clickety-clack of the wheels running over the rails. He would pull the curtain aside and gaze sleepily at the mysterious dawn mist lurking over the Erie Barge Canal. Their destination was Utica, where they would devour a special "Honnedaga breakfast" of cereal, thick cream, and fresh fruit in the magnificently restored train station. Transferring to the narrow-gauge Adirondack line to Forestport, the family was met at the end by an open Packard "touring car" with iced-glass windows. Although it was only twenty miles to Honnedaga, it was still several hours of travel. They rolled along on plank bridges and narrow rough roads, walking up some of the steeper hills that the loaded car couldn't manage. For the first eight miles they passed the scattered houses of lumber industry workers, then they moved on into the forest of the great three-million-acre Adirondack Park, protected since the late nineteenth century. Here they began to see wild game: turkeys, pheasants, deer, and the occasional bear. Finally they descended a steep hill to reach the lake, where they were met by an old launch from which Peter, the boatman, took them to camp.

Before the family arrived, the guides would already have "opened up" in preparation for them, laying good firewood on the porch of their cabin, hooking up the water line from the spring up the hill, and making sure that "Larry" (the two-seater toilet) was ready for use. Behind their camp was a tent for Flora and Joseph, who cared for all their needs and prepared fine French dinners served each night in front of a roaring fire. Also behind the camp was a large ice house, filled with ice cut during the winter. The cabin itself was simple, with an icebox in the kitchen, an old kerosene stove, and kerosene lamps along the wall and on the table. The family inhabited their rustic permanent camp for the entire month of August, enjoying immediate access to the pristine lake, seven miles long and one mile wide, as well as to the unspoiled forest.

Charlie thought Honnedaga a magical place. He filled his days with swimming, canoeing, fishing, and exploring the forest, where he and his sisters found caves, bear scat, beaver cuttings, and raccoons. Angel Bunny, alone with the children for most of the summer, took her family responsibilities seriously, even hiring a boy to prevent them from drowning in the lake. Her discipline extended to teaching the children to help keep camp, with Charlie and his sisters expected to sweep the camp clean, bring in fresh wood, and empty the slop buckets from each bedroom. Too, they had to fill the pitchers with fresh water and make their beds. Only then could they attend to their favorite chore: running to the lodge for milk, which they brought back in two-gallon cans.

Each evening after a fine dinner, they sat by a crackling fire while Charlie's mother read to them. Over the mantelpiece, someone had placed a broad pine plank with a quote from William Cullen Bryant's poem, "Thanatopsis": "To him who, in the love of Nature, holds communion with her visible forms, she speaks a various language." It was a clear statement of what the woods meant to Charlie's entire family. It was why Oscar had worked so hard to gain entrance into this exclusive club where his family could spend summers in a northern paradise. And it was why, eventually, all his children embraced the natural world in one form or another. Later, as evening coolness descended over the camp, the family would listen for a hooting owl, or the weird, wonderful, lonely call of the loon, a sound Charlie always associated with the northern woods.

Oscar came up for only one or two weekends a month, enduring a cruel schedule to reunite with his family. He would arrive well after midnight on Friday night, weekend at the camp, then leave Sunday evening, arriving back on Long Island early Monday morning. Despite his grueling schedule, Oscar believed in simplicity, and he managed to instill that in his son. When Oscar was in camp, father and son would sometimes hire a guide and venture out to one of the outlying camps to fish. They caught brook trout and slept in rustic shelters. For Oscar, Honnedaga was a place for restoration, for recharging, an island of constancy in an always-changing world: simple, special, elemental. Later, in Charlie's equally busy professional life, Honnedaga renewed the balance for him and his family, too. But this idyllic setting was also spectacularly exclusive, perhaps an escape from a complex, noisy, and messy world that was not as ordered and privileged as theirs.

But Honnedaga summers always came to an end and, after a ritual scrubbing in a tin bathtub by the fire, they would take the launch to the head of the lake, drive through the night to Forestport and then, at midnight, flag down the Montreal Express to New York. After the great train screeched to a halt, they tiptoed in, crawled behind the green Pullman curtains and drifted off into Honnedaga dreamland. When they awoke in New York City the next morning, summer was officially over.

Back at Kings Point, there were school, friends, and family traditions to enjoy. One of Charlie's favorite events was autumn winemaking. The Houstons bought dozens of crates of California grapes, and despite the Volsted Act making Prohibition the law of the land, merrily produced enough wine for the entire year. Another important tradition, Christmas, was reserved for family. It wasn't unusual to have twenty-five for Christmas dinner, with aunts and uncles, cousins, and grandparents all gathered at a table with a huge turkey at one end and a succulent ham at the other. The men frequently indulged in "Fish House Punch," a frighteningly strong concoction assembled on a base of rum and brandy. As a result, the final tree-decorating touches were often completed by the women and children as the men dozed contentedly. Christmas breakfast was a special event at which Angel Bunny always served oyster stew, a somewhat odd tradition imported from her Southern background. When she was a girl, a family friend had each year sent a barrel of oysters for Christmas. They would eat fresh oysters Christmas morning and, by keeping them on ice, oysters for the next few weeks as well. In addition to the oysters, the family enjoyed the trappings of a more traditional Christmas, with beautifully wrapped presents and decorations.

Even as the Depression came and went, there was no discernible change to the Christmas rituals for the prosperous Houstons. One year, Angel Bunny decreed that they should buy only inexpensive presents. This may have been simply for appearances though, for Charlie went to the "five and ten" store (Woolworth's) to pick up 5- or 10-cent price tags to attach to his more expensive presents. Even Oscar cooperated, enclosing a Woolworth's price tag in what was obviously a beautiful—and expensive—jewel necklace for his wife. Despite the family's comfortable economic status, there was clearly a certain level of discomfort in acknowledging it.

After World War I ended in 1918, Oscar became very involved with the War Claims made by individuals and companies against the German government for damage sustained during the war. It was a major undertaking and he worked hard at it. For his diligence, Oscar was eventually offered a federal judgeship. It would have been a prestigious position for him and would undoubtedly have changed all of their lives. But, while Oscar was a strong figure, in fact it was Angel Bunny who was in charge at Kings Point, and she persuaded him to turn the appointment down.

Throughout the 1920s, the family continued to prosper. But the long hours Oscar spent working left little time for the children. Charlie's memories of his father were vivid, yet somewhat wistful. Charlie's belief was that, because Oscar was unable to serve in World War I due to his bad vision and flat feet, he had a somewhat diminished sense of self. Ironically, this was a feeling Charlie would replicate when he was forced to remain on American soil during the next world war. Their moments together were fleeting, and Charlie saw Oscar as a complex, hidden, and busy man. As an adult, Charlie deeply regretted their lack of a close relationship, even while he understood the demands of his father's profession. Years later, Charlie's own children would express similar sentiments about their own complicated, famous, and distracted father. But like the young Charlie, they would accept their limited time with their father, acknowledging his other passions and responsibilities.

Despite Oscar's strong work ethic, when summer arrived he always managed a vacation, taking his family abroad when possible. Oscar believed that travel was a great educator, and he frequently told the children that while it was doubtful they would be left with a lot of money or property, he hoped to leave them with a rich heritage of travel. Their vacations, often imaginative and innovative, included a canoe trip through the canals of France and an attempt to retrace Robert Louis Stevenson's *Travels With a Donkey in the Cévennes*. For this adventure, they bought a donkey named Clémentine; however, they simply could not convince her to move. After a couple of days of frustration, they sold her and subsequently walked the route.

And so it was that in 1925 the entire family went abroad, embarking on one of the great steamships of the day, comfortably ensconced in first class, en route to Europe. After they visited Paris, his sisters, Bobby and Janet, went to stay with a French family at the spa village of Evian les Bains while Charlie and his parents walked in the hills for a week, ending up at Chamonix in the French Alps. They hiked along dirt roads from village to village, sleeping in small inns, carrying their lunch by day and dining well by night. The strenuous physical exertion, clear, bracing mountain air, delicious local cheese and bread, and constantly changing views enchanted Charlie. During that week of magical wandering, his most enduring images were of the abbey at Sixt, the Fer à Cheval cirque, and the Col d'Anterne, where they engaged a guide. They then crossed the Col de Brévent, where the guide uncorked a bottle of Asti Spumante to celebrate. From the summit of the pass they gazed directly at the enormous Mont Blanc massif before descending endless switchbacks to the valley floor. This trip marked the first time Charlie saw "real" mountains, and it made an indelible impact. He felt completely alive and invigorated by the experience and enjoyed a surprising kinship with his father that reflected their new common interest.

Chamonix in 1925 was just a small village nestled in the deep valley below Mont Blanc. Mountaineering attracted only a few outsiders then, but it was essential to the Chamonix economy. While in the valley, the Houstons visited the Hôtel Montenvers overlooking the Mer de Glace, from which many alpine climbs began. After wandering down to the glacier and absorbing the spectacular mountain and glacial scenery, they reluctantly prepared themselves to leave this mountain paradise. But their departure was unexpectedly delayed because of an accident; a climbing party had fallen and one young, badly injured man was brought back to the hotel. Charlie's mother helped care for him during the night until the small train could transport him back to Chamonix the next morning. The accident fascinated the impressionable Charlie, especially the weather-beaten climbers in their tweed knickers and coats, slung with ropes and ice axes. To reinforce his emerging interest in mountaineering, he discovered Geoffrey Winthrop Young's *On High Hills* in the hotel and promptly devoured it.

Despite the recent accident, Charlie convinced his parents to allow him to stay on a few days and climb a small mountain. His father, pleased by his son's emerging interest, hired a guide and a porter for Charlie to climb the Aiguille de l'M. It was a short and easy climb, starting well before dawn after a hasty breakfast of hot chocolate, bread, and honey. Charlie was excited—too excited—and his meager breakfast didn't remain with him long. In spite of his heaving stomach, he reached the summit, basked in the rising sun, and returned beaming proudly to his parents. It was with great sadness that he joined the rest of the family for their remaining days in Europe: he reluctantly attended *Aida* in Arles, plied the canals of Venice, and visited the glass-blowing artisans of Murano. Charlie's heart was back in the mountains—in the cold, clear air.

Returning to Kings Point was a distinct letdown. Charlie still missed his friends from Wooley's Lane, and he missed the mountains. He felt isolated, and strongly resisted his mother's advice to befriend the few nearby adolescents. Strangely, at one moment Charlie longed to be popular and sought-after, but at the next repulsed all advances, perhaps for fear of eventual rejection. Throughout his life Charlie rode this emotional pendulum, which caused him considerable turmoil and grief. He felt awkward and clumsy and shy. He was also afraid to dance, refusing invitations to parties and pretending an intellectuality he really didn't have. So he retreated to the swamps and tidal inlets near his house.

His parents became concerned. Worried about his isolation, his moodiness, and the quality of his education, they decided to send him to a private school. They settled on the exclusive Hotchkiss in Lakeville, Connecticut, a school with a fine academic reputation which was popular with wealthy and socially prominent New York families. Though their choice resulted in financial strain, they found it worth it to "save" their son. But Charlie's arrival as a sophomore in 1928 was an immediate disaster. Alliances and peer groups had already been formed and Charlie felt abandoned among strangers who were often casually cruel. "I was a total misfit," he recalled.

All new recruits were harassed by their seniors: they had to wear black ties, were forced to touch the walls while walking in the hallways, could speak only when spoken to, and faced trivial yet frequent insults. These meaningless rituals of school life were a severe blow to Charlie, who already felt inadequate because of his comparative lack of money and fashionable clothes. Private school had upped the ante once again, and he wasn't sure he was cut out for it. His first innocent adolescent homosexual encounters took place among the boys in his house, but even here he felt rejection.

Since sports were mandatory, Charlie reluctantly signed up for football. Certain elements of the sport attracted him: the autumn season, the chilly temperatures, the massive equipment, and the sweaty locker room. But he hated the battering that took place—and the aggression. As a result he was soon sidelined. He tried skiing, skated a bit, and in the spring tried track. But there was something lacking in his efforts—the competitive spirit.

Over the next two years, school improved slightly. He made a few friends, revitalized the dormant literary journal, and caught the attention of a superb English teacher who routinely invited a few students to his home for readings and discussion around the fire. It was through Mr. McChessy that Charlie learned to love great books, poems, and plays. It was a continuation of his lifelong passion for literature, set in motion at his grandmother's knee. He also organized a science club, something that pleased Oscar immensely.

For the next two summers Oscar arranged a position for Charlie as a research assistant in the Cold Spring Harbor Laboratory, helping a quiet young biochemist named Martha Washburn. Washburn was meticulous and patient and taught him how to be precise with his analyses. They studied calcium metabolism in cats; Charlie's job was to collect cat urine, feces, and blood—quite a different summer experience from that of his peers, who were gadding about, swimming, and sailing on the most fashionable beaches. As the lab was twenty miles from his home, Oscar bought his son a Ford convertible, which Charlie drove back and forth with pride. The car probably could have been a magnet for young girls, but even the flashy new soft-top could not eliminate his chronic shyness. Charlie was torn: "I wanted desperately to be like the others, to feel part of the social world they inhabited." But despite attending white-tie debutante parties and going to the speakeasies in New York, he always felt an outsider, and so increasingly retreated into the world of science.

Yet it wasn't science alone that diverted his attention away from the Long Island fashionable set; it was also the draw of the mountains. Oscar not only approved of Charlie's mounting interest, he too developed a growing fascination for climbing. In 1931 he organized another European trip that included an extended walk, this time through the Austrian Alps. They started in Innsbruck, where they hired a young guide, bought climbing gear, and headed off for a week in the Tyrolean mountains of Ötztal and Zillertal, walking from hut to hut, climbing summits along the way. It was a superb week; Charlie felt close to his father and was more smitten by climbing than ever. Oscar, sensing the infection, gifted Charlie another trip to the Alps, this time to Chamonix. There he engaged one of the great Chamonix guides to take his son up increasingly difficult snow and rock peaks. With each upward step, Charlie's confidence grew—not only as a climber, but as a young man.

THE HARVARD FIVE

I grew up exuberant in body but with a nervy, craving mind. It was wanting something more, something tangible . . . But you see at once what I do. I climb.

> —John Menlove Edwards

Despite having only average grades, Charlie was admitted to Harvard in 1931, something that was perhaps inevitable, considering his private-school education. As he explained bluntly: "I was a poor student—it [Hotchkiss] was a prestige school—it got me into Harvard with no difficulty at all." By now, Charlie had finalized his decision to study medicine, a natural progression from his earlier interest in all things living. He moved into Massachusetts Hall, one of the revolutionary-period buildings in the Harvard Yard, and he gradually became part of a tight circle of friends.

With his burgeoning interest in climbing and his recent adventures in the Alps, he joined the Harvard Mountaineering Club. At the rock quarries in the nearby town of Quincy he met many climbers, some quite talented. Many became his friends for life, and a group of them became known as the Harvard Five: Bob Bates, Ad Carter, Terris Moore, Bradford Washburn, and Charlie. Washburn was particularly popular since he had a car. Already a published author, with *Among the Alps with Bradford* under his belt, Washburn had earned enough money to buy a little Ford roadster. It was not unusual to see a motley group of climbers crammed into the car and its rumble seat as they headed off to the nearby crags. Bates, the son of a Pennsylvania professor, had spent his childhood summers in Randolph, New Hampshire, with his family, exploring in the woods while his father wrote books. Once he got to Harvard, it took no time at all for Bates to advance from walking in the woods to doing some serious climbing. Carter, from a New England blueblood family, was the linguist in the bunch. He would eventually take his language and climbing skills to new heights, editing the *American Alpine Journal* for many years. Moore's passion for Alaska ultimately saw him assuming the presidency of the University of Alaska. Art Emmons, another talented climbing partner of Charlie's, although not one of the Harvard Five, would soon suffer terribly for his passion, losing all his toes to severe frostbite on an expedition to Minya Konka.

They climbed routes that were considered some of the most difficult at the time, including Huntington and Tuckerman ravines on Whitehorse and Cathedral ledges, and on Owls Head. Together, they built the Harvard Cabin near Tuckerman Ravine on Mount Washington.

After his first year at Harvard, Charlie headed back to the Alps, this time without his father. The previous year he had met a lawyer and his girlfriend, Trudl, from Hamburg, and now, on his way to Chamonix, Charlie went back to visit them. He jokingly asked if Trudl would like to come climbing in the Alps. To his surprise, she said "I'd love to." The weather was atrocious in Chamonix, so after waiting around for a few days Trudl suggested something different—a float down the Rhine. What followed was six days of paddling, sleeping on sandbars wrapped in their capes, eating cheese and chocolate and crackers, singing, and telling stories. It was an idyllic adventure, marred only by glimpses of anti-Semitism in the form of anti-Jewish statements and swastikas scrawled on building walls.

Back in Chamonix, now alone and still waiting for decent weather, Charlie noticed one other person rattling around the hotel. Eventually Charlie approached him and offered, "I believe we speak the same language." The gentleman's response was a taciturn "Possibly." He turned out to be the distinguished British climber T. Graham Brown. The weather didn't cooperate, so both men went home without having climbed anything. But their meeting marked the beginning of a friendship that would eventually take them on great adventures in distant corners of the mountain world.

At Harvard, it was the slightly older and far more experienced Harvard

Five companion Bradford Washburn who most impressed Charlie. So it was with eager anticipation that Charlie accepted Washburn's invitation to join him on an attempt of the unclimbed Mount Crillon in southern Alaska in 1933. Washburn was already a well-known mountaineer, having previously organized an expedition to an unclimbed Alaskan peak, Mount Fairweather, so the invitation to join the trip was flattering to Charlie. This would be Charlie's first major climb. The 12,728-foot Crillon was an ambitious objective even for those with more experience, let alone for a group of college kids.

Washburn had a dominating personality and was a strong, powerful young man—a born leader. Charlie learned an enormous amount from Washburn about organizing expeditions and, more importantly, about what made up a well-functioning team. Four of the team were Harvard Five climbers: Ad Carter, Bob Bates, Washburn, and Charlie. To complete the group, Washburn invited his good friend Walt Everett, who acted as his assistant on the climb; Bill Child, a good friend of Bates from the University of Pennsylvania; and Richard Goldthwait, a young geologist. Each climber was chosen by Washburn primarily for compatibility, an important factor Charlie would remember, and emulate, in all his future expeditions.

Preparing for a major expedition was a new experience for Charlie, who was two years younger and subservient to Washburn in every way. He was particularly impressed with the older climber's meticulous approach: "It was an exact science with Washburn. Every item of food was weighed and bagged . . . sugar, cereals, dried fruits and vegetables were tied in small paraffin bags." Together with canned goods and biscuits, matches and candles, everything was loaded into individual bags sufficient for two men for three days. Down was not common in those days, except in their warm and heavy sleeping bags. Their parkas, called anoraks, were made of lightweight, tightly woven cotton and adorned with a wolverine-fur-trimmed hood. Under his anorak each man wore a sweater, a wool shirt, and a complete suit of woolen underwear. The climbers' trousers were also made of heavy wool. Their woolen gloves had canvas outers, complete with leather palms, and another small piece of wolverine fur on the back—useful for wiping their noses. On their feet were Barker boots, made of rubber with leather uppers fitted to "bear trap" crampons. They finished off their equipment list with skis, climbing skins, and goggles.

After all the equipment was purchased and packed, the party planned a departure meeting at New York's Grand Central Station. Charlie's family brought him to this grand leave-taking, but mistakenly ended up at Pennsylvania

Station instead. There ensued a mad dash across town with barely enough time to meet the others. Charlie's lasting memory of the event was of his mother, "distraught, clutching a box of cherries she had brought for my journey."

They boarded the train to Montreal, where they met the rest of the team, then headed across Canada by rail in the "colonist car," an old Pullman car with wooden berths and a small stove—nothing more. Rolling through the Canadian Rockies, they moved up top, enjoying the scenery and becoming fast friends. Charlie's excitement about Crillon was infectious, quickly making him a favorite on the trip—and not just with his teammates. At one of the many small country towns, the train stopped at the station café for a snack. The local waitress served up some pie and charged them each 10 cents a slice—all except Charlie. She charged him 5 cents, and told the others it was "because he's so cute." He may have been cute, but he was also the butt of their teasing pranks. Later in the journey, the team sent him off to search for a canoe, which they needed for the next leg of the journey. Unbeknownst to Charlie, they directed him to the red-light district, where the ladies of the house laughingly sent the young, innocent Easterner on his way.

Their arrival in the coastal city of Prince Rupert was, predictably, met with pouring rain. From Prince Rupert they took a two-day boat to Juneau, where they connected with a fishing boat to navigate the next 100 miles north along the Pacific Coast. The boat chugged into Lituya Bay and landed on Cenotaph Island, where they were hosted by an old hermit fur trader, Jim Huscroft. With widening eyes, Charlie observed a simpler and tougher lifestyle than any other he had seen: one full of chores, cutting and splitting wood, and hauling water.

The team had to first paddle ten miles up the bay to the snout of a glacier that would give them access to the Crillon area. It took an additional thirty-six hours of hard work to carry the canoe up the steep terminus of the glacier and across into the Crillon watershed. Arriving at a large body of water that lay between a steep slope and the flatter, severely crevassed glacier, they wearily dropped the canoe and their packs, looking at the water in dismay. How were they going to cross it? Sheer exhaustion had made them forget the canoe they had laboriously carried with them for just such a purpose.

They finally arrived at Crillon Lake—an intimidating place with massive chunks of ice calving in from the glacier. Nervous because of the obvious evidence of bears in the area, they huddled around a roaring fire. The next day they paddled across the lake and set up camp at the same spot used by

Washburn on his Crillon attempt the previous year. From here they would begin the arduous task of moving camps, food, and gear up the mountain, one camp at a time, until they were in position to try for the summit. They fondly called their base camp "Crillon Farms," as they planted lettuce, radishes and other vegetables, hopeful they might grow in the long summer days. The camp was comfortably situated among small trees, with a beautiful view of the lake. Their only problems were bears and mosquitoes, particularly the latter. Nevertheless, the team settled in for a long Northern summer.

Each day, rain or shine, they packed supplies up to the next camp, usually carrying eighty pounds on their backs. Charlie recalled reveling in "our youth and strength. It was tiring but exhilarating." There were many new things for him to understand: red snow, glacier worms, glacier fleas, glacial caverns, and mill wells. A special discovery was a place they called Cleopatra's Baths, a meadow of moss, muskeg, and scattered stunted trees, where small, deep, sun-warmed pools welcomed their aching muscles.

Their route threaded the glacier for ten miles, then over a high snowy pass, and up to an overhanging cornice, for which Washburn had brought dynamite—something the team teased him and Charlie mercilessly about. Charlie carried the caps and Bates carried the dynamite, making sure to keep their distance from each other on the way up. But in the end it wasn't necessary: the cornice was easily penetrated. Above the cornice they established a small high camp with several days of food and fuel. From here they hoped to cross the few remaining miles of snow plateau, climb the last ridge, and traverse to the 12,782-foot summit.

As the trip progressed, Charlie learned from Washburn the critical importance of sound leadership. Potential for a power struggle existed between the two, since both had strong personalities. Washburn recalled a small misunderstanding over some routefinding when he had to struggle to retain control of the situation. Despite the disagreement, Washburn contended that Charlie was the strongest climber in the group—much stronger than Bates. But Charlie insisted that he took a subservient role on Crillon, absorbing what he could from Washburn.

Finally, all six of them were crammed into the tiny high camp, poised for the summit. After a storm pinned them down for a day and night, it was decided that three would go for the summit and three would go down to their advance base camp; Charlie was one of the three who went down. A few days later the summit hopefuls returned, exhausted and disappointed that they had been forced to turn back only a half-mile from the summit, short of food and water. They subsequently packed up and skied down the valley, crashing through the breakable snow crust at every turn. Then it was Cleopatra's Baths and a hopeful visit to the gardens of Crillon Farms, where, alas, no lettuce had grown. Despite the lack of lettuce, the climbers ate well.

Charlie recalled very little disappointment of the summit failure, but rather enthusiastic wonder of life in the wild: "There followed a week of pure enjoyment. We went through lovely groves of immense arbor vitae with deeply worn bear trails down to the beach where we feasted on huge wild strawberries, so plentiful one could eat a quart almost without moving. We caught salmon in our hands . . . we chased a bear across the lake in the canoe . . . we paddled perilously close to the calving ice cliff so Washburn could get memorable photographs." It was a Northern paradise that each of them enjoyed in their own way. Bates hunted for goats, and the entire comical event was captured on film—and in Charlie's memory: "The sleeping goat, wakened by the first shot, staggered to its feet after the second, and came strolling toward the gun after the third. No blood!" The next day, Bates was much more successful, bringing back a goat that they roasted and ravenously devoured.

Eventually their food ran low, and it was time to leave. They had arranged a flight to take them out, but before they packed up their camp and left, there was one last chore to be completed: disposal of the latrine. Washburn decided that this was where the dynamite could finally be deployed, and deployed it was: "a tremendous blast sent crap high in the air . . . it rained for an hour!" The team found it a truly spectacular—and strangely festive— ending to the expedition.

Washburn and Everett flew out and the rest of the team stayed on at the beaches north of the bay, swimming, eating berries, grilling salmon steaks, and chasing—and being chased by—a mother bear and her two cubs. It was a summer that Charlie would never forget—carefree and wild. Jim Huscroft entertained them with endless tales of the North Country; for Charlie, it was his first taste of the North—and of expedition life. He was smitten.

))((

Charlie had found his tribe. He had discovered a physical activity at which he could excel and which set him apart from ordinary people. He seized upon this small group of like-minded climbers in order to avoid the strictures of the private Harvard clubs prevalent at the time. The club system was precise, elegant, and very structured, and although Charlie seemed welcomed by Boston society and a number of its attractive young debutantes, he was never fully accepted by, nor did he feel comfortable with, the top-tier "final clubs" at Harvard. They attracted boys from the wealthiest and most powerful Eastern families, boys whose futures as leaders were being defined by what they did at Harvard. Charlie was eventually invited to join a second-tier "final club," which he briefly did. He valiantly tried to fit in, drinking bravely with the others, but in reality it was a painful time. He instinctively disliked the self-serving and self-congratulatory atmosphere among the boys. Many of them moved on to have distinguished careers as politicians, financiers, and artists, buoyed by their Harvard years and the influential contacts made there. Charlie didn't feel that was his destiny.

Instead he joined the Hasty Pudding Club, a kind of Harvard amateur dramatic society. Its advantage was that it was somewhat less elitist and brimming with creativity. To his glee, Charlie became part of the Hasty Pudding touring musical show, which played in half a dozen Eastern cities. After weeks of rehearsals they hit the road, Charlie in the role of a chorus girl, clad in a long, elegant blue silk dress. It was a testament to his growing self-confidence that he could unselfconsciously enjoy the experience, feeling fully accepted by the other members of the club.

Charlie finally felt comfortable bringing his college friends to Long Island, and occasionally invited them to his youthful summer idyll, Honnedaga. One night, he and his friends found themselves at an overnight camp called Swanson's Camp. After an evening of hilarity, they were kept awake most of the night by a porcupine chewing under the cabin. As the host, Charlie announced that he would deal with the porcupine in the morning. Using a long pole, he bravely poked and prodded until the porcupine emerged from under the cabin, shaking his quills as he waddled. The entire group watched with interest as the porcupine climbed a birch tree to escape Charlie's harassment. Charlie went after him. The higher the two ascended, the more the tree swayed. Then it began to bend. From time to time the porcupine looked over his shoulder at Charlie, who continued coming up behind him despite their precarious positions. Suddenly the porcupine took defensive action, lifted his tail and emitted an enormous stream of green, fetid liquid. It cascaded over Charlie's face, hair, and clothing. Disgusted, Charlie retreated, further humiliated by gales of laughter from his friends. They took up sticks, warning him not to get close to them, and forced him down to the river to wash. He did so, but ultimately had to burn his foul-smelling clothes. The porcupine, having done his duty, ambled off into the woods, unaffected.

As Charlie gained confidence during his Harvard years, his personality evolved from that of an awkward adolescent to that of a socially adept young man. Still, his romantic efforts produced mixed results, and his attempts at sexual adventure were fumbling at best. He tried valiantly to keep up with his bragging college peers, but remained a frustrated virgin. However, he wasn't without dates. One particular favorite was Peggy Pearsall, a demure Boston debutante. On one occasion, Charlie squired her to the Cotton Club, the famous New York jazz haunt in Harlem. They sat down, ordered some drinks, and became vaguely aware of a black woman singing in a far corner of the room, accompanied by a piano. The singer finished her set and then began circulating throughout the room, eventually arriving at Charlie and Peggy's table. To Charlie's horror, she was stark naked. "She leaned on our table and she had these enormous breasts, which just dangled down on the table. Both Peggy and I just stiffened because she then began singing these filthy, filthy songs . . . it seemed to me it went on for hours . . . it might have been five minutes." The entertainer finally completed her song, and the horrified young couple gathered themselves, paid the bill, and fled.

Charlie loved Harvard. His years there were as fulfilling as his private-school years had been painful. He finally felt accepted for who he was, not for who he tried to be, nor because of his background. He also tasted alcohol and found himself at the center of some roaring drunken brawls. Somewhat a rebel, he was the ringleader of the student spring riots, for which he was placed on disciplinary probation for a year. But one thing that did not enter his consciousness was the emerging situation in Europe as Hitler marched inexorably toward dominance. He and his friends were blissfully unaware of what was happening.

The most important thing Charlie learned at Harvard was to study. He was exposed to fine teachers who steeped him in English literature and European art, subjects that remained precious to him. He struggled with advanced chemistry, and was aided by compassionate tutors. His grades gradually improved until he made the dean's list. But when it came to his extensive comprehensive examinations, he barely squeaked through.

Charlie wanted to do something worthwhile and meaningful that would have value to humankind. Did his professors infuse him with this desire? Or did it come from the casual acceptance that he and his fellow students had—that their lives would have meaning and importance? Many would, as they went on to have careers in the diplomatic field, or in prestigious law and banking firms.

Charlie struggled with his own identity, with his future, with his legacy. What would be his life's work? Would he do something important—significant? Did he have a talent? If so, would it be recognized during his life? There were early clues of his own future contributions. Even as a young student he took pride in his writing; he was meticulous with his words. But there were also omens—omens of a life tortured by ruthless self-assessment and the pursuit of unattainably high standards. When he was accepted into Columbia University's College of Physicians and Surgeons, Charlie felt ready to make his aspirations real.

But medical school would have to wait for one more great adventure. In 1934 Charlie's father proposed a climb of Mount Foraker, a 17,400-foot peak in a largely undiscovered part of the country. Foraker had not been mapped; few people had been near it, and none had described it. Oscar had only been able to procure a rough sketch showing approximate valleys and contours. Although he was not a serious climber, Oscar loved the idea of a remote expedition and he had confidence in the abilities of his son. His responsibility was to make all travel arrangements and pay for the trip, and Charlie's job was to pull the team together and plan the food and equipment.

For this trip the climbers once again used heavy down sleeping bags weighing seventeen pounds. They used a standard Logan tent as well as small emergency bivouac tents like those used on Crillon. They brought custom-designed one-piece coveralls made of double Grenfell cloth, complete with wolverine-trimmed fur hoods. The coveralls were windproof and tough, but terribly heavy. They used standard rubber and leather Barker boots that they could fit into crampons.

Washburn's Crillon trip had taught Charlie a lot about provisioning carefully—a methodology he brought to Foraker. Once again each bag was prepared to provision two men for three days, all packed in the basement of Lowell House at Harvard. As for the team, Charlie assembled an amiable group of climbing friends: T. Graham Brown, whom he had met in the Alps; Charles Storey; Chychele Waterston of Andover; the distinguished Alaskan hunting guide, Carl Anderson, from Anchorage; and Oscar. Notably absent was Washburn. Washburn would have loved to climb Foraker, but Foraker was extremely remote and therefore expensive, and while Charlie's father had money, Washburn did not. Instead, Washburn returned to Crillon for the third time, and this time he summitted. Washburn and Charlie never climbed together again.

After stitching together a combination of train and boat segments to Prince Rupert, Juneau, Anchorage and, finally, McKinley Park, the group took a rough road to Wonder Lake. Here, they met their horse pack train with its local wranglers. Charlie learned that horse travel wasn't as easy as it appeared: the horses ran away every night, it took till midday to catch them, and by the time everything was packed up, departure times were late in the afternoon. As a result, they traveled until one or two each morning, set up camp, and then repeated the process. The terrain was rough, with muskeg, bogs, ravines, and deep, swift rivers to ford. The mosquitoes were formidable.

Finally arriving at the most likely valley leading to Foraker, the team bade a fond farewell to the horses and arranged for a pickup in six weeks. From here they climbed a small hill that they named Spyglass; found their stupendous mountain; and began the series of long marches up the valley, ferrying loads as they went. It was a five-day trek to the base of the mountain, where they established a camp next to a pristine glacial lake they named Tranquility.

From the Tranquility camp they moved up a long snow ridge, encountering the usual challenges: bergschrunds, deep snow, and precipitous ledges. Above the bergschrund they couldn't find a place large enough for their tent, so they proceeded to dig a snow cave for shelter—Charlie's first experience at caving. At this point the climbing became more technical, and Oscar reluctantly realized that he was not up to this level of difficulty. So, together with Carl Anderson and Charles Storey, Oscar descended, while the rest continued up. Oscar was disappointed in his own performance, but was pragmatic enough to accept the fact that others were more skilled and able than he. Charlie experienced some pangs of guilt as his father, the expedition's visionary and patron, headed down, but he too was pragmatic, and his eyes were fixed firmly on the summit.

The three remaining climbers' work was not over, though. They made two more trips with food and equipment, caching them high on the ridge. There they met a steepening rock section that turned out to be only moderately difficult. It led them to an immense plateau that took twelve hours to cross. They finally summitted in twilight, at eight in the evening in cold, murky weather. In fact, it was so murky they weren't sure they had reached the true summit. They returned to their camp by 3:00 AM and resolved to take a rest day and then head back up to what appeared to be a second, more difficult summit. But one rest day turned into three, as a huge storm blew in and pinned them down. The weather finally cleared and they reached that second—and lower, as it turned out—summit, descending all the way down to advance base camp in one day. There they joined Oscar, who had been doing his own exploration in the next valley. They continued together down to base camp.

It was August 23rd—only one day before their horse wrangler's promised return date. Despite all they had to do, there was time to enjoy themselves and revel in their accomplishment. Charlie tagged along behind Carl as he stalked a herd of caribou, watching the hunter carefully choose a young and healthy animal before dropping it with one shot. That evening, before heading home, they all enjoyed a feast of roasted caribou, along with two bottles of whiskey brought by the wrangler. They consumed it all with gusto, toasting both the success of the climb and young Charlie's twenty-first birthday. The jolly party ended with most of them stretched out in various stages of alcohol-induced sleep. During the night, there was a terrific clatter. Charlie was tossed off his air mattress, thinking in his stupefied state that he would never drink again if this was what one had to endure. At dawn it all became clear. At some point in the night there had been a large earthquake and much of the earth around them had shifted.

The Foraker expedition was a milestone: the team had climbed the fourth-highest mountain in the United States. In the midst of an economic depression, their triumph was embraced by a public hungry for new hopes and dreams. It made major ripples in the media, appearing in a large article on the front page of the New York Times and many other newspapers. Undoubtedly this newfound fame would help create some of the opportunities that were to come Charlie's way in the not-too-distant future; the confidence he gained on Foraker would serve as a platform for more ambitious mountaineering undertakings in ever greater mountain ranges. It was a pivotal moment for a young man hungry for his next climb.

BLESSED GODDESS

The game is more than the players of the game, and the ship is more than the crew.

—Bill Tilman

Back in New York, Charlie found the first weeks of medical school exhilarating. He was lost in a sea of students in short white coats with armloads of notebooks. Medical school in the 1930s concentrated on the principles of anatomy, physiology, and pathology, rather than preparing students to take care of the sick. Anatomy came as a shock. Charlie's first impressions were of "cadavers covered with gray cloth . . . stretched on stone tables in a great room, an overwhelming, hushing first sight." The students' first response was discomfort; these shriveled brown carcasses had once been thinking, living beings with emotions like theirs. The bodies and the room were redolent with formaldehyde, a smell that soon penetrated every pore and marked the first-year students wherever they went. "We stank, all the time," said Charlie.

Four students were assigned to each cadaver, two to a side: the origin, insertion, and function of every muscle was to be seen and felt and memorized. As the dissection advanced they memorized the nerve supply and circulation to each muscle. Occasionally a surgeon would visit them and explain just how important their understanding of anatomy was and how an injury or illness might affect the function of the muscles and joints, which for the moment they saw only as dead meat.

Each instructor had his own style. Horatio Williams, the neurology professor, taught by relating his own self-diagnosis. When Williams began experiencing some difficulty walking, his doctor initially thought that he had multiple sclerosis. Williams lived in the country, and one day while looking out the window he noticed his cat staggering across the lawn. She was as unsteady on her feet as he was. As a doctor, he knew that cats didn't contract multiple sclerosis, so he talked with his doctor, suggesting that there might be something affecting both him and his cat. After some research, he thought of lead poisoning. When he checked his blood levels, it turned out that he did indeed have a high level of lead, which had caused peripheral neuropathy, similar to multiple sclerosis. After more investigation, he found that the steel water tank from which he drew his water had a layer of sediment with a high concentration of lead. Once he was properly diagnosed, he began to slowly improve. Charlie remembered this story and eventually put it to good use with his own patients.

Pharmacology had little relevance to the world in which the students would later practice, for all they had to work with at the time of their training was quinine, morphine, digitalis, and a handful of other rudimentary drugs. They were expected to give their future patients what limited medication existed, but relied heavily on the premise that the effect of the healing hand would be greater than the actual medication. It was training in the best possible old-school style, based on caring and compassion.

What excited Charlie and the other students most was their introduction to patients, the very anticipation of which made the students nervous, shaky, and sweaty. They were instructed to introduce themselves politely and, above all, be professional, wear a clean white coat and tie, and take on a respectful manner as they engaged in a systematic inquiry into the patient's present and past history. Dr. Dana Atchley, a quiet, gray, worried-looking man with a loyal and distinguished patient following, painstakingly taught them that taking medical history was a highly evolved art form, one they must master. Atchley insisted that an intangible, intuitive exchange with a patient was the essence of healing. He certainly convinced Charlie: intelligent listening became Charlie's strongest talent and probably earned him more love and respect over the years than did any other skill.

One of Charlie's first efforts at taking a medical history came courtesy of a deaf patient afflicted with syphilis. Patient interviews in the eight-bed wards were done with privacy in mind, with curtains drawn around each bed. It was in one of these fully-occupied wards that Charlie had to conduct his "private" interview. The first questions shouted into the deaf patient's ear were innocent enough. But then he had to probe further about the disease: When had he noticed the first chancre? When had the skin rash appeared? How had he contracted that (unmentionable) illness? The questions were shouted; and the answers, muted. Both patient and medical student were embarrassed, and the other patients were treated to a brief yet amusing interlude in their mundane hospital day.

In addition to the systematic inquiry taught by Atchley, the students were trained in how to conduct a physical examination. Here too Charlie was blessed with a superb teacher, Dr. Robert Loeb. Unlike the quiet, meticulous Atchley, Loeb was dramatic, brilliantly intuitive, ruthless in exposing shoddy work, and unforgettable at the bedside. His directions were clear: "Seek and ye shall find; seek not and you won't find a damn thing." The two professors' consistently high standards profoundly influenced Charlie, and elements of their highly contrasting styles could later be glimpsed in his approach, not only in medicine, but in other aspects of his life. He often appeared to swing quickly and effortlessly between the showman and the introvert.

Despite his commitment to medicine, Charlie had not forgotten his passion for climbing. In fact it was a growing distraction, one that presented some difficult decisions and negotiations—and a delicate balancing act. Early in his medical studies, Charlie managed to convince the school authorities to make a very unusual decision—to allow him to write his exams before the other students and leave six weeks early in order to travel to India for a climbing expedition.

※

"It's hard to believe how naïve and presumptuous we were," Charlie recollected. "Four American college kids: Ad Carter, Art Emmons, Farnie Loomis and I [plus Charlie's father, Oscar], inviting the best British climbers to join us on a major climb in the Himalayas." Admittedly, they had all cut their teeth on climbs in the Alps and Alaska, but this new plan was on a different scale. By 1932, three Americans had penetrated eastern China and climbed the 24,790-foot Minya Konka. One of those three was Emmons, who had spent several painful months in Tatsienlu, now known as Kangding, where his frozen toes had been amputated. It was Emmons who first talked to Loomis and Carter, all Harvard friends of Charlie's who had been contemplating an Alaskan climb; instead, Emmons talked them into the Himalayas. The three then came to Charlie, and in late 1935 they began planning in earnest for the 28,169-foot Kangchenjunga—third-highest peak in the world and as yet unclimbed.

Since Charlie was in his first year of medical school and Carter was working on an Alaskan survey with Bradford Washburn, Emmons and Loomis bore the brunt of the planning work, though Charlie's role was critical—his job was to entice some of the best British climbers to join their team. It all hinged on T. Graham Brown of whom Charlie thought highly. "I found him good company and a strong climber—though fifty-three. He [Brown] caught the others [the Brits] and we became a wonderfully happy group," claimed Charlie. After getting carte blanche to recruit other British climbers, Brown naturally thought of people who had originally been considered for Everest in 1933, but who had been turned down: Bill Tilman, Noel Odell, and Peter Lloyd. And so was born that eclectic team of four American college kids and four British Himalayan veterans. Plus Oscar. Once again, Charlie's father had his sights on a big peak and he wanted to climb it with his son.

After the team was assembled, however, the British members gently discouraged Charlie from attempting Kangchenjunga, suggesting that "it might be a bit much for us." The Brits offered the beautiful Nanda Devi as an alternative, which Charlie took as a generous gesture on Tilman's part, since Nanda Devi was generally acknowledged as "their" (Tilman and Eric Shipton's) mountain. Often referred to as "Blessed Goddess," it was the highest mountain wholly within the British Empire.

Extremely remote, beautiful and difficult to access, the 25,645-foot Nanda Devi had already attracted considerable attention: exploratory expeditions in 1883, 1905, 1907, 1926, 1927, and 1932 brought such experienced explorers as Longstaff, Bruce, and Ruttledge. All were turned back by a forbidding wall that completely surrounded the peak. Above this wall rose yet another wall, which in turn defined an enclosed basin called the Sanctuary. Finally, in 1934, Tilman and Shipton managed to penetrate the formidable Rishi Gorge into the Sanctuary. The gorge itself was several thousand feet deep and formed an intimidating wall of steep and inhospitable cliffs. The elusive Sanctuary was a place of rare bucolic beauty, with rolling meadows of flowers, grass, and herds of sheep and goats.

Although the American youngsters knew nothing about Nanda Devi, they were excited—and a little intimidated—by the greats who had agreed to join them. Noel Odell was known for his extraordinary accomplishments on Everest in 1924, as well as his climbs in the United States while working as a professor at Harvard. Bill Tilman was already a legend not only for his climbing but for his extensive explorations. It was a powerful group. They promptly changed their name from the Harvard Kangchenjunga Expedition (HKE) to the British American Himalayan Expedition (BAHE).

Charlie was understandably concerned about the height of Nanda Devi, so in preparation he read as much as he could on the effects of altitude. As well, he contacted Dr. Ross McFarland, an altitude expert, and convinced him to take him up to a simulated altitude of 28,000 feet in a low-oxygen room. Charlie couldn't know it at the time, but this was the beginning of an interest that grew and developed far beyond the current expedition.

They assembled the best equipment they could find: light wool sweaters from Shetland, Grenfell cloth parkas with wolverine fur around the hoods, leather boots with Tricouni and hobnails from London. Their food included sun-dried fruits and vegetables from Massachusetts, cereals, meats, pemmican, and special treats. They agonized over every culinary detail, little suspecting what Tilman's reaction would be. All the logistics had to be organized months in advance, as there were no computers, fax, or email connections.

Separately, each member of the team made his way to India. On the boat trip over, Brown and Odell observed Charlie's father, Oscar; both came to the conclusion that he was not fit for the climb. While still on the boat, Odell had the cruelly unpleasant job of telling Oscar that he should not go into the Sanctuary because of the danger and the technical nature of the terrain. Charlie felt terrible. Oscar had paid Charlie's way and had brought the entire family over to India. "My father took it quietly but he never forgave Odell—he was clearly heartbroken." Yet again, Oscar had envisioned an ambitious alpine objective, only to be turned back from the actual climbing because of his physical limitations. It didn't diminish his chosen objectives, but it did place his judgment of his own physical capacity into question. Or perhaps it demonstrated that Oscar was motivated by his aspirations for Charlie rather than for himself.

When Charlie landed in Bombay, he described the experience as "pure Kipling!" Later, on subsequent travels to India, Charlie would come to reject this kind of colonial romanticism, but in 1936 Charlie's reaction was a typical one, intoxicating while it lasted. In the Taj Mahal Hotel, high ceiling fans rotated lazily, creating an illusion of coolness in the steaming heat. Turbaned barefoot servants in spotless, starched white uniforms sped about. "The white man was king; India his servant. British supremacy was so natural, we never dreamed we were seeing the last years of imperialism," Charlie recounted. Everywhere he went the British ruled, taking their supremacy for granted, "bumbling but kind, arrogant yet concerned, exploiting the endless wealth of India, yet curiously protective." Charlie accepted the British Raj and was blissfully unaware of the downsides of colonialism. What he failed to notice were the stirrings of independence, the work of a small yet passionate group whose efforts to free their country would see most of them eventually in jail. Charlie saw only Kipling's Raj: "Firm but benign, enlightened yet archaic, and above all, self-serving and paternalistic."

The seven members of the team converged on July 6 at the Forest Bungalow in Ranikhet, Garhwal (the eighth was on his way from Shanghai). The Brits and Americans were finally together. Charlie remembered the atmosphere: "We [the Americans] were all quite shy. I think they [the Brits] were uncertain as to what these puppies were up to. It was sniff, sniff, sniff." Charlie was initially somewhat intimidated by the wiry, focused, and powerful Tilman. Although Tilman exercised great economy in words and action, what he did was achieved with minimum effort and maximum impact—an impressive man. It was also the first time that Tilman glimpsed the food supplies organized by the Americans. Tilman was of the opinion that all tinned food tasted the same; likewise for cereals. Therefore, having an assortment was simply a waste of space. Charlie remembered that "with grunts and scowls he ruthlessly bagged and scrapped half of our treasured food; thus we could leave Ranikhet with six Sherpas and only thirty-seven Dhotial porters." Charlie protested a bit, particularly when some of his favorite luxuries got scrapped, but Tilman didn't bother to argue; he just continued to pillage the food stores. There was some idle speculation that the leader of this purge—Tilman—should also be scrapped, or at least bagged, but they grudgingly accepted his decision.

Despite the simplified rations, Charlie was extremely happy: "The march in was pure joy . . . leeches, rain, broken bridges, and leaking tins—nothing mattered when we were traveling the beautiful and romantic hills where our early heroes had climbed." They enjoyed breathtaking views from the 11,000-foot Kuari Pass, visited Badrinath, bathed in hot springs, and were tended by the Sherpas in the tradition of the British Raj: bed tea at dawn, again on the road an hour later, a civilized pause for lunch and tea, and camp by mid-afternoon. The Americans initially insisted on carrying their own packs, but the Brits knew better.

Charlie Houston's father, Oscar, as a young boy with his best friend, Johnny

Charlie Houston with his stuffed dog (1916). The dog was once lost in the Catskills and returned when his parents offered a reward.

Charlie Houston on his swan rocker (1915). He had this swan rocker for many years, and it served several other children.

Boat transport to the Honnedaga summer camp

*Charlie Houston in a sailor suit at age 7
(1920)*

*Charlie Houston and his sister Barbara
(1920)*

Charlie Houston's youngest sister Janet (1925)

Charlie Houston exploring a serac on the Mer de Glace in France (1925)

Charlie Houston with his long ice axe on the Mer de Glace (1925)

Charlie Houston lounging on the lawn at his home, the Hutch, in Long Island (1938)

Charlie Houston filming on the Mesizl Moraine, the Mer de Glace, France (1932)

Houston family dinner at the Hutch (1940)

Nellie Houston (Angel Bunny) at Honnedaga (1949)

Oscar Houston at Honnedaga (1949)

The Brits may have had some inside knowledge about tents as well. Charlie had arranged for the same McKinley tents that had proved very functional on his Alaskan trips. What he hadn't bargained for were leeches and driving rain. As the tents filled with water and blood-sucking insects, Charlie became the butt of merciless teasing from the Brits. "Were they equally good in snow? Was the rain in Alaska very dry?" they asked. Fortunately, the tents performed much better as they gained altitude.

It was on the journey to base camp that they began to know each other, walking by day and talking in the evening. T. Graham Brown, a physiology professor in Cardiff and a Mont Blanc fanatic, talked about the Alps, always with a pipe attached to the corner of his mouth. The "pups" talked about Alaska, trying to establish their turf—trying to impress the Brits. Tilman described these sessions in his book *The Ascent of Nanda Devi* with "that distant country Alaska, of which we had already heard more than a little." Tongue in cheek, Tilman recounted how, according to the Americans, Alaskan glaciers grew to ominous lengths, the trees grew branches of ice, the temperatures descended below recorded depths, the grizzlies were as large as elephants, and the mosquitoes were not much smaller! Odell turned out to be a wonderful companion—quiet, smiling, always cheerful, and rather slow. Charlie's memory of Odell prompted an amusing speculation: "He took a long time to get going in the morning . . . meticulous with his packing . . . always the last to get going . . . and of course that had happened on Everest when what's his name [Mallory] took Irvine instead of him . . . should have taken Odell . . . they might have done it."

In addition to enjoying the fascinating countryside, the eight men amused themselves by fantasizing about "the Great Game" being played out between Britain and Russia to determine who would control Central Asia. There were apparently a couple of dozen British officers who were attempting to infiltrate the Karakoram and up into the interior of what is now Tajikistan. Many of them were captured and killed. At the same time, Russia was sending similar spies into the south, trying to find the best route into India. It only added to the excitement.

When they reached the great Rishi Gorge, the Dhotial porters balked: the Rhamani River torrent was too strong and they didn't know how they would make the crossing on their return. Tilman rigged a spectacular and frightening rope pulley that worked—just. But the porters didn't trust it, and left, leaving the team with some tough decisions to make about their supplies. Tilman pragmatically took over. "Nothing but chemicals," he muttered as he culled the food supplies once again. Charlie was too much in awe of this strong, silent man to protest much. All agreed that Tilman's decision to eliminate food was prescient when, two days later, each team member sweated loads through the gorge. Charlie recalled it as a formidable place, where "the Rishi has carved a canyon in places 10,000 feet deep through the rim of mountains that encircle Nanda Devi; the walls are steep and slippery rock and grass, interrupted by cliffs." They made several carries each day through this treacherous terrain, finally cresting the rim for their first glimpse into the Sanctuary. There it was, Nanda Devi, towering in the center of a pastoral, rolling meadow. Relaying loads through the grass and flowers and up through the moraines, they finally reached their base camp on August 7.

Above them was 8,000 feet of mountain, so foreshortened they couldn't even begin to guess the route. For the next week they carried loads ever higher, stocking camps and fixing ropes as handrails in some places; mechanical ascenders such as Jumars were unknown at the time. The rock was precipitous and crumbling, interspersed with steep-sided snow ridges. By August 14th they were camped at 21,000 feet. An early casualty was a tin containing all the tea, which had been placed on a rock and slid off into oblivion. "It was life's blood to the Brits, though less so to us," said Charlie. Much more serious was the condition of one of their Sherpas, Kitar, who developed dysentery on the march in, and who remained in base camp for the rest of the expedition.

The methodology of their climb could be categorized as "modified siege tactics." They inched up the mountain, one camp after another. They were a small, vulnerable party, without radio and a long and difficult way from help. Complete self-sufficiency brought a level of conservatism not present in today's expeditions. For six weeks they made decisions by consensus. But it gradually became clear that when they were high on the mountain they would need a leader to make some tough decisions. So they held a secret ballot and Tilman was chosen—an obvious choice considering his experience. On August 21st, while huddled storm-bound in a tent, they asked him to choose two teams to go for the summit. Tilman proposed that Odell and Charlie be on the first team, with Lloyd and Loomis next. Yet Brown argued that he was the most fit, had the most experience, and should be the one to team up with Charlie for a summit attempt. At this time Brown was clearly suffering from oxygen deprivation—he had turned cyanotic and seemed confused to the other climbers—yet he kept insisting. But the decision had been given to Tilman, and Tilman chose Charlie and Odell.

The 25th dawned with crystal skies. Despite a lot of new snow, they all climbed to 24,000 feet, where Odell and Charlie were left to make a high camp. Charlie remembered the following events clearly: "The next day we two climbed steadily up the steepening face to a ridge. By early afternoon we were making slow progress, feeling the altitude in waist-deep snow. We continued to 25,000 feet where an easy snow slope led to a rock wall and the summit. The weather was perfect, the view magnificent and we were joyfully confident." But it was getting late and they decided to return to their bivouac; climbers did not climb at night in those days. Their plan was to move their camp a bit higher and to go for the summit the next day. They celebrated that night with some corned-beef hash. Charlie was preparing the meal and served Odell first, not noticing that the bottom of the tin had been punctured. As Charlie consumed the contents at the bottom of the tin, he was the most affected by what turned out to be severely contaminated meat. Two hours later he was violently ill, vomiting and wracked with diarrhea, crawling over Odell in order to get outside the tent. It was a long night for both of them.

The next day Odell managed to communicate with the others lower down the mountain that Charlie had a problem. Tilman recounted: "We were startled to hear Odell's familiar yodel, rather like the braying of an ass." Tilman and Carter understood Odell to be saying "Charlie is killed," so they immediately climbed up to where the two were. To their relief, Odell and Charlie were both alive, although Charlie was very ill. Odell had in fact yelled "Charlie is ill," causing confusion, particularly for Carter, who was accustomed to people becoming "sick" rather than "ill." Charlie was led down to the next camp, and Tilman replaced him up high. The next day, Tilman and Odell moved the camp 500 feet farther up. On August 29th they reached the summit; Tilman later wrote: "I believe we so far forgot ourselves as to shake hands on it." He felt badly for Charlie, referring to his illness as a "miserable turn of fortune for him, robbing him as it did of the summit."

In the meantime, Charlie and Brown's descent to base camp was a near disaster. "I was feeling pretty feeble and he was not thinking straight," Charlie recalled. One of them slipped, the other was pulled off—it was a near-fatal accident. Once they were safely back at base camp on August 31st, the air felt thick and rich, filled with all the smells missing at higher altitude. It was warm and dry and there was room to walk about without ropes. That night they ate fresh vegetables and new potatoes baked in a wood fire, smothered in real butter. "We were young, tough, strong; we had reached our goal, and we ate this simple fare and could have conquered the world," Charlie remembered.

But their rejoicing was severely dampened by the death, from dysentery, of Kitar. They buried him at base camp, with a service and a carved slab to honor him. Meanwhile, a runner carried a cable to the *London Times*: "Two reached summit August 29th," purposely vague as to who had made it to the top. The team was determined to not give out names. This was the highest mountain thus far to be climbed in the world, and the public interest was enormous.

Tilman and Charlie, along with Pasang Kikuli, decided to leave the Sanctuary via Longstaff Col to the east, while the others returned the way they had entered. They awoke on the morning of September 2nd to cold, driving rain. Breaking camp was a grim affair. The porters departed and Charlie, Pasang, and Tilman were left to have one last meal. They kicked the dying embers of the fire and finally hoisted their heavy packs. "To me there is always something very final, terribly final, about breaking camp, especially in the mountains. It is as though you were cutting off one more piece of home and security and further advancing to something quite unknown," Charlie explained.

The journey that followed was challenging: even Tilman described it as "a little dicey in places." In horribly cold rain that finally turned to wet snow, they slithered and clawed their way up and over the moraines. As they ascended they began to struggle with a deep, wet snowpack that had them floundering up to their waists. The second day was no better, with more soggy snow on even steeper terrain. As they labored higher the view improved—and the avalanche hazard increased. Finally they reached the top of the pass at 19,000 feet. The clouds immediately moved in, obscuring their views. With only a crude map of the area, they descended quickly, desperately looking for a decent place to camp.

The next day they walked down the valley, moving from glacier to moraine to gravel, and finally to grass and flowers and life. Tilman selected one side of the riverbank to walk down while Charlie and Pasang chose the other. Charlie and Pasang chose wrong. At the end of the day, Tilman sauntered into the village of Martoli, where he was soon joined by the villagers in laughing and eating. Meanwhile, Charlie and Pasang clung precariously to the cliffs on the wrong side of the gorge. After a miserable night by the raging torrent, they were rescued by local shepherds, who brought them back across to Martoli on a rickety bridge. Here they were greeted by Tilman and the villagers with large mugs of villainous Tibetan beer. That day a band of Tibetan traders arrived in town. Included in the group was a girl who entertained them enthusiastically with her dancing. Much of her gyrating was directed at the terribly embarrassed Charlie, who later realized it was his sweater—not him—that was the main attraction! The villagers rolled about in gales of laughter as Charlie disentangled himself. "Finally, stuffed with *chapattis,* dizzy with *chang,* we escaped from this village and stumbled down to the main road."

Tilman described the entire experience in words that resonated for Charlie, and many future international teams of climbers: "It was but a short three months that we had met, many of us as strangers, but inspired by a single hope and bound by common purpose. This purpose was only achieved by teamwork, team-work the more remarkable on account of the two different nationalities . . . the Americans and ourselves do not always see eye to eye, but on those rare occasions when we come together to do a job of work, as, for example, in war or the more serious matter of climbing a mountain, we seem to pull together very well. Where each man pulled his weight each must share the credit; for, though it is natural for each man to have his own aspirations, it is in mountaineering, more than in most things, that we try to believe, 'The game is more than the players of the game, and the ship is more than the crew.'"[2]

By September 12th they reached Ranikhet, just in time for Charlie to take the train to Delhi and catch the twice-weekly flight to Europe and the boat home, arriving only slightly late for medical school.[3]

Upon his return to medical school, Charlie had some catching up to do with his studies. In fact, it's doubtful he ever completely caught up. But he struggled hard, not only with the medical studies but also with the distraction of fantastic memories of his summer adventure in India. He did finally settle down, moving on to hematology, histology, embryology, and the other coursework.

The years of basic science thankfully passed, and the clinical years commenced. It was what Charlie and the other students longed for. They began to meet more patients, slowly mastered their inhibitions, and learned how to examine naked bodies without embarrassment. For Charlie, the most traumatic, fascinating, and intoxicating subject was obstetrics. The obstetrics "rotation" required that four or five students live in a dormitory off the obstetrics wing to be on call twenty-four hours a day for what seemed like weeks. They worked, ate, and slept in their white scrub suits, snatching whatever sleep they could. Night and day were indistinguishable, although it seemed that the deliveries always came at night. They were expected to calm the women, some of whom screamed for hours before delivery, and others remained eerily quiet in their terror. It was Charlie's first serious introduction to the female anatomy and to the intimacies of what happened after what was still for him the mystery of intercourse. It resonated profoundly for him: "It was the first real step to the sanctuary of medicine, more dramatic, more dangerous and more revealing than any other experience. It seemed the gateway to real life."

In contrast, psychiatry seemed completely useless to the young medical student, possibly due to inept teaching methods. In one class, patients were marched out onto a platform to demonstrate schizophrenia and manic depression. Although the patients were blissfully unaware of the attention, the students squirmed uncomfortably. The classification of psychoses and neuroses was medieval; treatment was pitifully feeble. Charlie's assigned psychiatric patient was a young girl obsessed with the idea that her nose was growing ever longer and longer. He dreaded visiting her in the locked ward and felt he had absolutely nothing to offer her. Shock therapy was used, as psychotropic drugs were still a thing of the future and psychosurgery was experimental. Charlie felt that he had neither the sensitivity nor the intellectual depth to understand the subtleties of psychiatry.

For most of his fellow students, surgery was where they wanted to focus their attention. Students were allowed to "hold hooks" or be second assistants in the operating room for minor operations, although they were frequently scolded or cursed by the surgeon. Charlie, along with the others, quickly learned which surgeons were competent and which were "phony solicitude masking incompetence." He felt there was too much concentration on "fixing" things: removing a diseased organ or readjusting an abnormal function manually, rather than the softer, caring, compassionate bedside approach taught by Atchley.

To learn about infectious diseases, they were taken to nearby hospitals to observe measles, scarlet fever, chicken pox, diphtheria, typhoid, and paratyphoid fever, all extremely dangerous afflictions at this time before antibiotics and vaccines had been developed. Seeing the actual pathology left indelible impressions, invaluable later in his career. For tuberculosis, they were taken to Seaview Hospital, a sanitarium forty minutes away. Dr. Loeb carefully taught them every aspect of a careful chest examination. Modern medicine would see the addition of X-rays and, eventually, MRIs to this type of physical examination.

Charlie then had his first exposure to the famous Bellevue Hospital—the shabby, ancient, crowded home for the destitute sick, where some of the most distinguished doctors practiced. It was a prized internship and an invaluable training ground. For Charlie, and many of the other students, it was their first exposure to the hopeless poor. The majority of patients at that time were Irish or Italian, with a scattering of Chinese. Despite the anguish of the diseases, Charlie was surprised that Bellevue somehow remained an island of optimism.

For one afternoon each week they rotated through out-patient clinics where they saw patients with skin problems, asthma, emotional stress, and gynecological complaints. One clinic, thinly disguised as "dermatology," treated patients with long-standing syphilis. Many of the patients had tabes dorsalis, a neurological condition brought on in the late stages of that disease (or as a result of dementia or heart disease), and the prime learning experience for the students was how to do a spinal puncture, commonly called spinal tap. By frequent "tapping," progress of the disease could be measured. The spinal fluid was tested using the colloidal gold curve, protein and cell count and Wasserman, medical processes that could track the progression of the disease in the central nervous system and in the brain. The disease was treated by an alternating schedule of bismuth and arsenic injections, painful intramuscular shots usually given weekly. There was no mention of gonorrhea, and sexual practices—as a cause—were not explored. Rheumatic fever was also quite common at the time, and without antibiotics available the results were devastating—usually permanent heart damage.

The days of training were the best days— exciting, exhausting, frightening, but intoxicating. There was so much to learn. Although much of the detail that they learned was irrelevant to future patient care, the discipline, the methodology, and the experience with patients was crucial to their future. Above all, it was an intensely rewarding time for Charlie. There was only one problem: something was missing after Nanda Devi. Charlie had tasted the excitement of the great ranges—and success. He desperately longed for more.

FIVE MILES HIGH

In true mountaineering, the summit is not everything; it is only part.
—Charles Houston

An eager Charlie had but a short wait for his next chance at a major expedition. In 1937, the American Alpine Club obtained permission to attempt K2, the most remote of the great mountains and the second highest in the world. K2 had seen several previous attempts, the most determined of which were by the Italians. But now it was the Americans' turn. Initially the American Alpine Club wanted Fritz Wiessner, arguably the country's leading climber, to lead the expedition. When Wiessner declined, Charlie was asked to take his place. This was intended to be a reconnaissance climb in preparation for Wiessner's serious attempt to follow in 1939. Though Wiessner ostensibly stepped down because of business commitments, privately Charlie wondered if he was increasing his odds for success in 1939 by declining the 1938 climb. Charlie was not alone in those thoughts. Still, this was heady stuff. K2, second only to Everest in elevation, virtually untouched—"beyond the passes," as Kipling had written. Although it was clearly a reconnaissance attempt, Charlie admitted: "Secretly, however, each of us hoped that ours would be the group that reached the summit."

His experience gained on Nanda Devi made the planning easier, except for the personnel. Because none of Charlie's Nanda Devi companions were able to join him, the recruiting process became somewhat frustrating. After the third potential teammate begged out because he had committed to Wiessner for the following year, Charlie lost his patience. In a letter to Bates, he confided: "Wiessner has asked him to go next year and Bill [House] thinks that would fit in better with his career. Bill makes number three that is not coming with us because Wiessner has extended hope of next year to him. I am so damn mad at Wiessner I have been aching to write him a fiery letter all day, but hope to restrain myself."

The first to sign up for Charlie's reconnaissance expedition was his good friend Bob Bates, despite some feeble protests about having to postpone the completion of his Ph.D. studies. Next was Dick Burdsall, summiter on Minya Konka. And finally, having convinced his boss to grant him a leave of absence, there was Bill House. Then came Paul Petzoldt from the Tetons, a well-known guide and a good friend of Farnie Loomis. The British government arranged for a transport officer named Captain Norman Streatfield, a veteran of the harsh, romantic northwest frontier of India. Charlie's Alaskan climbing companion Bradford Washburn was not invited, perhaps to avoid a potential clash of wills. It was a small group, and some suggested that it was too small and weak for such a great challenge. The team simply ignored the naysayers.

Possibly the most interesting—and potentially explosive—member of the team was Petzoldt. Almost from the start there was tension between Petzoldt and the rest because of his comparative lack of money. In Bates's words, "Paul was always trying to scam money and Paul thought Charlie had a lot of it, so he was a natural target." It was understood that Petzoldt's way was being paid by the others—in fact it was paid by Farnie Loomis—but Petzoldt expressed disappointment that he wasn't being paid an additional fee to be there: "I probably thought at the time, Jesus, these guys are getting a helluva good guide for nothing!" In fact, Petzoldt's favorite description of Bates and Charlie was that of "two Eastern nabobs" clearly in need of a guide. The rest of the team did not see Petzoldt as their guide.

Another point of tension was style. Petzoldt was dismayed to learn that the team planned to attempt K2 without any climbing hardware: no pitons, hammers, carabiners, or pickets. Petzoldt disagreed, and did something about it. He scrounged together what little money he had, and while in Paris purchased a selection of hardware that he thought would give them at least a fighting chance on K2. The pitons remained a point of debate between the two, as Charlie alternately referred to them as "iron ware" and a "cog railway." Charlie's style was austere, heavily influenced by the traditional Brits, though he would eventually acknowledge the usefulness of the hardware in protecting the climb, particularly high on the mountain.

The difficulties between Petzoldt and Charlie weren't only about style and money; they may also have stemmed from a difference in social standing. Although Charlie admired Petzoldt as a climber and found him to be a superb companion on the mountain, Petzoldt's first wife, Patricia Bernice Petzoldt, later reported that he felt he had not been treated as an equal by the "Eastern elitists." Just before leaving for Asia, Petzoldt had apparently discovered a memo in the American Alpine Club files in New York questioning whether this "Wyoming packer and guide" would conduct himself in a socially acceptable manner, particularly as the team was planning to visit with the British and French alpine clubs. Charlie himself had once referred to Petzoldt as "a blue collar guide."

Charlie and his team combined planning techniques from their Alaskan climbs with the Spartan approach taught by Tilman. Bates and Charlie put together the food; Burdsall researched what scanty information he could from existing maps and literature and acted as expedition treasurer. Using a highly scientific approach, Bates and Charlie dropped biscuits from second-story windows and left them out in the rain in their effort to find the perfect one: a biscuit that would travel well and not absorb too much moisture. They searched out woolens in the Shetland Islands and windproof suits and lightweight sleeping bags from London. The trip was budgeted at $9,000, and generous donors provided the funds. Charlie's medical-school exams delayed his departure, so he left later to meet up with the rest of the climbers on May 9th.

Charlie landed in Karachi and boarded a train to cross the Sind desert in order to meet the team in Rawalpindi. There he disappeared into the alluring smells and sights and sounds of the bazaars, inhaling the acrid smoke of burning dung and the pungent aroma of Indian tobacco. He wandered among the booths displaying sweets, coconuts, fruits, vegetables, and cheap Western goods. He was joined by ambling cows, munching at will from what the food stalls had to offer. Flies were everywhere. Beggars, brightly sari-clad women, half-naked *saddhus,* and men in long-tailed white shirts thronged the narrow alleys. Everywhere people jostled, gesticulated, shouted, and cried out strange atonal sounds to advertise their wares. Charlie was dazed by the romance of it all and, once again, was reminded of Kipling: "I was *Kim* . . . I was living in Kipling's India; indeed I was on my way to the very land described in *The Man Who Would Be King.*"

Then it was on to Srinagar, where a massive packing job awaited them for the next stage of the journey. The description in Bates's and Charlie's post-expedition book, *Five Miles High,* illuminates the prevailing cultural attitude: " . . . we stowed the Sherpas in two lorries crammed with crates and bundles, arranged ourselves more expansively in two cars, and began the 180-mile drive to the Vale of Kashmir." [4] After three entertaining days in Srinagar, they took trucks to road's end, where, together with six Sherpas, a cook, and a cook's helper, they loaded twenty-five ponies for the long walk in. Before leaving Srinagar, Charlie received one last letter from his parents that elicited this emotional response from him: "You can't realize how very much I love you. If any one could have better parents, I don't see how, for you both are more than I deserve." But he was also eager for what lay ahead of him: high passes and entry into Central Asia, where no more than a hundred Westerners had ever traveled. He was twenty-five years old; he was strong and motivated; the world lay before him.

The 350-mile approach march took thirty-one days through hot, dry, spectacular country. It was tremendously exciting for all of them, traveling through this wild and little-known region. The scale was difficult to comprehend at first, and it was obvious that invasions and warfare were an ongoing fact of life here. First they climbed over the snow-covered Zoji-La Pass into Baltistan, past a white marble-like rock carved with the initials "H.H.G-A, 1861-2-3." This was the spot where Henry Godwin-Austen had allegedly passed.

Along the way they used the horses, not just for packing loads, but also for riding. Charlie admitted in a letter to his parents that he quite enjoyed riding; it gave his blisters a chance to heal and offered a much better view of the country. On the ninth day of their march, as they followed the mighty, muddy Indus a thousand feet above the torrent, one of the ponies slipped on the trail and plunged into the river, taking all of the cook's bedding with it. Luckily, the animal and the gear were eventually saved. Occasionally they were surprised by lush, green oases perched in this vertical desert, the results of generations of hand-dug irrigation ditches. The climbers were regarded as curiosities, but welcomed as friends. In addition to the tiring, satisfying, long day's travel, they enjoyed polo where the game had originated, dances, and dinners. Each day they knew each other better, as they dreamed and planned together: "We were inspired by a single hope and bound by a single purpose." The team appeared to be getting along well. In a letter sent to his family, Charlie exuded praise: "Petzoldt has turned out to be a gem, House is extremely good, and Bates and

Burdsall you know already. Stratified [sic] has turned out far better than we hoped: he is very keen and full of energy."

This journey was in sharp contrast to the much shorter march into Nanda Devi in the Garhwal, where the constant rain created lush forests, towering trees, large streams, and acres of flowers. In contrast, Baltistan was dry, predominantly sand and rock, with towering ocher cliffs. Flowers were rare, and water even rarer. Where the Garhwal had been soft and seductive, inviting rather than threatening, Baltistan was hard and wild.

Although the travel was strenuous, they enjoyed luxurious treatment at each camp. Upon arrival at a suitable camping site, each climber would "plant" his ice ax on his preferred tent spot and then retire to a shady nook to await the arrival of the coolies, who would erect the tents. "It was really Millionaires' Row in expeditioning," Charlie recalled in *Five Miles High*. They were often the recipient of massive bouquets of domestic flowers from the locals, who would then lobby the expedition coolies for the privilege of assisting with the tents. And so it continued: blowing up the air mattresses, laying out the sleeping bags, arranging their private things, even taking off their boots. Even in the relatively privileged backgrounds of the climbers, such devoted attention and luxury seemed almost excessive.

On May 25th they reached Skardu. At a dinner one night with the Tehsildar, the governor of the province, the conversation turned to geology, a particular interest of Bill House's. House commented on the irrigation ditches they had observed that day, and wondered aloud what happened when they ran dry. The Tehsildar told the team that the ditches were fed by glacial melt; when a glacier dried up, they simply "manufactured" a new one. This was done by dispatching villagers to two other glaciers—one male and one female, where they would carve off large blocks of ice, deposit them in a suitable location for a replacement glacier, cover them with charcoal, thorns, and hides—and wait. Within no time (actually twenty years or more) a new glacier would emerge.

They finally reached Askole, a mere huddle of poor stone huts. Despite the poverty, they were greeted warmly with offers of delicious apricot pits, eaten like almonds. Here they found men who were eager to help them on the next leg of the journey, but caught only rare glimpses of the mysterious Muslim women with their pale faces and Grecian noses, draped with Greek coin jewelry. They felt as though they had entered a place with a deep and unfathomable past.

Then disaster hit: Petzoldt, their biggest, toughest team member, became delirious with high fever and crippling back pain. After two days of observation and attempted treatment, Charlie, who was still a medical student, admitted he had no idea what the problem was. Finally they agreed that Petzoldt was too ill to travel and that Charlie should remain behind with him. On June 5th the rest of the team headed off. Charlie walked along beside them for a mile or so, and then returned to his duties with Petzoldt. The memory was painful: "If Paul recovered we would try to catch up with them; if he died—well, I would bury him and hurry on to them." In a letter to his parents, Charlie admitted he wasn't sure he would see the others again. Much later, Charlie concluded that the symptoms almost certainly indicated dengue fever.

In addition to administering to Petzoldt, Charlie became swamped with medical requests, healing as best he could the sick who appeared from miles around. "I've seen a baby who doesn't eat, but vomits 9-inch worms, a man with a broken back, another with terrible callous growths on his hand, another with ringworm, others with ringing in their ears, trachoma, stomach ache, vomiting blood, epilepsy, fever . . . " he wrote home. To some of these patients he offered good solid treatment, but to others simply placebos. Nevertheless, as the only physician he had no idle moments.

Petzoldt slowly improved and, though he was very weak, he and Charlie finally left Askole and caught up with the others. His temperature had reached 105 but he had survived the crisis, giving Charlie at least some of the credit in a letter to the American Alpine Club: "I feel very lucky that Charlie was able to pull me through so quickly." His greeting to the other climbers was more to the point: "Charlie fixed me up. How's the food holding out?" Together as a team now, they reached the huge Baltoro Glacier, initially unimpressive and ugly, but soon its magic was revealed: "Like imagined castles, cathedrals and towers, separated by valleys of ice, the beautiful granite stood many thousands of feet above our heads. We were in the land of Giants. Rounding the corner at Concordia, the vast amphitheatre where half a dozen glaciers meet, we saw our beautifully symmetrical pyramid, towering two miles above its base and awesome even twenty miles away." They set up camp and paid off their porters, using an ingenious system to arrange for their return. They simply gave the leader forty-five stones and told him to throw one away each day and come back when they were all gone.

With six weeks ahead of them their assignment was overwhelming: examine the mountain and find a route for the 1939 team. It was an intimidating place. In his letter home, Charlie wrote: "The mountain looks grand, grand but pretty damn high—12,000 feet above camp!" The broken cliffs and jagged icefalls above the base camp, continuously showered with avalanches, were unthinkable as a route. Farther to the east the face fell in a steep, unbroken avalanche slope 10,000 feet to the glacier. Twice they went west, taking several days to cross a dangerously crevassed glacier, climbing to 22,000 feet on the Savoia Pass, only to be turned back by steep, green ice. Two other pairs of climbers went five miles east toward Windy Gap, attempting a route on the Northeast Ridge. But after reaching 22,000 feet, they too turned back.

By June 27th they were discouraged, having examined all the routes they thought feasible at that time. In a letter home Charlie admitted: "I must tell you that this is a bigger, harder mountain than any of us realized before—and it will take a better party than ours a much longer time than we have left, in order to get anywhere at all."

Despite the worry and disappointments of not finding an obvious route, the team performed as well as they could. Charlie relied on Bates as his "main aid and counsel," although admitting that he was "not too strong on hard climbing." Bates, for his part, had complete confidence in Charlie as a leader, feeling that he was fair and caring. Petzoldt was turning out to be a fine climber and route finder, although he had some troubles with acclimatization, needing several days of rest at base camp before moving high on the mountain. Streatfield was great in camp as a worker and a companion, although also not a strong climber. And Dick was "the most patient, long suffering and willing man of all," Charlie enthused, although pointing out that he, too, was not a strong climber.

The biggest disappointment was House. In his letter home Charlie pointed out: "[House] is continually complaining about the lack of food, and demands much more than we are able to provide. He is a very fine climber, but his choice of routes is poor and he takes far too many chances. In addition, he has frequent depressed spells during which he is very bad company." Years later, Charlie wondered if House had been suffering throughout the expedition with various stages of altitude sickness. Despite the problems with House, Charlie knew that his skills were instrumental in overcoming one of the cruxes of the climb, what came to be known as "House's Chimney"— a vertical crack in a great cliff, about 150 feet high, up which it was necessary to wriggle.

After summing up the situation with his group, Charlie was forced to admit that "we have a very weak party for so big a job." But he added: "There are many redeeming features—the chief of which is that we realize our weakness and pull together very well." Throughout it all, Charlie refused to take credit as the leader, referring to himself simply as the organizer.

They decided that the East Ridge, explored by the Italian Duke of Abruzzi thirty years earlier, offered the most promise. They dubbed it the Abruzzi Ridge. For the next twenty-five days, they struggled up to the final summit pyramid. As each party found a suitable campsite, others packed loads to stock each of the seven camps with fuel and food. They leapfrogged up the mountain, enduring severe blizzards interspersed with unbearably beautiful days of bright sun and the infinitely dark sky seen only at altitude. At the top of the Black Pyramid, Charlie and Petzoldt stopped a moment to enjoy the view. "After a restful cigarette, which seemed especially welcome at these high altitudes, we turned again to our task."

His memories of the upper reaches of the mountain were precise: "These were wondrous days with moments of incredible beauty, hours of fatigue, and seconds of panic when stones whirred like shells about us." The route was unceasingly steep, becoming more difficult and dangerous as they went higher. They had little rope to fix, only a few pitons, and mechanical ascenders were still unknown. Finally, with the party completely intact and still strong and motivated, July 20th found Petzoldt and Charlie established in Camp VII on the lower edge of the great snow shoulder. The rest of the team returned to lower camps to wait their turn at a summit attempt. It was then that they realized a horrible mistake: the match supply had remained at Camp VI. Charlie and Petzoldt had a total of nine matches. That night they used three. The next morning, three more. Only three remained.

"We climbed steeply, then across a gentle slope to the foot of the final barrier—1,500 feet of rock and ice cliffs. I could go no farther; Petzoldt was a bit stronger, but the summit was beyond us then," Charlie recalled. Exhaustion had descended upon him. He stopped for about fifteen minutes, struggling with his racing pulse and his overwhelming emotions of regret and relief. "I believe in those minutes at 26,000 feet on K2, I reached depths of feeling I can never reach again," he wrote. Petzoldt climbed down to him and they returned to their camp. Two more futile attempts with matches and finally, with the last one, they lit their stove, melted water, cooked a meal and went to bed. Without matches they knew they had to go down; without matches they could not melt water—the critical element to remaining high. And so they descended, with the intention of having another team take their place.

The weather thickened, and very aware of the climbing difficulties still below them, they were not ready to temp fate further. By July 25th they were all safely back at base camp. Then the weather improved, causing a point of disagreement between Charlie and Petzoldt. The latter subsequently maintained that weather was never a factor in their decision to descend. Their cable, sent from Skardu on August 3rd said simply: "EVERY ONE WELL SPLENDID TRIP REACHED TWENTYSIX THOUSAND FEET REACH SRINIGAR SIX DAYS CHARLES."

Charlie's task had been to find a feasible route for the 1939 expedition; nobody had expected them to get that high. Charlie summed it up: "We just kept going until we ran out of matches."

They reached Skardu over the Skor La and climbed to the flower-strewn meadows of the great Deosai plateau. With great sadness, they sat and gazed down at Kashmir in the distance: their journey's end. In the following years, Charlie and Bates reminisced many times, speculating what it would have been like if they had reached the summit. Charlie remained convinced that his life would not have changed much, other than delaying by a couple of years his entry into medicine: "It would not have created an enormous stir because back in 1938 the Himalayas were not such a big goal . . . it would not have made a Hillary of us." Besides, in 1938 there were other world events brewing that would soon take center stage—events that would lead to war.

Perhaps because he was stronger high on the mountain, Petzoldt thought that if they could have pushed a bit harder, they might have summited. But Charlie insisted they had done the right thing; they had quit as it became dusk. "You didn't go climb at night in '38—not on that kind of mountain," he said. There was occasional criticism of the team for not having made that final all-out attempt on the summit. In modern times, they quite likely would have done so. But Charlie expressed the view of most of the team when he said: "We lived to climb again, for many years. In true mountaineering, the summit is not everything; it is only part." Years later, at Telluride's mountain film festival, on a panel with several American K2 climbers chaired by K2 summiter Rick Ridgeway, Petzoldt brought it up again. He said that he had been opposed to the decision to go down, and that the decision had been taken because Charlie wasn't feeling well. Ridgeway looked over at Charlie and raised his eyebrows. Charlie said nothing. He was hurt and angry, but he didn't respond.

When the team reached Kashmir, a surprise awaited them: the Germans were there, fresh from their unsuccessful Nanga Parbat expedition. They appeared to be "swaggering" a bit, although they tempered their gait somewhat when they learned what the Americans had accomplished. Determined to impress, the Germans threw a cocktail party for the less-experienced, naïve Americans and proceeded to get them "drunk as skunks," Charlie recalled. Not to be outdone, the Americans decided to host their own event on their houseboat. Yet because the entire team had just received a series of medical injections for their ongoing travels, they were unable to drink alcohol for forty-eight hours. Bill House solved their dilemma with Planter's Punch for the Germans and iced tea for the Americans. Charlie recalled the event with glee: "It was a very successful party. Some of the Germans even fell off the houseboat. Paul Bauer said he couldn't remember a thing!" The young Americans savored their revenge.

The trouble with Petzoldt was not over, for though they separated after the expedition, an incident occurred that would forever dampen any friendship between the two. Petzoldt decided to stay on in India, where his curiosity about Indian mysticism led him to an ashram in Kashmir. An elderly American doctor named Dr. Barker invited Petzoldt to visit the community, and Petzoldt quickly settled in as his assistant, even helping him on a few surgeries. Shortly after, Petzoldt was joined by his first wife and things quickly began to deteriorate. Unlike her husband, she was openly skeptical about the beliefs and traditions of the ashram, the inevitable friction becoming most evident with Dr. Barker's wife. One evening Petzoldt himself made a derogatory comment, causing an uproar that ended in a wrestling match between Petzoldt and one of the ashram followers as they struggled for control of a shotgun. The Indian threw the gun out of the window and ran out. Petzoldt followed and unexpectedly ran into Barker, who was just entering the room. Barker grabbed Petzoldt, who threw him aside and ran out without looking back. The doctor fell to the ground, hit his head, and subsequently died. Petzoldt was initially charged with manslaughter but was eventually acquitted. Regardless, an English intelligence officer recommended that the couple leave the country immediately. Back in the United States, Charlie received an urgent cable from the Consul General requesting money. Together with his father, he quietly made the necessary arrangements for Petzoldt to return. Charlie never completely forgave Petzoldt for not thanking his family for helping him out in this moment of need. Petzoldt claimed ignorance on the source of the money, but the friendship subsequently withered, even though they managed to put aside their differences later in order to work together on the expedition book.[5] It was yet another example of the gulf that separated Petzoldt and Charlie.

As it turned out, the attempt on K2 was only part of a much bigger adventure. Charlie and the rest of his team, excluding Petzoldt, decided to take a slight detour on their way home, through Afghanistan and Persia. They each had about $175 for the journey, which they thought would take about five weeks. Their itinerary took them from Peshawar to Kabul to Teheran, then on to Baghdad and Damascus and finally Europe.

Their entry into Kabul on August 22nd was in the company of three unwanted officials who had attached themselves to the travelers: one was a man who insisted on inspecting their luggage; the second wanted their passports; and the third demanded a tax for no explainable reason. When Charlie and company refused to cooperate, all three piled in on top of the luggage. They escorted them into Kabul and ultimately succeeded in walking away with the money they had initially demanded.

After exploring the city, the Americans arranged to leave Kabul in a regular mail lorry packed with humanity and freight, as would be almost all their conveyances in the weeks to come. The rough roads resulted in frequent repair stops, where Charlie would take the opportunity to throw out his sleeping bag on the sand, catching an hour or two of badly needed sleep. Strangely, the rough, rutted dirt roads changed dramatically whenever they arrived at rivers, as the Germans had recently built modern, three-lane steel bridges across many of them—an omen of the impending war.

And so they progressed, through Ghazni, Kalat, Gereshk, Farah, Sabzawar, and Herat. The scenery was grand: vast, dry expanses, rugged hills, and spectacular sunsets. Perhaps it seemed grander because of the perpetual emptiness in the pit of Charlie's stomach. His diet throughout the weeks consisted primarily of melons, grapes, and tea. On very lucky occasions, he managed to find a rice pilaf in some unlikely village.

Eventually they reached the no-man's land between Afghanistan and Iran, then Mashhad, Tehran, Khanaqin, and Kirkuk, where they took a train to Istanbul. When Charlie finally arrived in London, his clothes were in rags, his shrunken stomach was a fraction of its former size, and he was desperately short on sleep. But what remained were a multitude of impressions, mannerisms, customs, and visions of the mysterious lands through which he had traveled.

Upon their return to the United States, House, Petzoldt, and Bates joined Charlie at Honnedaga to begin work on their account of the expedition, published under Bates's and Charlie's names as *Five Miles High*. It was a time of reminiscence, collaboration, and sometimes frustration, as they each had their own creative style—and their own version of what had actually happened on the climb. Charlie insisted that they share authorship because, in his opinion, the trip had had no real leader: they had shared a true sense of democracy.

The 1938 expedition would prove, in many ways, the greatest of Charlie's life. He had embarked on an adventure as bold as one could imagine—the equivalent of a moon launch for that time. The fact that they had failed to summit K2 didn't appear to ruin the expedition for Charlie. "We had thoroughly scouted this magnificent mountain, found a reasonably safe, though difficult (for the times) route and had come amazingly close to summiting." History too would color the unforgettable trip that followed K2, through an unknown and unspoiled Afghanistan. For the world was crumbling, and would, in fact, never again be the same.

On his long overland voyage back from India, Charlie began to be aware of Hitler's plans to conquer the Middle East and Asia. Traveling home through the Balkans and Italy by train that September, Charlie sensed the fear and paranoia sweeping Europe. But despite this exposure, he never suspected that his own country would be caught up in the firestorm. Throughout 1939, he, like many of his countrymen, thought Hitler an unimportant blowhard and accepted Chamberlain's "Peace in our Time" declaration of September 1938. When war burst out the next fall Charlie was so fully immersed in the hospital that he thought of little else. Like many in the West, he slept through the gathering storm.

SOUTHERN BELLE

How beautiful this would be if I could only share it with someone.
—French artist Samivel's caption for a
lone person viewing a sunset

With the dramatic K2 expedition and medical school behind him, Charlie began a two-year internship. Interns lived in the hospital, each with a small room, sharing a hallway and bath with someone in an adjoining bedroom. They ate in the staff dining room. Their meal tickets were provided, as were their white uniforms and laundry. They earned the princely sum of $6 a month for what Charlie recalled was a "wonderful romantic life." They were on duty days, except every second Sunday, and were on call every second night. Charlie felt that internship was like being in the service of a great church. He cherished the single-mindedness of those years. "Our whole lives and energy and mind and emotion were given to caring for the sick, to learning our profession, polishing skills."

For the first six months, interns were responsible for much of the laboratory work done on their wards: drawing blood, running urine and stool analyses, and taking blood counts and sedimentation rates. Rounds were made at ten every morning by the attending physician and a senior professor. Charlie remembered these as serious rituals. The house officers, head nurse, and students stood nervously in the proper pecking order, focused on the attending physician in his long white coat.

Charlie's first independent diagnosis was made while assisting George Perera, one of the attending physicians. A sailor had been admitted with a dangerously high fever, but nothing diagnostic was found from his history or the physical examination. Charlie then ran urine and blood tests and thought he noticed something strange in a few of the red blood cells. This was achieved by a tricky process known as "pulling" a slide: blood had to be drawn between two paper-thin cover slips that, at an exact moment, were quickly pulled apart. If done correctly, a thin film of blood covered each slide and a clear picture of red and white blood cells could be seen.

After carefully examining the sailor's slides, Charlie recognized what he was looking at: malaria. He rushed to Perera with his conclusion, and Perera agreed. This was his first case of many where sailors brought malaria back from the tropics. It had now become impossible to completely ignore the war, even though it still seemed worlds away.

Pneumonia cases also provided the interns with opportunities to practice a dramatic and sometimes life-saving lab test. The patients always seemed to be admitted at night, and Charlie loved to describe the process, now so archaic that many doctors have never even heard of it: "Half asleep, I would be handed a sputum cup with some nasty stuff in it and told to 'run a mouse.'" This meant finding a pneumococcus and determining which of some twenty-five types it might be. First he would take a tiny amount of the ugly sputum, dilute it a bit with saline, and carefully inject this into the abdominal cavity of a laboratory mouse. There, the bacilli, if present, would rapidly multiply. Four hours later, he would draw a few drops of fluid from the infected mouse's abdomen and place a drop on a glass slide. This had to be carefully mixed with a drop of antiserum of one type of pneumococcus. If the two matched, then a slight swelling could be seen in the capsule of the pneumococcus. Once the swelling occurred, Charlie would rush down to the ward and report the findings. The patient could then be given the curative antiserum. But it wasn't always curative; pneumonia still killed twenty-five percent of its victims.

As a young intern, however, Charlie didn't always make the right call. One day he was visited by two strangers in long white coats who asked if he had any cardiac patients on his ward. Charlie admitted that he did—a couple of cases of rheumatic fever and a couple of patients with terribly damaged heart valves. "We would like to run a test on one of them," they suggested. Charlie was protective of his patients and pressed for more details. "We have this long thin tube that we slide into a vein in the arm and slip it slowly up into the heart so we can measure pressure and gas content in the pumping heart," they explained. Charlie exploded, "That's ridiculous. I certainly won't let you do that on my patients"! They left. Later he learned that they were André Cournand and Dickinson Richards, future Nobel laureates for their work in cardiac catheterization.

Charlie was protective of his patients in part because of the fear of infection on the ward. In those days before common antibiotics, only a few chemicals were effective against infection. There was sulfanilamide, which turned the lips purple. Sulfathiazole and sulfadiazine were less toxic and slightly more powerful—but not powerful enough in many cases. In rheumatic fever victims there was often subacute bacterial endocarditis (SBE), a growth of infected tissue on a heart valve caused by the infection, which would break off and lodge in the brain or elsewhere in the body. Rheumatic fever was always fatal and there was little to be done for these patients other than to let them die in peace. Thankfully, with the introduction of penicillin, this became a treatable disease.

One of the more daring processes that Charlie was required to learn during his surgery rotation was "direct transfusion," a procedure that demanded skill and a highly attuned team. One would draw blood into a 100-ml syringe and pass it to a second person, who injected the blood into the recipient's arm through a large needle held in place. The syringe than went to the third member of the team, who rinsed it carefully and gave it to the leader to draw more blood. The trick was to keep the rhythm so that neither the donor's nor the recipient's veins would clot.

Everyone was meticulous about removing every tiny bubble from an injected solution. One day Charlie was a member of a "direct transfusion" team when he was handed a syringe to be injected. Too late, he realized it was empty. Before he knew it, he had injected a full syringe of air into the patient. Charlie and the others gasped with horror, but the patient just coughed slightly and showed no other troublesome signs.

Charlie's precociousness, too, often emerged on the ward. Though it sometimes caused him difficulty, one day it may have saved a life. A woman was admitted with a blood count showing very few platelets, causing her to bruise and bleed easily. A quick search for the cause revealed that she had recently colored her hair with a dye that had a benzol base, a chemical very toxic to platelets. They determined this as the cause, and settled in to wait for the toxic effects to wear off. But she grew rapidly and steadily worse; hemorrhages appeared everywhere, including in her brain. She became paralyzed and, finally, comatose. The family pleaded with Charlie to do something.

In fact, Charlie had a theory about what was wrong: there was a remote chance that she had idiopathic thrombocytopenia, a blood problem that could be cured by removing the spleen. He presented the theory to his colleagues but found no support. Nevertheless, he wouldn't give up and arrogantly contacted the revered Professor of Surgery Alan Whipple. Late that evening, Whipple agreed to see the patient. Charlie remembered it clearly: "I can see him today. He was dead tired, sat holding his head in his hand . . . . I told him the story and why I had called him . . . after a long pause Dr. Whipple agreed to do it, saying 'If the family understands the risk, I cannot refuse this patient surgery.'" He performed the surgery the next morning, and a week later the woman walked out of the hospital. Although Charlie's youthful obstinacy didn't endear him to the rest of the medical staff, it gave him the confidence to trust his instincts. These instincts would be honed by training and observation and, increasingly, experience. Each successful diagnosis reinforced Charlie's motivation for studying medicine in the first place: to heal. But he admitted to an additional incentive: "There's an ego satisfaction; no doubt about it. There's a great gratification of the ego when you lay on a hand and a person gets well. It makes you feel important; it makes you feel big; it makes you feel strong and there's a sense of heroism when you touch someone and they get well."

Despite the intoxication of healing people, Charlie did have a private life. He was surrounded by a bevy of gorgeous young nurses in crisp white uniforms and perky little caps. For a time he pursued Doris, a buxom blonde secretary. After some attempts, he finally convinced her to accompany him to Great Neck to go sailing in his sister's small boat. Disappointingly, there was a strong cold wind blowing when they reached the dock. A few friends showed up and discouraged them from heading out. When Charlie ignored them, they eagerly stayed on to watch the inevitable disaster. Even before starting out, Charlie managed to fall overboard in the process of securing the dinghy. More determined than ever, and despite the mounting wind, they managed to get the sails up, slip the mooring, and sail off into the brisk wind—and the gathering dusk. Very quickly Charlie realized that he couldn't handle the wind, and Doris was completely inexperienced. With great difficulty he made it back to the mooring, but not before falling in once more. It was all very entertaining for his friends; Doris, however, declined his future invitations.

Then, in his second year as an intern, he met someone special. Her name was Dorcas Tiemeyer, and Charlie was smitten. She was quick, witty, imaginative, and dedicated to nursing. As a head nurse she was in charge of twelve beds in her main ward and six more in that adjoining. She exuded competence and a kind of toughness, and had a sharp tongue yet a surprising, wry sense of humor. Charlie recalled, "Her subordinates jumped when she said jump—and so did I." After some fumbled attempts he persuaded her to go out with him. Dorcas shared a small apartment with another nurse, and when her roommate was away she and Charlie would take advantage of the privacy. Charlie earnestly tried to seduce her, but she would have none of it. Although Charlie courted her vigorously, he worried about his parents' acceptance of her and was equally anxious about meeting her family. Sensing that this relationship was serious, he also worried about the practicality of earning a living for the two of them, since he had always been fully supported by his parents.

But he enjoyed being with Dorcas and was convinced they were well matched. "We laughed a lot and talked about medicine and poems and books . . . she was imaginative and curious and willing to try anything," he remembered with pleasure. On warm summer evenings she would make picnic suppers which they would enjoy on the palisades across the George Washington Bridge. Or they would go to the Cloisters, an art gallery and park. They shared a love of poetry and sailing, and soon began to spend all of their free time together. Dorcas was well aware of Charlie's addiction to climbing, and seemed to accept it as his overriding passion. Finally, he took her home to Oscar and Angel Bunny, and was relieved when they accepted her immediately. Oscar, in particular, was taken with her, so much so that when her apartment was robbed and a favorite ring was stolen, he sent her an exact replica with a note enclosed—supposedly from the repentant burglar. Dorcas grew even more upset as she imagined being stalked by the burglar. Poor Oscar had to admit to his generous action, no doubt endearing himself in the process.

During this heated courtship, across the ocean the Germans were making aggressive movements toward their neighbors. When war came to Europe in 1939, Charlie paid little heed, although he did remember being at Honnedaga Lake with his mother during the Battle of Britain, Angel Bunny huddled obsessively over a tiny radio, listening for reports of the battle. His parents took the war seriously and worried about the safety of their British friends. They worried that Britain would perform badly and that the United States would get drawn into the war on a defensive basis.

Then, on Christmas Eve, 1940, Charlie invited his parents to the hospital to watch the seasonal ritual of nurses caroling throughout the wards. Singing softly, they transported tiny lighted candles in a solemn procession along each floor and down the stairwells. Charlie's memories of the scene were vivid: "The world seemed to be falling apart, but the songs, the sentiment of the season, and the lovely young faces and voices—well, it was devastatingly beautiful." He and Dorcas decided it was the perfect moment to announce their intention to marry. His parents were overjoyed.

The visit with Dorcas's family, however, was more difficult. Her mother, an educated and cultivated person, accepted Charlie warmly, but her father was unimpressed, even hostile. Her younger brother simply teased and joked, and her older sister was overly protective. Ultimately, Charlie found her family uninteresting. Possibly responding to this northern boy's complete lack of interest, they never warmed to him. Charlie was determined to have very little contact with them after they were married, and this is exactly what happened: "I never saw them again, except for a half hour at our wedding." His justification was that Dorcas had outgrown her family.

Despite their excitement at the prospect of a life together, they had to temporarily keep their plans secret; they both wanted to continue working in the ward and this was not possible if they were a couple. Charlie was profoundly satisfied, working to heal and save lives with someone he loved so deeply. Dorcas would call every morning at seven to wake him, and leave him love notes throughout the day, disguised as reminder slips. Despite their attempts at subterfuge, in fact it was an open secret, and their newfound happiness was noticed and enjoyed by all their colleagues.

By 1941, with Hitler's many triumphs, it finally began to dawn on Americans that the German dictator might actually win the war. At that point Charlie tried to join the Red Cross, hoping that he and Dorcas might get married and go to England together. But the Red Cross was not interested in married couples, and Charlie would not go without her.

Instead, that July, they went down to the "Little Church Around the Corner" in New York, and, with only their parents and two close friends, held a ten-minute ceremony to launch their married life. Charlie's father generously bankrolled them with $5,000 to get started, and their first purchase was a Mercury convertible costing $1,100. Immediately after the ceremony they headed west, bound for Wyoming. Upon reflection, Charlie was amazed at their insensitivity: "We left all the people that we invited to the wedding standing on the sidewalk as we drove off . . . no reception, no nothing. Got married and left." Staying in modest motels that cost them $2 or $3 a night, they made their way west, reading *John Brown's Body* aloud to each other each evening. Charlie described their state of mind as "incredibly naïve, oblivious of the rest of the world, unconcerned about our future, enjoying each other completely." Of course they were well aware of the carnage across the sea, but this was their time—their private oasis of newly wedded bliss—its temporary nature very likely adding to the poignancy.

When they reached the Tetons in Wyoming, they went immediately to Jenny Lake, where they floated down the clear, cold streams, camped in the little tent left over from the 1938 K2 expedition, and met up with one of Charlie's Harvard climbing friends, Betsy Cowles. Dorcas turned out to be a very promising rock climber, a pursuit she probably would have taken up more seriously had the war and child-rearing not intervened. They climbed as well with John Case, a well-respected American climber who wandered into their camp one night. Among their ascents was the Exum Ridge of the Grand Teton. Because of routefinding problems on the lower part of the ridge, they found themselves in an electrical storm within a couple of hundred feet of the summit. Ice axes humming, they carefully distanced themselves from the dangerous tools and waited for the worst of it to pass. Due to the various delays, they were overtaken by darkness while on the climb and spent the night spooning each other on a narrow ledge, looking down at a cheery campfire that Cowles had lit in the valley below. In fact this was the only time in Charlie's climbing career that he was inadvertently benighted in the mountains.

They remained in the Tetons for four weeks. Each night they were awakened by bears raiding the cold spring where they kept their supplies. Charlie would get up, yell, and throw things at them, not fully comprehending the size and nature of the creatures. And each day they would head off on another climbing adventure.

One day Charlie received a letter from home stating that his commission in the Navy had arrived and he was to return at once. The summons was not unexpected, but with some trepidation and with very little remaining money, they headed east, camping out each night and eating sparingly to minimize costs. Credit cards were still a thing of the future, and they needed what little cash they had for gas. It was the end of a halcyon summer, a contented period of love and companionship, and the beginning of the reality of war.

HIGH FLYERS

Risking your life fighting for what you believe really is, at least I believe, the ultimate test of a human being.
—Charles Houston

I t was late summer in 1941 when Charlie and Dorcas headed east for Washington, where Charlie was to learn more about his commission with the Navy. He was referred to Captain J. C. Adams by Dr. Ross McFarland, the man who had taken Charlie up to a simulated 28,000 feet in preparation for Nanda Devi. Adams wanted to discuss a number of topics: mountains, climbing, his experiences at altitude—and aviation. It was a decisive conversation that would influence the next stage of Charlie's life. At the end of their discussion, Adams ordered Charlie to attend flight surgeon school, after which he would be in charge of one of their new altitude training units. Charlie looked at Dorcas and said, "Boy, the Navy is pretty great!" It looked like a promising start to his military career.

The war was going badly in Britain, but Charlie was more concerned with the change in his life: new uniforms, packing up their few belongings, and the long drive south to the Pensacola Naval Air Station in Florida, where he would receive his flight training. During this time, his parents regularly invited visiting young British naval officers to their home on Long Island for meals, or for a weekend, providing a steady flow of up-to-date information on the war. The visitors certainly impressed Charlie's youngest sister, the flamboyant Janet, for she eventually married one of these young ensigns.

Back in Pensacola, Dorcas found a small cottage on a narrow inlet, and there they set up their first home together. The cottage was small and infested with cockroaches, scorpions, and lizards. But it was home to the young newlyweds. They spent much of their spare time on the beach, lounging in the tepid waters of the Gulf of Mexico.

Flight training was a breeze, if somewhat dull for Charlie. As in the first two years of medical school, much of what these prospective new pilots was taught held little relevance to the real world. Charlie sensed that the student pilots were being hurried through their training, but if it was because of an impending war he was still unaware of that. By November, classes had accelerated and word went round that trouble was brewing. After their formal graduation on November 30th, students were ordered to stay in close touch by radio and telephone. It was implicit that war was imminent. Then, over cocktails one Sunday afternoon, the phone rang: Pearl Harbor had just been bombed. The magnitude of the attack was not fully appreciated, but the situation sounded grim. By dawn the next day, Charlie and Dorcas were on their way to Norfolk. By the time they arrived, Roosevelt was calling on Congress for a declaration of war.

Charlie's initial duties were in the dispensary, doing physical examinations, inspecting the kitchens and dining rooms for cleanliness, and examining men sent in by the Shore Patrol for drunkenness. One evening a young lieutenant aviator arrived in the dispensary, distraught, with a story that on first glance seemed straight ahead: "I picked up this woman on my way to town. Gave her a lift. On the way she went 'down on me,' and I think she bit me or something. It's been bleeding and running ever since." It was Charlie's first exposure to oral sex and he was completely puzzled, but his hospital corpsman knew immediately what had transpired and attended to the officer's needs. Charlie found a copy of Kraft-Ebbing's text on sexual behavior and read with disbelief, shock, and disgust about the strange variants in conduct.

One night while Charlie was on duty, a seaman came in with an acute earache. The standard procedure was to pierce the ear with a needle in order to drain out the pus. Charlie was in the middle of the procedure when the lights suddenly went out. The emergency lights kicked in, but a quick survey of the base revealed that every light was down. Charlie immediately abandoned the poor seaman and prepared for the sudden influx of casualties he was sure was imminent. "Suddenly we heard sirens and saw a flood of car lights," Charlie recalled. "The casualties must be arriving!" And sure enough, a group of Shore Patrol dragged a bloody sailor into the small operating room. There was an overwhelming smell of bad whiskey about the man, who was snoring loudly. Next arrived four very drunken men, just as the lights went on again. The "attack" turned out to be a fight that had broken out among the sailors in a bar just next to the base. In their hurry to escape the police, they had crashed into a utility pole, cutting off all power to the station. Charlie went back to the earache.

Yet, despite these mundane casualties, the nation was at war and the atmosphere on the base reflected the tension and horror. Tankers and freighters were torpedoed every night, clearly visible as they burned and sank only a few miles offshore. Exhausted, shipwrecked sailors were brought ashore to the hospital. Charlie attended to them at the dispensary while Dorcas did her duty with the Red Cross. The air station buildings had machine guns on their roofs; line officers wore side arms and there were constant rumors that the Germans were landing.

Four months passed rapidly, and in March Charlie received orders to report to the Jacksonville, Florida, Naval Air Station. Once again, Dorcas found a place for them to live, this time in a grand old home owned by an aristocratic widow, Mrs. De Souza, who "kept her silver polished, served formal tea each afternoon, scrubbed her gardenia leaves with soap and water, and shampooed her hair with eggs to keep it lustrous." Charlie was convinced she was half mad, but in a delightful way. The war news was sporadic: the papers carried little solid news, the radio was limited, and there was no television. They heard about the landings on Guadalcanal, but not how desperate it was. The good news still overshadowed the bad.

In Jacksonville, Charlie was assigned to the altitude unit under Regular Navy Lieutenant McCaffrey, who "knew little and cared less, but thought aviation would serve his career well." McCaffrey appeared to be afraid of the decompression chamber. Charlie's job was to "take them up" to 16,000 feet and to teach them how to use their oxygen equipment, ten student pilots at a time. The equipment was rudimentary—a rebreather in which oxygen was supplied and recycled through a soda lime canister to remove carbon dioxide. After each 16,000-foot experiment, a report was required for each man's reaction, along with a recommendation about his future flying ability, completely based on this one experience.

Flyers turned purple or white and became groggy and uncertain, often fainting in the process. McCaffrey was afraid of what he saw and ordered the chamber be reduced to 14,000 feet, but without adjusting the reports. Charlie objected, pointing out that McCaffrey was lying to Washington. McCaffrey countered with the likelihood that nobody was reading the reports anyway. But Charlie insisted on reporting the falsehood. For this indiscretion he was put on a summons and called before the admiral, who read all the statements on both sides and informed Charlie he'd been charged with insubordination and recommended for a court martial. Charlie was stunned and pleaded his case once again. The result was a reduction in his charges from court martial to "discourtesy to a senior officer," and Charlie was confined to quarters for five days. Yet, while still confined to quarters, he received an order promoting him to full Lieutenant.

Charlie returned to the unit fuming, feeling self-righteous about having been treated badly. To his immense satisfaction, a few months later McCaffrey was transferred to the Aleutian Islands. Despite his problems at work, Charlie and Dorcas enjoyed their private time together, often wandering along an unspoiled stretch of coarse sand bordered by spectacular magnolia trees, known as Vero Beach. Though time would reveal that seven saboteurs had landed on that very beach and subsequently been captured, there was no publicity. Charlie still thought little of the war, protected as he was in his research capacity.

Late that summer Charlie received orders to report to the Naval Air Station north of Miami at Opa Locka. Here, Charlie was in command of the altitude training unit, work he found exhilarating. He did his most productive work at Opa Locka. Gradually the war became more real to him. He witnessed a few unbelievably young—yet wise and war-weary— pilots coming to train pilots who were equally young—but still naïve.

Dorcas again found a little house for them, this time in the sleepy suburb of North Miami. There in that hot and humid climate they enjoyed a tiny garden shaded by coconut and mango trees. They lived simply, as rationing was in full force and many foods were unavailable. Dorcas transferred her earlier nursing commitment to homemaking. While she ensured that Charlie's home life was as perfect as possible, her care and attention left him free to concentrate on his work with the Navy. And now they had something new to occupy their thoughts—for Dorcas was pregnant.

By 1943, aircraft could fly higher than pilots could tolerate, so altitude training became increasingly important. Charlie seized this opportunity and created his own unique training program. He installed a new, much larger decompression chamber that could reproduce 40,000 feet of altitude in five minutes, or could drop to forty degrees below zero in ten. He developed new and innovative demonstrations in cold, thin air.

One of the pilots presented Charlie with a practical question: "What do I do if I have to cough or blow my nose at 25,000 feet?" Going down was obviously not the answer. Charlie decided it was time to learn—and to demonstrate—just how much time the trainees would have before lack of oxygen adversely affected them. Without letting his superiors know of this particular experiment, Charlie asked one pilot on each training ascent to take off his oxygen mask at 20,000 feet, but to replace it as soon as he felt the effects of hypoxia.

After a few experiments, he drummed up the courage to inform the executive officer of these deviations from protocol, who simply warned him to be careful. His reports eventually made it all the way to Washington; the response was quick, warning him of the risks, but implying enough approval that Charlie was encouraged to continue. However, he also knew that if anything went seriously wrong, he would be held completely responsible; his experiments were clearly outside the established protocol.

Charlie's next step was to install a gun ring in the chamber. He then built a small, flyable model airplane, which the trainee could "fly" with stick and rudder. The gunner would be placed in the gun ring, told to take off his mask, and ordered to "fire" at the target specified over the headset. Again, the gunner was told to replace the mask the instant he felt any problems, but as Charlie remembered, few did; most "crashed" without replacing their oxygen mask. The demonstrations were nothing short of spectacular. They soon became a routine part of altitude training and Charlie was credited with many new and revealing innovations.

In return, some of the pilots tried to teach Charlie to fly. But he admitted: "I was inept, tending to land many feet above the ground." After a disastrous incident in the Everglades where his plane began to roll, hit a fence, and subsequently turned over, he gave up flying permanently. But he frequently flew as a passenger in the rear seat during the fighter trainer flights, usually getting very sick in the process. Charlie's constant goal was to achieve a sense of realism; he wanted to feel what being sick in combat might feel like. He soon realized that above 35,000 feet even 100 percent oxygen was not sufficient. So he tried to develop a pressurized mask to take the pilots higher. He was convinced that altitude training was a crucial and important component of combat preparedness, and so were his superiors in Washington.

But sometimes, in his darker moments, he asked himself if his experiments were a simple rationalization for remaining safe and comfortable, far from the terrors of war.

During Charlie's stay in Miami, his crew tripled in size and they ran more than 50,000 aircrew and pilots through the program. Soon the chamber was used not only for training but for a new research project assigned from Washington. Their task was to explore ways of counteracting the effects on pilots who lost their oxygen supply at great altitude, an assignment that appealed to Charlie: "It was a chance to do a small research project and to help save lives." Barry Commoner had previously developed a maneuver called Emergency Pressure Breathing, in which the subject was told to take a deep breath, compress his lungs by trying to breathe out against pursed lips, and then relax. The rationale was that this would increase the pressure of oxygen in the lungs and enable survival if repeated several times a minute. But the procedure was hard to do and even harder to teach. Eventually Charlie determined that over-breathing—a form of hyperventilation—rather than pressurizing, was the answer to improved blood oxygen and, ultimately, survival. After dozens of successful runs in the chamber, Charlie received approval to make some flights in a B-24 Liberator Bomber.

Now they would actually *be* at 25,000 feet. Charlie would tell the pilot, gunner, or other crew member to remove his oxygen mask, over-breathe, and then do his regular job for twenty to forty-five minutes. "It was pretty spectacular," he explained. "Those who breathed normally collapsed in less than two minutes, but the over-breathers went on for half an hour and said they could go longer." The data was undeniable: controlled hyperventilation worked. Over-breathing subsequently became standard training for those whose duties took them to very high altitudes, and it undoubtedly saved lives.

But Charlie longed for action. Having heard hair-raising tales of the experiences of flight surgeons on carriers, he begged for sea duty. His commanding officer refused. For a few weeks he was assigned to a fighter squadron, but the combat-wise pilot did a quick assessment of Charlie and soon had him returned to the altitude chamber. For Charlie, this rejection was traumatic, proving to him that others felt he was incompetent for combat duty. In reality, it was because he was doing the best work he could back in the chamber. Intellectually he understood this, but emotionally he felt separated from the action—and useless. "Risking your life fighting for what you believe really is, at least I believe, the ultimate test of a human being. I never had that chance."

By the end of 1943 the tide had turned in the Pacific war. Brave young pilots who had gone off to Guadalcanal, to carriers, and to desperate landings
on other islands were coming home. Many of their friends had been killed,
and the wise-eyed veterans were changed men. Having seen too much death
and defeat, they were drained, prematurely old. Charlie and Dorcas came to
know several soldiers, but Charlie felt ill at ease with these seasoned war-
riors, and friendships did not flourish. There was simply too much discrep-
ancy between their life experiences: "I remained the novice outsider." Like
his father, who similarly had not enlisted in World War I because of his eyes,
Charlie always felt that each was "less of a man for this." His lack of combat
duty and his having never lived on the edge during the war instilled a certain
amount of insecurity in Charlie—even feelings of cowardice.

Then Charlie was dealt a deeply personal, unexpected blow. His good
friend Dr. Payton informed him that the unborn child in Dorcas's womb was
anencephalic—the sterile, detached term that the medical profession uses for
a baby that is alive, but with no brain, and no hope of surviving after birth.
After much hand-wringing, Charlie decided not to tell Dorcas, but to let the
delivery proceed. She continued, happily anticipating the birth of their first
child. Angel Bunny came down in anticipation of the birth and Charlie felt
he had to tell her the truth. After the easy delivery, Charlie and his mother
broke the news to Dorcas. They told her that the cord was wrapped around
the baby's neck. It seemed the best thing to do at the time in Charlie's mind,
and he thinks Dorcas never learned what really happened. Though it was a
brutal shock, Dorcas was young and resilient and after a time of grief seemed
to recover her hopes of another child. In fact, she quickly became pregnant
again, and in the summer of 1945 their daughter, Penny, was born.

Despite the personal tragedy of their lost child and the subsequent ela-
tion of a newborn, Dorcas visited her own family only once after the war. As
she and Charlie grew closer, she grew increasingly distant from her family,
eventually losing touch with them completely. It was Charlie's family traditions that permeated their household, and it was the Houstons who became
Dorcas's extended family. Unlike Angel Bunny, Dorcas did not maintain a
strong decision-making voice in her marriage. Gradually, she became completely absorbed by Charlie and his family, and the strength of their family
traditions increasingly muted—and finally silenced—her former life. Even
for the times, this seemed an unusual situation, and likely spoke to the overwhelming influence of Charlie's strong personality.

Charlie was ambivalent about her complete absorption into his family: "I think Dorcas must have covered her hurt very deeply because she appeared unmoved when her father died. . . . In a certain sense, I robbed her of her family, but in another sense I saved her from an unpromising life." Dorcas may have had mixed feelings, too. She certainly would have realized very quickly the strength of the Houston family unit, and very likely found it attractive, even supportive. But Dorcas, a product of her own family background and nursing education, was clearly not an "unpromising" person, or she would not have caught Charlie's eye. Surely she must have regretted the separation from her family and any thoughts of young Penny being deprived of contact with her grandparents. Regardless of her own private misgivings, Dorcas seemed to accept her new role, devoting herself increasingly to becoming an ideal wife for her complex, intelligent husband; a good mother for her new daughter; and a suitable daughter-in-law for Charlie's parents.

Professionally, Charlie's blunt honesty and uncompromising standards continued to cause him problems. One apparently obnoxious ensign clashed repeatedly with Charlie, who by then had been promoted to lieutenant commander. Charlie thought that his own elevated rank would protect his actions, and naïvely wrote a frank, and he thought accurate, fitness report on this brash young man who so irritated him. Charlie's superior told him that wouldn't do. Charlie and the young ensign subsequently had an ugly disagreement, after which Charlie reluctantly sanitized the report, and the young man was transferred. He didn't think much more of it until thirty years later when he met the man at a medical conference. The former ensign greeted Charlie warmly, telling him that he had inspired him to study medicine; Charlie had been a role model for him, and his brutally frank comments had changed his life.

This "happy ending" was important to Charlie, a man who above all else craved being valued, being needed. Even as he barreled ahead with unpopular actions, he was confident others would eventually understand his reasoning—and ultimately agree that "all was for the best." For this outcome, he relied on his own powers of persuasion, as well as his good moral compass. But he was conflicted. Although he was devoted to his work and family, he was sensitive to even small slights and jealous of those who rose faster than he did, and he felt unable to compete. Painfully aware of these insecurities, Charlie felt it imperative to do something he considered grand and meaningful with his life, in an attempt to quiet those voices and firmly establish his value.

In 1945 it became clear that the war was winding down. In the Pacific, island by island, the Japanese were eliminated. In Europe, the dramas of Stalingrad and Leningrad, of Egypt and Tunisia, of Anzio, Dunkirk and Bastogne and the battle for Berlin were all over. Charlie learned of Hiroshima and then, soon after, Nagasaki. Europe was won, and the war was over. His war research complete, Charlie needed a new project. It turned out to be one of the proudest accomplishments of his life.

OPERATION EVEREST

I bought the food, but they cooked the meal.
—Charles Houston

In 1946, after a brief stint supervising an electronics lab in Pensacola, Charlie was back where he wanted to be: doing research. This time he worked under the leadership of an energetic and imaginative cardiologist, Ashton Graybiel. Graybiel ran the research division loosely, encouraging his small crew to be productive in whatever way they wished. Without any specific project in mind, Charlie returned to his emergency breathing procedure, with a particular interest in quantifying the relationship between pulmonary ventilation and arterial oxygen saturation: "I tried to figure out how a burst of increased pressure in the lungs could—or might—increase the oxygen pressure in the blood: did this push a chunk of oxygen into a bit of blood; did this richer blood affect the whole; was the immediately-following blood actually poorer in oxygen?" Together with his associate and a few volunteers, they began breathing different air/nitrogen mixtures while measuring blood oxygen saturation. The experiments produced some interesting and dramatic results. When pure nitrogen was breathed, the subject passed out immediately: "It was just whamo!"

The research team soon learned that the volume of air they breathed—

pulmonary ventilation—had a direct and immediate impact on blood oxygen. It was clear that hyperventilation alone improved oxygen delivery; pressure was not needed. Their findings were new to the field, and they published a small paper on the subject.

With this new information, Charlie began scheming about simulating a climb of Mount Everest. He was curious to know if humans could survive without supplemental oxygen on the world's highest summit, where air contained approximately a third of the oxygen pressure at sea level. The program came to be called "Operation Everest," and looking back, Charlie felt it was one of his best achievements, partly because it was imaginative and unusual for the time, but even more because of the opportunities it created for others in years to come. In addition, the program provided some relief for his disappointment, even shame, about the war. Charlie had no idea at the time how Operation Everest would affect his own career, but even in 1946 he knew they were on to something important, both for medicine and for mountaineering.

The history of mountaineering medicine is a long and colorful one, going back as far as the ancient Egyptians, who thought illness was an imbalance between the temporal and spiritual worlds. But it was the Incas, living high in the Andes who understood something called "environmental aggression" and who maintained two completely separate armies, one for high altitudes and one for sea level. They had strict laws controlling migration between high and low altitudes. And through their religious practices, they became competent climbers, often going above 18,000 feet for their sacrifices to the gods.

There were numerous examples of loss of life to altitude in important historical events. Alexander the Great lost thousands of men when he crossed 14,000-foot passes on his way to India. Hannibal's men and elephants struggled through the highest passes in the Alps, and Marco Polo too noted the effects of altitude. General Du Qin had urged the Chinese Emperor not to send envoys to Kashmir because of the perilous nature of the Silk Road: "Travelers have to climb over Mount Greater Headache, Mount Lesser Headache, and the Fever Hills. . . . " Buddhist pilgrim Too Kin, wandering Asia for fifteen years seeking enlightenment, wrote a very early description of high-altitude pulmonary edema (HAPE): "A white froth came from his mouth and he said to Fa-Hsien, 'I cannot live any longer.'" Neither Too Kin nor General Du Qin understood the illness that afflicted them; they attributed it to poisonous emanations from plants and minerals.

On the North American continent, Cortez's men climbed Mexico's 17,802-foot Popocatépetl to obtain sulfur to make gunpowder in 1532 and reported that "a fog-like curtain blurred our eyesight. This was an effect of the rare air brought down on us by a mountain demon. . . . " Sixty years later, the Jesuit missionary Acosta wrote about a sickness he suffered while crossing the Pariacaca Pass in the Andes: "When we come to ascend the highest point of the mountain, we feel an aire so . . . subtile that it is with much difficulty we can breathe. . . . "

Mountain sickness had different names, depending on the continent and the mountain range; it was known as *tunk, bis, dum, mundara,* or *damgiri.* An entire mountain range was named after its effect: the Hindu Kush means "Hindu Killer." Then, in 1640, with the invention of the barometer, it was discovered that higher air was actually thinner and lighter.

The intersection between mountaineering and medicine began in 1787 when the physicist and geologist Horace-Bénédict de Saussure made the third ascent of Mont Blanc. In his description of the experience, he explained: "The sort of weariness which proceeds from the rarity of the air is absolutely insurmountable . . . since the air had hardly more than half of its usual density, compensation had to be made for the lack of density by the frequency of inspirations. . . . " Although de Saussure was capable of describing his symptoms, it was Thomas Beddoes who explained them ten years later, purporting that muscular exertion must expend a great deal of oxygen, which the rarified atmosphere couldn't supply, simply because the high atmosphere contains a far smaller proportion of oxygen than do lower altitudes.

As mountaineering increased in popularity, and because many climbers were also physicians, the numbers of theories abounded, many of them bizarre: some blamed earth's magnetism; others blamed rhubarb, marigolds and heather; still others were sure it was minerals under the rock that were to blame for mountain malaise.

Physiologist Dr. Paul Bert clarified the problem when he began to study "barometric anoxemia" in a decompression chamber in 1863. From his studies in the chamber, as well as stories he gathered from hundreds of travelers to the high mountains, Bert compiled *Barometric Pressure,* the first bible of altitude physiology, conclusively stating that it was lack of oxygen, not plants or minerals, that caused mountain sickness. He did not go unchallenged.

Mountaineer-doctor Angelo Mosso had studied the sickness in a decompression chamber on top of Monta Rosa, concluding that over-breathing at altitude was the cause. This led to more studies, including a lab near the summit of Mont Blanc, where unsuspecting squirrels were forced to run laps on a wheel, first in the valley, then up on the summit, and finally back down in the valley again.

Yet another theory emerged, this one from astronomer Jules Janssen. Janssen was convinced it was exertion, not lighter air, that caused mountain sickness. To prove his theory he had forty-two men pull him up a mountain on a sled. Janssen felt fine; the forty-two men did not. A young Chamonix doctor, Etienne Jacottet, rushed up the mountain to join Janssen, became severely ill, and died shortly after of high-altitude pulmonary edema (HAPE). Poor Jacottet became possibly the first martyr to high-altitude science.

As the nineteenth century came to a close, it was more or less accepted that decreased oxygen pressure on the high mountains was the true cause of altitude sickness. Meanwhile, a very high mountain in Nepal was found to be over 29,000 feet high. The logical question emerged: could man climb that high without supplemental oxygen?

In 1913 Thomas Ravenhill, a doctor for a mining company above Ollague, Chile, recognized altitude illness in the miners and described it vividly and clearly in his clinical report: Altitude research in the Andes was born. By 1935 the basic effects of hypoxia were identified and the changes in blood, acid-base balance, metabolism, and renal function were well described. Then World War II, with its high-flying fighter pilots, stimulated much more hypoxia research than had been done over the preceding thirty years. Much of this new research was done by Charlie.

Thanks to the result of his experiment in a decompression chamber prior to the 1936 Nanda Devi expedition, Charlie had already made the link between hypoxia and high-altitude climbing. Charlie was cautiously confident that an acclimatized man could go as high as the summit of Everest, although he felt it would be at the very limit of consciousness.

In January of 1946 he broached his idea about acclimatization, first to some friends, then to Graybiel, and finally to the senior medical officer. They were mildly enthusiastic and recognized it as a reasonable way to keep the command functioning in innovative studies. By February 14th he had received permission to conduct " . . . a study of acclimatization at high altitude in the low pressure chamber . . . " And by April 25th approval arrived from the Bureau of Medicine and Surgery in Washington "to obtain data on the respiratory and circulatory changes which occur during acclimatization to altitudes of 25,000 feet, and higher. Four subjects would live in the low pressure chamber for approximately thirty days during which the chamber would be slowly decompressed to simulate increasing altitude to 25,000 feet or above." Charlie's unofficial agenda, although he didn't put it in his letter, was to see if people could survive on top of that high mountain in Nepal—Everest. Up until that time, almost everyone believed that if you went that high without supplemental oxygen you would simply die.

Charlie was surprised that there appeared to be no strings attached to the study. Nor were there any limits on cash or resources. He attributed this relatively free hand to his good track record with the Navy, despite some turbulence early in his military career: "I think they recognized I was, let's say, sometimes a loose cannon, but mostly pretty productive." Now he had to move quickly, for the entire experiment was expected to wrap up early in August. His first task was a trip to Washington, Philadelphia, New York, and Boston to speak with some of the leaders in physiology—men such as Bruce Dill, Glen Millikan, Leslie Nims, John Fulton, and Magnus Gregersen. Some were immediately enthusiastic, others more cautious. But they all agreed that it was worth trying.

Next Charlie had to assemble his research team. He chose Dick Riley because of his distinguished reputation as a physiologist and physician. Lieutenant Commander Margaret Haley, a nurse-dietician from the Navy, was assigned to the project because food would be a major factor in keeping the subjects motivated to continue. Two outstanding laboratory workers, Frank Consolazio and George Selden, were seconded from the Harvard Fatigue Laboratory to do the painstaking blood analyses required.

But the biggest challenge was finding subjects: "Could we find men willing to live in this steel box for five weeks?" Charlie wondered. The answer was yes. One single announcement brought enough volunteers to choose from—four, plus two alternates, just in case. They weren't climbers, but were military and medical personnel. According to Charlie, they were just ordinary kids with no specific interest in climbing. Charlie simply explained what he wanted to do, and why, and told them that there would be a few painful procedures and lots of boredom. Such was the extent of the prescreening for research candidates.

They set up a kitchen inside the lab with special foods, despite the wartime rationing that was still in effect. Large trash cans of hot water were taken into the chamber each evening in order to provide the volunteers with bath water. They found a portable toilet. The one thing they could not provide was privacy; in the ten-by-twelve-foot room it was simply impossible. And as they went higher in simulated altitude, Charlie anticipated that this lack of privacy might become an issue as they each reacted to the discomfort in their own way.

An unfortunate complication was the time of year: they would be operating during the hurricane season, when power outages were common. Even a brief power outage would force them to bring the chamber down to sea level. Clearly an auxiliary power supply was essential. Public Works loaned them two generators, each the size of a school bus. During the first test run all the fuses blew, and the team discovered that special wiring was needed to run the ventilation pumps. It was a complex combination of equipment, operators, and conditions. Everything needed to function for one month— without a flaw.

Charlie explained the dangers: "It was known that long residence at altitude might enlarge the heart and could actually lead to heart failure. We knew that blood pressure in the pulmonary artery increased at altitude, and we expected this in our subjects." But was it reversible? Would it cause enlargement of the heart? The most important thing was safety: to this end, a trained hospital corpsman would be on duty day and night, the technicians would take four-hour watches, an engine room engineer would be on duty all the time, and Charlie planned to move into a small room adjoining the chamber for the duration of the experiment.

One of the doctors would examine the subjects each day, checking heart and lungs, pulse and blood pressure. Charlie explained that "although altitude illness had been described a long time ago, we didn't know anything about pulmonary or cerebral edema which later became infamous as HAPE and high-altitude cerebral edema (HACE). Our fears were based on ignorance and thus all the more powerful. We simply were not sure what might happen."

After three days of trials and mistakes, on June 30th they closed the door of the chamber and, without ceremony, started the long "trip" to—they hoped—the top of Everest. The plan was to climb a few thousand feet each evening, believing that this would give the subjects the night to adjust and so be stabilized by the next day. Years later they realized that this was not the best possible plan—it was much safer to sleep low and climb high during the day. During and after measured exercise on a cycle ergometer, they collected samples of lung air, arterial blood, and urine from the subjects. They took frequent electrocardiograms as well as occasional chest X-rays in order to observe the effect of oxygen deprivation on the heart.

They hoped to make a continuous picture of how the body changed during acclimatization to increasing altitude. No studies had yet been done under such controlled conditions, and none had gone so high. As the experiments progressed and the subjects went higher, the men began to look very drawn, though they claimed to feel well. Their nighttime breathing was often shallow and irregular, and even though Charlie remembered this periodic-breathing phenomenon from Nanda Devi and K2, it was still disconcerting to observe.

At 18,000 feet they decided to allow the subjects two days' reprieve before the next increase in altitude, allowing more time for acclimatization. The subjects immediately reported feeling better because of the hiatus. Interestingly, it wasn't just the subjects who were hurting; some of the scientists and crew, including Charlie, began to experience painful side effects from going in and out of the chamber. Because of the reduction in air pressure, they began to develop joint and bone pain, commonly known as "the bends," as nitrogen bubbles formed in their bodily fluids. Then Charlie experienced a severe headache, accompanied by loss of vision for thirty minutes. He didn't mention it to anyone, but learned later that he wasn't the only one with these symptoms.

Above 20,000 feet a new anxiety surfaced. "What would happen if we had to bring one of the subjects back to sea level because of an emergency?" Charlie wondered. "Would the man stop breathing?" They learned the answer soon enough. High-intensity lights used for filming inside the chamber blew a fuse, plunging the entire chamber into total darkness. Two crewmen were inside with the subjects. One could not attach his oxygen supply quickly enough, lost consciousness, fell into the other crewman, and knocked him down. The second man immediately called for a crash dive–depressurization. The crash dive was completed, and thankfully both men continued to breathe.

Conversations within the chamber were entertaining, since the four subjects began as complete strangers. There were heated arguments about the relative merits of Oregon and Texas, the talents of the girls in each subject's home town, and the size of fish. Amazingly enough, two of the subjects smoked—inside the chamber! One of the men built model airplanes, one carved wood, and the others read. "With three good meals a day, and a hot bath in the trash can every other night, and then a movie arranged by the Red Cross, their days were full," Charlie explained.

By the third week, Operation Everest had attracted a lot of attention: the local paper did a story, the air station journal carried daily reports, and officials arrived from Washington, along with distinguished scientists from many parts of the country. One admiral commented, "This is the first time I've ever talked with heroes while they were being heroic." At 22,000 feet they produced a dramatic demonstration of the value of acclimatization. A hospital corpsman was brought up from sea level, wearing oxygen, and then told to get on the bicycle and begin pedaling, but now without his oxygen mask. Despite his orders to replace it immediately if he felt anything wrong, in less than a minute he collapsed and had to be revived with oxygen. This was immediately followed by one of the acclimatized subjects climbing on the cycle and pedaling happily without an oxygen mask until he was finally asked to stop. It was a very vivid demonstration of the benefits of acclimatization. Life in the chamber was never dull. One day, while the pressure corresponded to that at 22,000 feet, the lights went out. One of the technicians in the lock lost his oxygen mask and fainted. They had to "crash" the lock down very quickly to revive him.

Finally, on July 30th the "dash for the summit" began, and the chamber was raised from 24,000 feet to 29,000 feet over a two-hour period. The atmosphere was tense. Once each hour, the subjects cycled for five minutes. Their pulse was taken, their heart activity was recorded on the electrocardiograph, and they were asked to give spoken recordings of their sensations. A thousand feet short of the top, two subjects asked for oxygen. This was a critical moment because nobody knew what would happen to a man who had been starved for oxygen for weeks and then given pure oxygen. Would he stop breathing? Would he be intoxicated? They watched closely as the subjects' faces turned from a deep purple to a healthy pink glow. They reported feeling fine, except for a feeling of pressure inside their skulls. Charlie breathed a sigh of relief, knowing now that using oxygen in an emergency was not dangerous.

The others continued cycling. At 27,500 feet one man became dizzy and nauseated. He ceased cycling, slowly returned to his bunk, and asked for oxygen. Although he momentarily lost consciousness, he too recovered quickly with the mask securely attached to his face. But two of the subjects cycled on, slowly and laboriously. The chamber reached 28,000 feet, then 29,000 feet, and finally the altimeter needle topped out at 29,025 feet, where they stayed for twenty-one minutes. In fact, it was closer to 30,000 feet, because as Charlie later learned, aircraft altimeters are calibrated somewhat differently. They had proven that an acclimatized man could survive higher than Everest, breathing only air, but it appeared he could not do much strenuous physical exercise at that altitude.

This ground-breaking experiment was completed seven years before Everest was climbed—*with* oxygen—and thirty-two years before Everest was climbed *without* supplemental oxygen.

Although Charlie's mountaineering question had been answered, there remained a major uncertainty for the Navy: had this degree of acclimatization increased a man's tolerance for even greater heights—*while* breathing oxygen? They were interested in the military application of this knowledge. So on July 31st two of the subjects, carefully fitted with standard oxygen masks, started up to 35,000, and then slowly to 45,000 feet. At 48,600 feet Morris complained of abdominal gas pains, and the chamber was lowered to 45,000 feet. A second attempt again caused pain. The other two subjects then tried it; the chamber was once again slowly taken up to 46,000 feet and then, finally, to 50,255 feet. Both men were alert but reported a slightly dizzy sensation. As the ascent ended, everyone breathed a sigh of relief as the chamber was brought down and the connecting door was opened.

Not yet finished, the team next set out to determine the maximum altitude at which the subjects could do physical work efficiently. Two men were taken up in 500-foot increments while breathing oxygen and exercising. At 46,000 feet both felt they could continue indefinitely; at 47,000 feet they felt they would be limited to a few hours of work, and at 48,500 feet their limit was about thirty minutes of physical labor.

The building was overrun with photographers long before the chamber door was opened. The men stepped out to a barrage of flashbulbs, handshakes, and congratulations from a distinguished group of visitors. All were bearded, and somewhat thinner than thirty-four days earlier, but they were in excellent health and their spirits were high. The entire team looked back at the previous month with pride as the final entry was made in the log: "Pumps secured, lights and communications secured—Chamber secured."

"It had been a big venture into a largely unexplored world and we had reason to be satisfied," Charlie said. "We had shown that the altitude of Everest was not lethal—though close to man's limit, and we had demonstrated that acclimatization would indeed increase a pilot's ceiling, breathing oxygen." All the data had been recorded daily on a master chart and it now remained to be analyzed and interpreted. From these data came several articles giving physiologists new insights into man's ability to acclimatize. It had been an exciting period for Charlie. He had full responsibility and authority for the project and was able to command help wherever he needed it. A handful of people caught the spark and worked very hard to ensure success. "To others I might have been a bit vague about the goals, but in my mind I wanted to know if a man could live and move about on top of Everest." Now he knew.

Charlie Houston as a Lieutenant in the USNR, Jacksonville, Florida 1942

Dorcas Houston at Honnedaga

Charlie and Dorcas Houston on Gulf Beach, Florida (1945)

1933 Mt. Crillon team shot: Charlie Houston, Bob Bates, Bill Child, Brad Washburn, Walt Everett, Ad Carter. Bradford Washburn photo

Mt. Crillon ice cliff, with Charlie Houston climbing on top of Bob Bates while Ad Carter waits below (1933). Bradford Washburn photo

Mt. Crillon - hauling loads across the glacier (1933)

Team photo for Mt. Foraker: Charlie Houston, Chychele Waterston, Charles Story, T. Graham Brown, Oscar Houston and Carl Andersen (1934)

T. Graham Brown and Chychele Waterston on the summit of Mt. Foraker (1934)

Nanda Devi team photo: Bill Tilman, Farnie Loomis, Graham Brown, Peter Lloyd, Ad Carter, Noel Odell, Art Emmons, Charlie Houston (1936)

Tilman with hat and pack on the way to Nanda Devi (1936)

Climbing through the gorge headwall towards Nanda Devi (1936)

Walking into the Nanda Devi Sanctuary (1936)

Nanda Devi after the trek out: Bill Tilman, Pasang Kikuli, Charlie Houston (1936)

LET GO WITH BOTH HANDS

Yet each man kills the thing he loves, By each let this be heard,
Some do it with a bitter look, Some with a flattering word. The
coward does it with a kiss, The brave man with a sword!
        —Oscar Wilde, from "The Ballad of
        Reading Gaol"

After the war years, during which he had worked on high-altitude research, Charlie needed to find a job. He desperately wanted to practice medicine, because that's what he had been trained to do, and both he and Dorcas wanted to move to New England. At the same time he was under considerable pressure to stay on with the military and become part of a still-secret task force that would go to Bikini, an unknown atoll in the Pacific, for a nuclear test. He was tempted, but his heart was set on a medical practice, and he and Dorcas wanted to set up a traditional home. By the fall of 1945 his discharge papers were signed, their belongings were packed, and he, Dorcas, and Penny headed north to Exeter, New Hampshire.

Since 1940, Charlie had known he wanted to make this move. A well-respected physician, Henry Saltonstall, had corresponded with him during the war and was now living on a large farm near Exeter. Saltonstall had talked with a group of doctors about forming a group medical practice, and

Charlie was interested—but apprehensive. His war experience had been interesting but it had taken him out of routine medical practice. He hadn't done a sick call in four years. During that time the age of antibiotics had dawned and new medications and diagnostic methods had emerged. Feeling the need to retrain himself, he decided to take an unpaid, informal externship at Bellevue Hospital in New York to relearn the practice. But instead of seeing the kind of illnesses and people he would probably encounter in a country practice, Charlie was exposed to exotic problems, major illnesses, and a rushed outpatient service where he had barely five minutes to see each patient, rarely one he had seen before. Charlie felt the entire experience was a mistake, explaining, "The medicines, the tests, the procedures were strange. The patients were indigent, often foreign, as frightened of me as I was of them. The wards were crowded and dingy and there I saw a wild assortment of problems, most of which I didn't think I'd ever see in Exeter." He yearned for a routine practice.

During his Bellevue stint, Charlie, Dorcas, and Penny temporarily moved back to the Long Island family home. Charlie commuted to New York with his father, thinking it would provide them an opportunity to get reacquainted. The experiment didn't work. "We just didn't talk," he said. Instead, Oscar was drawn to Dorcas, spending hours talking with her in the evenings, answering her many questions and becoming very close to her in the process. Charlie became increasingly depressed. It soon became obvious that it was time to move to Exeter, ready or not.

Exeter in 1947 was a town of 5,000 people. An additional 20,000 lived in the surrounding areas. Because the region appeared to be underserved by the five overworked doctors, Saltonstall and Charlie reached an agreement with two resident physicians, Oscar and Louis, to form a group practice. Oscar and Louis wanted help and were willing to share patients and, to a limited extent, their incomes. They found a splendid house on the main residential street, bought it for $9,500, hired an architect to redo it into offices, and named it the Exeter Clinic.

This was an idea ahead of its time. In 1947 the American Medical Association still frowned on partnerships, categorizing them as a form of socialized medicine. Nevertheless, the doctors forged ahead, agreeing to share expenses equally and to divide the net income. For the first three years most of the income would go to the two established doctors, but by the fourth year the plan was to share equally, regardless of who earned what. It seemed a simple formula. "It was naïve and idealistic—and it worked remarkably well for ten years," Charlie commented. "Can you imagine doing anything like that today?"

The clinic formally opened in March, 1947, and Charlie and his family moved into a tiny apartment in Saltonstall's barn. Eventually the strain of the cramped quarters became too much, especially later in the year after their son, Robin, was born. And so they began looking for a house. Though their savings were almost gone and Charlie's salary was precariously small, they fell in love with a brick house dating back to the War of 1812, on three acres of land with a spectacular view. It was a treasure. After some skillful bargaining they managed to convince the bank to lend them $13,000, and the house was theirs. But first of all they needed a well. They watched anxiously as the drill bore slowly through the rock, foot by foot, dollar by dollar, until finally they reached an acceptable flow of water at the $700 level. After extensive remodeling, they moved in.

Charlie needn't have worried about his ability to practice medicine. He had been well trained under Drs. Atchley and Loeb and he was excited to see patients and to apply his skills to the real world. He scorned the patent medicines that were stock in trade for country doctors, convinced that listening to the patient, thorough examinations, and reassurances healed best. He was in his element: "Medicine in that era was not a way to a good living; it was an art form, a skill, a talent to be used." Charlie clearly had those talents, for he quickly developed a small but devoted following.

He had many interesting, and sometimes frightening, experiences. One of them almost ended his Exeter career. The patient's name was Everett—a farmer with severe rheumatic heart disease common in New England at the time. He had had heart failure and was bedridden at home, with huge swelling in his legs and fluid in his abdomen and lungs. Charlie adjusted Everett's medications and added a kidney stimulant (diuretic) to drive out the fluid. He even took a sterile set of instruments to Everett's home to draw off fluid from his lung cavity and his abdomen. After he was fully digitalized the patient slowly improved. But Charlie was convinced that Everett's wife, Eliza, didn't like or trust him, although she couldn't deny her husband's improvement.

"We didn't have too many tools then, but one of the best diuretics—salyrgan—was effective but painful when injected into the muscle," Charlie explained. So instead, he gave it by vein twice a week. One day Charlie read a brief medical letter warning that intravenous injection of this particular drug might cause sudden death. Rarely—but possible. Charlie thought it over and concluded that the risk must be very small. Besides, Everett was so thin there wasn't much muscle left in which to inject a needle. So he continued with the veins.

After several weeks Everett was well enough to come to Charlie's office for the injection. Eliza insisted on joining him in the examination room, much to Charlie's irritation. Even though Everett was much improved, Charlie thought that another injection might help. "I prepared the syringe, set the tourniquet and turned to inject, and then Everett fell back—dead." It was indeed fortunate that Eliza was there watching. She could see that the needle hadn't touched his skin. "If I had been two seconds faster, nothing could have persuaded me—or Eliza—that I hadn't killed Everett . . . it was a narrow escape."

With the advent of readily available antibiotics and steroids, medicine was being propelled into a new era. It was at a medical convention in Atlantic City in 1949 that Charlie first heard of cortisone, touted for its miraculous affect on arthritis, asthma, lupus, and even psychoses. But as doctors saw the spectacular benefits of penicillin and cortisone, some began using them indiscriminately. It was eventually proven that if cortisone was given in full doses for too long it could cause irreversible loss of calcium from the bones and destruction of cartilage, as well as various other side effects such as euphoria. Antihistamines were also coming into vogue, offering relief from the common cold. In order to try and keep up-to-date with the changes in medicine, Charlie took a day off every two weeks to go to Boston to make rounds with one of the great Boston professors, Dr. Chester Keefer. It was Charlie's way of ensuring that he was, in fact, practicing good modern medicine.

The routine in Exeter was seldom dull. Charlie would start at the hospital, where he usually had a few patients. Then he would head out on house calls, driving twenty to thirty miles around the country and visiting patients or just stopping by for coffee and a visit. It was the best way to understand how people lived, why they got sick, and sometimes why they didn't get well. "I loved the house calls, but at $5 for each one, they certainly weren't cost effective," he said. In contrast, office calls were calculated on a sliding scale: $2 for those without much money, and much more for those who could pay. A visiting consultant shocked them all with the prediction that soon, "hospital rates will rise from $5 to $5.50 a day." Charlie earned what would now be considered a pittance. In his first year of practice in Exeter, he earned $2,200: the next two years, only marginally more.

Afternoons were devoted to office hours, then a hurried dinner at home, more office hours, and hospital rounds from 7:00 PM to 10:00 PM.

He maintained this grueling schedule five nights a week at first, then gradually cut it down to three. With each of his appointments Charlie tried to allow plenty of time to listen and explain. "People liked that," he recalled. "Today one of the most common complaints is that doctors simply don't listen to what patients want to say."

Night calls usually involved a trip far out of town, and they were usually serious in nature. One such call occurred during a snowstorm, when Charlie was completely snowed in, sitting snugly around a fire. He remembered it vividly: "The phone rang: one of my favorite patients with high blood pressure was having a bad nose bleed." For the next hour Charlie tried to stop the bleeding with a variety of suggestions over the phone, but nothing worked. Finally, at about one in the morning, he decided that he had to go, so he called the highway department, who agreed to meet him with a snowplow on the main road about two miles from his house. Carrying his black bag, he skied down the hill in the dark, rode the plow into town, picked up some special instruments at the clinic, and packed the patient's nose at her home. Then, just before dawn, he had to climb back up the hill, feeling quite heroic!

Charlie was occasionally viewed as an intruder—and even a threat. This may have been because he openly scorned the poor work he sometimes saw. To be fair, he was equally as admiring of those who performed well. His clinic comprised an eclectic collection of colleagues: "One of the local doctors was a not so secret alcoholic . . . another was beloved, gentle, dedicated, and totally incompetent. The most flamboyant of the local doctors was noisy and rough and not very able." Charlie remembered the day when his colleague came roaring into the nurses' station asking, "Charlie, what the hell can you do for poison ivy?" before promptly dropping his trousers, revealing an immense rash covering his thighs and genitalia to all assembled, including the horrified nurses.

Socially it was a somewhat quiet existence, although the community was filled with interesting people. Exeter Academy was a fine, well-endowed private school that resulted in a town full of highly educated faculty, including his previous climbing partner, Bob Bates, now an English professor. Although Charlie and Bates remained friends, Charlie categorized it more as an action-oriented friendship, best on a mountain, rather than a close, confiding kind of relationship. A favorite with Dorcas, Bates had one weakness—women—and several sobbing, heartbroken women found their way to Charlie's and Dorcas's shoulders. It didn't terminate their relationship with Bates, but it did strain their friendship, with Charlie and Dorcas finding Bates's behavior irritating.

One day Bates called Charlie with a puzzling situation. One of his students from the academy had a note from his doctor stating that he was not to engage in any athletics whatsoever because of a "bad heart." The boy didn't appear sick to Bates, so he asked Charlie to have a look at him. George Russell was thin, but well-built. Charlie examined him and could only detect a very slight, insignificant heart murmur. He concluded that George could probably try some reasonable sports. He passed this on to Bates, who immediately took him out rock climbing and, later, skiing. Young George then went on to join the rowing club, took up wrestling, and eventually became captain of the wrestling team. He subsequently went on to Stanford and became captain of that esteemed institution's wrestling team. He was headed for the Olympics as a wrestler and, were it not for a broken shoulder sustained just before the competition, would have competed at the highest level. Charlie often wondered what George's family thought of a small-town country doctor overruling that original diagnosis. When he asked the boy, he answered, "Well, the fact was that my family was too poor for me to come home at Christmas that first year and when I finally got home, I looked so much better that they never thought to challenge this new approach." George eventually became a very successful businessman and generous philanthropist who insisted that Charlie had saved his life. Years later Charlie laughed at this story and at countless others where a patient felt he owed his life to Charlie: "I get a lot of credit for those things, don't I. That should get me through the pearly gates!"

SOUTH SIDE OF EVEREST

Gather Courage. Don't Be a Chicken Hearted Fellow.
                    —Motto at the school in Dhankuta, Nepal

It was a beautiful spring day in 1950. Charlie, Dorcas and their children were enjoying a leisurely picnic on the grounds of their Exeter home when Charlie received an exciting call from the world-famous traveler and writer Lowell Thomas with an invitation to go to Tibet. Thomas had fallen and broken his leg when he had been there in 1949, and wanted a doctor to accompany him this time as a safety measure. While at a party in New York, Thomas had asked Dr. Magnus Gregersen, one of Charlie's former teachers, for the name of a doctor with mountain experience in Asia, and Gregersen suggested Charlie.

The unofficial rationale behind Thomas's invitation was much more intriguing. Deep in northwestern Tibet, a radio operator, Robert Ford, was functioning as the sole information source for the free world, even as communism was increasing its stranglehold over Asia. Ford had severe, crippling arthritis, and a "miracle drug"—cortisone—had only recently been proven to assuage his form of the disease. George Merck, owner of the company that produced the drug, had agreed to give Thomas a large supply of the costly medication; it was Charlie's mission to deliver the drug to Ford and cure his arthritis, enabling him to continue his clandestine work. Thomas didn't clearly explain just how this meeting would be arranged.

Dorcas was not pleased with the scheme. Not only was the Exeter Clinic just getting established, Charlie would be away for at least six weeks, leaving her with two small children. Plus, Dorcas knew there was real danger associated with this expedition. Disappointed, she had been operating under the misguided impression that Charlie had settled down with his thriving medical practice, their two children, and their friends. She thought that mountains were a thing of his past. After all, it had been almost twelve years since he'd gone to the Himalayas. But Charlie could not be swayed. Few Westerners had visited Lhasa since Francis Younghusband was there at the beginning of the century, and it was known to be a mysterious place of great richness, both culturally and economically. He even convinced himself that it would be a first-hand opportunity to see Tibetan medicine from the inside. He would be in one of the most fabulous cities on earth, on the far side of the Himalayas, engaged in secret service for his country—and paid at that! It was an irresistible, romantic, and even glamorous notion, one that contrasted sharply with his ordinary life. He was being asked to be a player in that "Great Game" as described by Kipling. On July 6th he flew to Washington, where he met Lowell Thomas. They were ushered in to see Dean Rusk, then assistant secretary of state. During the consultation with Rusk, word suddenly came down that the Communists were in Lhasa. Permission was abruptly withdrawn; the trip was off.

The letdown was tremendous. Charlie's Exeter practice, which had previously seemed fulfilling and rewarding, suddenly appeared dull and drab. How could it compare to delivering a miracle drug to a lonely and distant spy? Meanwhile, Charlie's father had been quietly planning another grand adventure—this time a visit to Nepal, which at the time was almost completely closed to outsiders. Oscar refused to discuss exactly how he had obtained permission to visit the country, particularly a part that was perilously close to Tibet. Yet somehow Oscar had secured the necessary documentation to mount an expedition to the south side of Mount Everest. When the Lowell Thomas trip to Tibet fell apart, Charlie's father approached him: "Son, I have permission to walk to the base of Everest across Nepal, and if you would like to go along, why not join us. . . . If you could take time off to go with Lowell Thomas, you can do so to come with me."

This idea was even more intriguing to Charlie. As far as he knew, there were almost no explorers who had penetrated even close to this area. Joseph

Hooker had been allowed to cross the Nepalese border from India on his way to Tibet in 1848 and had marched about thirty miles into the country, gazing at the hill village of Dhankuta, but that was the extent of his permission. The next visitor was Doctor Dillon Ripley from the Smithsonian Institute, who in 1949 had traveled about fifty miles beyond Dhankuta. But he was sure that no Westerner, and certainly no mountaineer, had ever seen the south side of Everest.

Again, Dorcas protested. The Korean War had taken everyone by surprise in June; Asia was in turmoil. Many thought that another Great War was inevitable. Air travel to Asia was scarce and uncertain, and China's role in Tibet was unclear. The area they were proposing to visit was unknown. Nepal itself was still remote and unexplored and had only recently opened its doors to foreigners. Charlie desperately wanted to go. With Tibet closed to climbing, the southern approach had suddenly become very important. Besides, he explained to his skeptical wife, his father was sixty-seven and should not be in that wild and remote country without Charlie at his side. In the end, Dorcas reluctantly acquiesced.

From the beginning their adventure was envisioned not as a climbing expedition but rather an exploratory reconnaissance. In fact Charlie hadn't climbed for several years. The team comprised an unusual assortment of people. Andy Bakewell was a wealthy St. Louis family friend who had become a Jesuit and was now stationed in Darjeeling. He had extensive mountaineering experience, knew India well, and spoke Hindi. Betsy Cowles, the experienced climber with whom Charlie and Dorcas had climbed on their honeymoon, also accompanied them. Oscar, Angel Bunny, and Cowles set off for India in August, arranging to meet Bakewell and Charlie in Kathmandu. They were all entertained royally by the prime minister in Kathmandu and were among the first few Americans to sign the register at the American embassy.[6] Angel Bunny continued on traveling in India, accompanied by her servant, Solomon.

Kathmandu was still a relatively small city of 100,000, with few outside influences. Cowles described the city smells as "marvelous," emanating as they did from "eucalyptus, mint, spice and the Far East"[7]—a pleasantly nostalgic thought, considering the more modern stench of diesel smoke in that Himalayan city. In Kathmandu they happened to meet Bill Tilman, Charlie's Nanda Devi partner, who had just returned from a wild trek in the Annapurna region. Tilman probably knew more about the Himalayas than any living person, so, not surprisingly, Oscar immediately invited him along. Charlie was ecstatic. He and Tilman had bonded well on Nanda Devi, and there was no doubt that Tilman added much-needed strength to the team.

From Kathmandu, they boarded a narrow-gauge train for the forty-eight-hour trip to Jogbani on the edge of Nepal. Then it was on to Delhi, where they ran into a character who called himself Frank A. C. Thomas. Thomas was very keen to be invited along, claiming to have traveled throughout the area they planned to visit. He professed to speak Nepali and Tibetan fluently and tried to convince them that he would be an invaluable asset to the team. Intuitively, Charlie's father resisted, adding that if the Nepalese granted him separate permission, he could join them. Thomas persisted, but Oscar held his ground, not trusting the oleaginous Thomas.

They passed back into the forbidden kingdom, unencumbered by passport checks or border guards. Tilman joined them, and for thirty miles they jostled about in a huge truck along a crude track. Then they began to walk. Up one jungle-choked ridge, down to a river, up another ridge, and then down again. As they were traveling on a major north–south route, they passed hundreds of heavily laden coolies with everything from salt to oranges to brightly colored cloth in their straw baskets. When the small team stopped, even for a minute, they were immediately surrounded by a curious, polite crowd craning for a better view of the odd looking strangers. Finally, after dropping down to the Tamur River, crossing it on a suspension bridge and then ascending about 3,000 feet, they reached the first Nepalese village, Dhankuta, which they described as "the dream town of all our lives." Here in the neat, whitewashed village with well-swept cobbled streets, they were greeted by the mayor and a local teacher, who invited them into the school. In crude script above the door was written the school motto: "Gather Courage. Don't Be a Chicken Hearted Fellow." They immediately adopted it as their expedition slogan.

After a night camped on a small knoll near the village, the trek began in earnest. Charlie's memories were vivid: "We started late next morning, climbing to the top of the ridge—and gasped! Below us fell a series of cultivated terraces down, down to a silvery river, and beyond this, foothills faded into the distance. Impossibly high above them were snow white summits, riding like clouds above a blurred horizon." They continued on to the Arun River, one of the great torrents that cut through the range from Tibet. Here they walked upstream for a few marvelous days: "Up in the chilly pre-dawn, after our Sherpas brought hot tea to each of us, breakfast of hot cereal and *chapattis*, and then off with our little caravan bringing our baggage behind.

By noon we were ready for a picnic lunch, by four we were ready for tea and rest where our Sherpas had decided to set up camp." On hot days they would cool themselves with a quick dip in the river. It was truly idyllic. In fact, Tilman later described the trip as a "great picnic, bumbling through Nepal, a land of unbelievable beauty, freshness and excitement."

During the ten-day trek they became very close. Charlie's father husbanded his strength for, at his age, the great climbs and descents were difficult. But each day he grew stronger. Tilman, a lifelong misogynist, almost deserted the expedition when he first realized there would be a woman along: "Hitherto I had not regarded a woman as an indispensable part of the equipage of a Himalayan journey but one lives and learns."[8] For several days he walked ahead or behind, sulking—or so they thought. Cowles reassured them that she would soften him up. Sure enough, soon they were walking together, eating together and obviously enjoying each other's company. They were even spotted holding hands occasionally, although Charlie maintains there was nothing more than friendship involved. He was convinced that Tilman simply enjoyed Cowles because she could do whatever Tilman could do. Romance wasn't in the picture.[9]

In truth, Cowles was irresistible to everyone, including Oscar, who appreciated her ability to do things with him that his wife could not—like walking to Everest. In fact, Oscar apparently became somewhat agitated when "Tilman took up with Betsy." Although Oscar's "nose was a bit out of joint," he managed to contain his irritation. Charlie, too, admired Cowles's physical prowess, although he never made any comparison to Dorcas, who, regardless of her ability or interest in going to Nepal, had not been invited on the Everest trek. Of course she was also busy with family responsibilities back in Exeter.

Cowles was particularly good with the women and children who clustered around her at every stop along the trail. Tilman made bread every few days, kneading the dough in a plastic bag in his pocket while he walked, and baking it on an open fire at night. Although the Sherpas referred to his bread as "foot-bread" because his boots were always covered in flour, Tilman insisted that he did not use his feet in the making of it. The forests had yet to be depleted by the massive tourism influx, so they never hesitated to have a wood fire each night. The Sherpas prepared hearty meals of local chicken, flour, and vegetables. "It's hard to explain what a marvelous time this was for all of us," Charlie explained. They felt completely isolated from the outside world, and happy to be so.

They eventually entered Buddhist country, and finally descended into the Dudh Kosi valley, which they knew came directly from Everest. Here the natives looked Tibetan and there were few signs of Western culture. Neither saw nor ax appeared; all the work appeared to be done with the *kukri*—a short, curved knife. The strong and sturdy local people were clad in felt leather boots and heavy, homespun coats and pants. The women also often wore attractive silver and stone jewelry. Here too the explorers saw Tibetan refugees who brought terrible tales of torture, oppression, and what amounted to virtual elimination of their country. As they drew closer to Tibet, they wondered just how safe it would be. In his diary Charlie worried about ever being allowed to return. By November 14th they were at the foot of a steep hill that led up to Namche Bazaar, the last real village before the border with Tibet. Somehow, using their crude and rather vague map, they had found the way and would soon see the great mountain.

The day was cold, darkening early with a thick layer of clouds that obscured any remaining sunlight. About a mile before the town, a reception committee, complete with a herd of small Tibetan ponies, came out to meet them on the trail. After being convinced to mount the ponies, they rode into Namche, where they found row upon row of stone houses, firmly shuttered windows and doors, and a reassuring feeling of strength and toughness.

Their arrival in Namche coincided with market day, and the town was crowded with hundreds of people from miles around. "Here we were near forbidden Tibet, within reach of Everest, surrounded by people who had never seen a foreigner. Heady stuff!" remembered Charlie of the experience. They erected their tents on a terrace next to the headman's house and were immediately invited in for a wicked brew of yak butter and strong, salty tea, a concoction they just managed to choke down. It was their first look at the inside of a Sherpa house, which they found fascinating—and smoky.

The next day they crossed the river and climbed up through freshly fallen snow to the Tengboche monastery. "We weren't prepared for this," admitted Charlie. "It was larger and more elaborate than expected . . . the lamas came running out to greet us . . . we were in a dream place, welcomed guests where none had come before." Even the taciturn Tilman was moved.

They were taken to a small stone house attached to the monastery, in the middle of which was a kind of fireplace. Down a steep set of stairs was a crude toilet. That night's rest was frequently broken as each of their uneasy digestive systems demanded repeated trips up and down that stairway. The next morning one of the lamas woke them by lighting the fire and serving them a drink of strong *rakshi* (distilled liquor) to launch the morning. The startlingly clear day revealed the sight they had come for: "Then, forty miles away, bathed in sun was the great wall of the Everest massif, not beautiful but majestic." Cowles described their view: "There is something profoundly moving about having the biggest hill on earth right in front of you, yours to see day after day, in all the lights and in all the moods." One of those moods was illuminated that evening when, long after all the other peaks were shrouded in darkness, Everest was afire with the late-evening light of the setting sun.

Charlie's eyes were drawn elsewhere: "It's awesome, but the really beautiful peak seen from the monastery is Ama Dablam. It's like the Matterhorn, just as sheer and sharp but ten thousand feet higher and pulls your attention from all else, even the scores of other peaks near and far." They could see no feasible route up the mountain.

But they were not there for Ama Dablam; their job was to explore Everest. On November 16th, 1950, Charlie, Tilman, and one Sherpa set off to go as far as they could while the others remained at Tengboche. They had exactly six days during which to examine the unexplored south side of the mountain. They knew their impressions would be cursory at best, but they were determined to learn what they could and bring back as many good photographs as possible.

Neither Tilman nor Charlie was absolutely sure of the best way to get past the wall that shielded the lower part of the mountain, but finally they chose left as the best option. They hoped to pass around the western end of Nuptse and enter the Western Cwm in order to examine the South Face of Everest. First they had to cover the forty miles to the wall. They walked past two tiny villages, Pheriche and Phalang Karpa, beyond which the yaks were taken to graze. They camped in a field and the next day came to a great plain below the slopes that hid Everest. The plain was covered with dwarf juniper and contained a few rock-walled corrals. The air was cold and clear with no clouds to be seen. They were completely surrounded by magnificent, unclimbed, and unnamed peaks.

The next day they left Pheriche and continued north and around the corner to catch their first glimpse at the high cliffs that form the border with Tibet. They stumbled up the moraine and then on the glacier that falls from those cliffs, hoping to look more closely onto the face of Everest. Both Charlie and Tilman were tired, feeling the altitude, and uncertain. They crossed the glacier and crawled up steep slopes until Charlie's headache and fatigue overcame him. There, on what has since become known as Kala Pattar, he took photos of the chaotic ice that falls from the valley below Everest, the Western Cwm. Meanwhile, the indefatigable Tilman continued up the moraine in order to look into the icefall. At that point they turned back, not having seen quite as much as they had hoped to but at the end of their strength, both nursing blinding headaches.

That night they lit a huge fire beside their campsite, and so began an evening Charlie would not forget: "Tilman talked as he never had before. . . . For the first time this silent man told about adventures not told anywhere else. It was almost as intoxicating as had been our sight of Everest." Tilman told tales of Sinkiang and Hunza, about suffering alone in his tent with malaria in Sikkim, about his adventures with Shipton. In fits and starts, with long silences in between, he told of the war and of fighting with the partisans, about being wounded and twice being decorated. He finally told Charlie that this would be his last trip into the mountains, saying only that he was now too old. Tilman later articulated this sentiment in *Nepal Himalaya*: "The best attainable should be good enough for any man, but the mountaineer who finds his best gradually sinking is not satisfied."[10] In retrospect, after significant research in altitude-related illnesses, Charlie was sure that Tilman was suffering from cerebral edema. They had both gone up too high, too fast.

But they still had a job to do. They were here to learn more about Everest: was there a direct route from the floor of the Western Cwm? Was there a way over the Lho La, which in turn would lead to the North Col route? Were there other ways of ascending the mountain, such as the western shoulder?

The enchanting night over, they headed out early to gain some higher ground. After climbing steadily up the Khumbu Valley, they finally reached the lower end of the Khumbu Glacier. Slipping and sliding on a combination of ice and scree, they encountered hundreds of pure white pinnacles, many over 200 feet high, reminding Charlie of the "ice ships" of the Baltoro Glacier in the Karakoram. They had one more day to explore—November 19th—and disappointingly it was cloudy. After crossing the Khumbu Glacier, they reached the west side of the valley and could now clearly see the Lho La at 20,000 feet and Changtse at 24,747 feet. They could also see the West Peak of the mountain, which hid what they knew would be the final ridge to the summit pyramid. Across the North Face they could pick out the First and Second Steps as well as the final pyramid. Surprisingly, both the North and South Faces were relatively free of snow, and from this observation Charlie thought that the autumn might provide a more favorable climbing season, although he acknowledged the disadvantages of the colder temperatures and shorter days. They could see that the South Face was steeper than the North, but they could not see much of the Western Cwm, and so determined that passage up the Cwm would be difficult, if not impossible. Even though they could not see it, they came to the conclusion that the headwall leading up to the South Col between Lhotse and Everest would not be a reasonable route. (This of course became the standard route on Everest.) They did not dismiss these routes completely, but their evaluation was based on their knowledge of the already-discovered, and satisfactory, Northeast Ridge route. These seemed like poor cousins in comparison. As Charlie explained: "If some of the world's finest climbers have failed on a route which is not exceptionally difficult, who is likely to succeed on one which is more difficult and uncertain?"

In their subsequent reports to the climbing community, neither Tilman nor Charlie gave much encouragement for an approach on this side. Meanwhile, the northern approach through Communist-dominated Tibet was closed for the foreseeable future. And although the southern approach was shorter, lay in fertile, populated country, was warmer and sunnier than the forbidding north side, and provided a comfortable base camp, there simply was no obvious, feasible route up the mountain. Back home, Charlie wrote in the *Appalachian Mountain Club Newsletter*: "From where I sit today, thousands of miles and many months distant, with my mind's eye I can recall that view, pour [sic] over the pictures, and persuade myself that some route may lead to Everest from the deeper recesses of the west cirque; we could not see it then, and the chances are small."[11] Charlie wryly recalled that it was to Tilman that the Brits went for information about the area; surprisingly, they never contacted Charlie. To be fair, Tilman was much more accessible to those British climbers than was Charlie, who was halfway around the world. Charlie went on to claim that the Brits rarely even acknowledged their 1950 exploratory expedition. But laughingly he added: "I lost no opportunity reminding them that my father's expedition was there long before they were!"

While Charlie and Tilman were exploring a possible route up the south side of Everest, the rest of the party remained back at the monastery, where they were entertained in a spectacular manner: music, dance, food, and revelry. Oscar captured the unique traditions on film: massive brass gongs, spectacularly colorful costumes, intricately designed prayer *katas,* the drone of prayers, and frighteningly real masks.

When Charlie and Tilman returned to the monastery, they tried to convey their emotions of being in such a wild place, of the magnificent beauty, and of wandering freely among the towering peaks. They were pleased with what they had seen, but not completely satisfied that they had done a proper job of it. "We were just too sick," Charlie remembered, referring to the effects of altitude. The fourteen-year-old abbott blessed them and then allowed them to photograph and film him. In a moment of generosity, Charlie bestowed upon him his hat, which the abbott gleefully accepted.

The march out was a model of efficiency, as they were all in superb condition. One by one, they bid farewell to the familiar valleys and passes, to the *mani* walls and *chortens*, and to the Buddhist prayer flags fluttering in the high alpine breezes. Mile by mile, they steadily descended, until they were greeted by warm valley breezes and the welcome sight of flowers and fruit. Just before they arrived in Dhankuta, a messenger from the mayor arrived. He announced that there had been a revolution in Kathmandu and advised them to take an alternate road to the border. While they had been leading a life of seclusion and tranquility in the high valleys of the Solu Khumbu, the rest of the country had taken a startling turn.

They felt despondent as they left behind this land of beauty and apparent innocence. To Charlie and his little band of explorers, it still appeared a Garden of Eden, and they couldn't help but ask themselves whether they were going *back* to civilization—or leaving it.

A small mystery remained. Just before the messenger had arrived, Charlie had discovered something unusual on the trail—an empty film box, and not the kind used by his team. They speculated wildly about how it got there and finally concluded that it couldn't have been anyone other than Frank Thomas. They queried the messenger and learned that a foreigner and one Sherpa had indeed passed through Dhankuta a few days after the Houston team. Sure enough, when they rendezvoused with their pre-arranged car at the trailhead, out stepped Thomas.

"He was very glad to see us—but it wasn't mutual," Charlie said. "He put off all our questions, and when we plied him with *rakshi, we* were the ones who got drunk!" They did, however, learn the story of how the Nepalese king had taken temporary refuge in the Indian embassy in Kathmandu, of his escape into India, his abdication of the throne, and the new assertiveness of the Nepalese Congress Party. What was completely unclear was who had masterminded the entire thing. On the train back to Delhi, Thomas grilled them intensively until, finally, Oscar put his foot down and said no more questions until Thomas told them something of himself. When he finally out of Tibet by private plane.

Once they were in Delhi, Thomas's network of contacts became even more intriguing. He first suggested that he knew the Maharajah of Darbhanga's private pilot, who could fly them over Everest, giving Charlie the ultimate Everest photographs—from the air! But when they checked in with the American ambassador, he pleaded with them to drop the idea; the area was simply too sensitive. Then Thomas proposed a flight over K2 instead. Charlie got very excited. For five days they arranged the details, but eventually the Indian intelligence officers protested loudly, and again the American ambassador suggested they drop it, hinting that there were aspects of Thomas that were suspicious and sordid. "You must remember that in 1950 much of Asia was in flames," recounted Charlie. "The Chinese were rampaging throughout Tibet, killing lamas and plundering monasteries. North Koreans were bloodily beating United Nations troops—mostly American—and it seemed possible that China would join and force us out of that hapless land . . . on top of that was a revolt in Nepal of unknown dimensions." They wisely abandoned the K2 plan, but this was not the last Charlie would hear from Thomas.

For Charlie, the adventure was still not quite over. The group split up, with Bakewell heading back to his home in Darjeeling, Tilman to London, and Charlie's parents and Cowles to Hong Kong. That left Charlie in Delhi waiting for a flight, which after a few days finally appeared. Shortly after leaving the ground, the plane suddenly lost one engine. "I was sitting next to a famous *New York Times* journalist, Bill Costello, who said very calmly, 'This is it' and we braced for an instant crash. Somehow the pilot held the plane steady, and he slowly, delicately turned back and landed." When the pilot emerged from the cockpit, he was wringing wet with sweat, and his dark, northern Indian skin was as pale as pale could be.

A relief plane eventually arrived and Charlie wrangled a flight as far as Karachi, where he was welcomed by Ambassador Warren at the embassy. Charlie arrived late in the evening, exhausted, rumpled, and covered in dust and sweat, just in time for an elegant dinner party. He was seated at Mrs. Warren's right and instantly became the center of attention for the many diplomats assembled as they quizzed him into the early-morning hours on Nepal and his Everest journey. The next morning Ambassador Warren tried to entice Charlie with a trip to Gilgit. Though he was sorely tempted, Charlie chose the next flight back to Europe.

When he returned to Exeter, Charlie was queried by many. Now that he'd done the reconnaissance trip to the south side of Everest, why did he not organize an actual climbing expedition? He had made inroads with the government in terms of permits, they had found a possible way, why not try it? But Charlie simply wasn't that interested in Everest; another mountain held his heart. "We had been very close to the top in 1938, and the tragic debacle of 1939 still angered me." K2 was his dream.

Charlie's wanderings through that remote part of Nepal did not go unnoticed. Shortly after his return, two men in suits arrived at his Exeter medical office, asking to speak with him. In truth, they were CIA operatives there for a debriefing: where had he gone; what were the people like; what were the travel routes; were there any other foreigners; what were the major rivers. One operative questioned him while the other guarded the door. In the end, they gave him directions to a drop box where he was instructed to contact them if anything new came up, or if he remembered any additional details. As they left, they swore him to secrecy.

The intrigue over, Charlie attempted to focus on re-establishing his medical practice and being with his family. Back in Exeter, Dorcas had been managing their home with quiet precision and had quickly become known as the best cook in town. Her dinner parties were formal affairs with fine wines accompanying carefully prepared dishes. With the beautiful china, linens, and Murano glassware that Charlie was to inherit from his mother, her dinner parties were even more elegant. Dorcas being a perfectionist in all she did, chose her guests carefully. Eight seemed to be the perfect number. Dinner was always preceded by cocktails and hors d'oeuvres, and Dorcas kept a notebook of all her parties, indicating who was invited, what was served, what people enjoyed, what they talked about, and who got along with whom. Then she and Charlie rated the dinners. Dorcas's ratings were always lower than his: "We had one D, a couple of C's, but most of them were B or A−," he recalled. Her dinner invitations were coveted, but also a bit feared, since Dorcas could be intimidating in her pursuit of the perfect evening.

Her female guests often asked for her recipes, but after a couple of disappointing experiences, Dorcas politely declined. As she explained to Charlie: "One thing I can't stand is when people serve one of my dishes and give me credit for it and it's poorly done." Even more irritating for Dorcas was when they served her dishes and *didn't* give her credit for them. Later, Charlie with a trip to Gilgit. Though he was sorely tempted, Charlie chose the next flight back to Europe.

When he returned to Exeter, Charlie was queried by many. Now that he'd done the reconnaissance trip to the south side of Everest, why did he not organize an actual climbing expedition? He had made inroads with the government in terms of permits, they had found a possible way, why not try it? But Charlie simply wasn't that interested in Everest; another mountain held his heart. "We had been very close to the top in 1938, and the tragic debacle of 1939 still angered me." K2 was his dream.

Charlie's wanderings through that remote part of Nepal did not go unnoticed. Shortly after his return, two men in suits arrived at his Exeter medical office, asking to speak with him. In truth, they were CIA operatives there for a debriefing: where had he gone; what were the people like; what were the travel routes; were there any other foreigners; what were the major rivers. One operative questioned him while the other guarded the door. In the end, they gave him directions to a drop box where he was instructed to contact them if anything new came up, or if he remembered any additional details. As they left, they swore him to secrecy.

The intrigue over, Charlie attempted to focus on re-establishing his medical practice and being with his family. Back in Exeter, Dorcas had been managing their home with quiet precision and had quickly become known as the best cook in town. Her dinner parties were formal affairs with fine wines accompanying carefully prepared dishes. With the beautiful china, linens, and Murano glassware that Charlie was to inherit from his mother, her dinner parties were even more elegant. Dorcas being a perfectionist in all she did, chose her guests carefully. Eight seemed to be the perfect number. Dinner was always preceded by cocktails and hors d'oeuvres, and Dorcas kept a notebook of all her parties, indicating who was invited, what was served, what people enjoyed, what they talked about, and who got along with whom. Then she and Charlie rated the dinners. Dorcas's ratings were always lower than his: "We had one D, a couple of C's, but most of them were B or A−," he recalled. Her dinner invitations were coveted, but also a bit feared, since Dorcas could be intimidating in her pursuit of the perfect evening.

Her female guests often asked for her recipes, but after a couple of disappointing experiences, Dorcas politely declined. As she explained to Charlie: "One thing I can't stand is when people serve one of my dishes and give me credit for it and it's poorly done." Even more irritating for Dorcas was when they served her dishes and *didn't* give her credit for them. Later, Charlie

acquiesced, the story was too smooth—too plausible—and Tilman suspected a hoax. Thomas was too informed, too well-traveled, too fluent in
remote dialects, and too familiar with remote and forbidden lands. He also
knew too much about the soon-to-be-aborted plan to spirit the Dalai Lama
out of Tibet by private plane.

Once they were in Delhi, Thomas's network of contacts became even more
intriguing. He first suggested that he knew the Maharajah of Darbhanga's private pilot, who could fly them over Everest, giving Charlie the ultimate Everest photographs—from the air! But when they checked in with the American
ambassador, he pleaded with them to drop the idea; the area was simply too
sensitive. Then Thomas proposed a flight over K2 instead. Charlie got very
excited. For five days they arranged the details, but eventually the Indian
intelligence officers protested loudly, and again the American ambassador
suggested they drop it, hinting that there were aspects of Thomas that were
suspicious and sordid. "You must remember that in 1950 much of Asia was in
flames," recounted Charlie. "The Chinese were rampaging throughout Tibet,
killing lamas and plundering monasteries. North Koreans were bloodily beating United Nations troops—mostly American—and it seemed possible that
China would join and force us out of that hapless land . . . on top of that was a
revolt in Nepal of unknown dimensions." They wisely abandoned the K2 plan,
but this was not the last Charlie would hear from Thomas.

For Charlie, the adventure was still not quite over. The group split up, with
Bakewell heading back to his home in Darjeeling, Tilman to London, and
Charlie's parents and Cowles to Hong Kong. That left Charlie in Delhi waiting
for a flight, which after a few days finally appeared. Shortly after leaving the
ground, the plane suddenly lost one engine. "I was sitting next to a famous
New York Times journalist, Bill Costello, who said very calmly, 'This is it' and we
braced for an instant crash. Somehow the pilot held the plane steady, and he
slowly, delicately turned back and landed." When the pilot emerged from the
cockpit, he was wringing wet with sweat, and his dark, northern Indian skin
was as pale as pale could be.

A relief plane eventually arrived and Charlie wrangled a flight as far as Karachi, where he was welcomed by Ambassador Warren at the embassy. Charlie arrived late in the evening, exhausted, rumpled, and covered in dust and
sweat, just in time for an elegant dinner party. He was seated at Mrs. Warren's
right and instantly became the center of attention for the many diplomats assembled as they quizzed him into the early-morning hours on Nepal and his
Everest journey. The next morning Ambassador Warren tried to entice Charlie

collected her most successful original recipes into her own, personal cookbook that was lovingly handed down to family members and close friends. Called *Mem's Specialties*, it featured such mouthwatering dishes as "Angel Bunny's lamb stew" and "Ambrosia chocolate mousse chantilly."

It wasn't just the creation of good food that intrigued Dorcas. She also experimented with something quite revolutionary at the time: freezing food. She would cook two casseroles, freezing one for future consumption. She experimented with different ingredients and various techniques, capturing all of her research into a massive document that Charlie didn't discover until well after her death.

In Exeter, Dorcas also embraced the "May Bowl," an annual get-together first held just before World War II at Great Neck with Charlie's parents. Charlie and Dorcas continued the tradition, each May throwing an elaborate garden party for approximately thirty people. It was always a combination of old friends and new acquaintances, as one of the objectives of the party was to introduce the possibility of new friendships. One of the highlights was a special punch composed of dry white wine and a secret herbal ingredient that Charlie transported from the Great Neck garden to each subsequent home. Dorcas carefully evaluated each May Bowl party, based on quality of food, weather, conversation, and potential friendships formed. It quickly became a much-sought-after invitation.

Then, quite unexpectedly, her family responsibilities grew with the arrival of Peggy Tenduf-La, a young Tibetan woman from Darjeeling who was sponsored by Oscar Houston and Lowell Thomas to come to the United States to attend medical school. Peggy, nicknamed Tenki, arrived on December 19th, 1951, at the age of nineteen. She flew into New York absolutely transfixed with what she saw—thousands upon thousands of houses lit up with what she would later learn were Christmas lights. It appeared a fairyland to Tenki. After a hurried visit with the senior Houstons at their splendid home in Long Island, she went on to Radio City Music Hall, where she was interviewed by Lowell Thomas. The entire family then came up to Exeter to spend Christmas with Charlie's family, where Tenki remained.

On one of Tenki's first evenings in Exeter, the Houstons received an invitation to one of the town's most exclusive social events of the year: black tie for the men, evening gowns and gloves for the ladies. The Christmas decorations were brilliant and the food was delicious. Tenki entered in her exotic Tibetan dress, looking ravishingly beautiful as she charmed the entire room. Most thought she was a princess. Within twenty-four hours Exeter was abuzz with the rumor that Charlie, the Himalayan traveler, had brought her over as his Asian mistress.

As the Houstons settled into family life, canoeing proved a favorite summer pastime. An avid canoeist since his boyhood, Charlie still managed to frighten himself on a regular basis, sometimes in the company of his family. One warm summer day they found themselves quietly floating down a small stream when suddenly they were surrounded by bushes alive with spiders—all kinds of spiders—and their associated webs. As they tried wildly to brush them away, hundreds fell into the canoe, absolutely terrifying the two children and greatly angering Dorcas. On another occasion, Charlie attempted to run an impressive rapid just north of Exeter in full view of his family and several colleagues. He quickly lost control, landed broadside on a rock island, dumped the canoe, and swam down through the rapids, all the while chasing his rapidly filling canoe. When he finally caught up with it, conveniently pinned against a rock, it was with dismay, but with much delight for the onlookers, that he discovered it was bent into a perfect U shape.

A more serious incident began innocently enough when one hot July day Charlie took Robin and his friend Dulcie Lynch canoeing. They floated along a tranquil, slow-flowing stream with less than a foot of clear water gliding over light-colored sand. As Charlie stopped to take a break on shore, the two six-year-olds waded out into the stream to play. Charlie's attention momentarily lapsed, and suddenly he noticed that they had disappeared. Charlie leapt into the canoe, pushed as fast as he could, and managed to reach their last-seen point. He searched frantically for Robin, found him in very deep water, and grabbed him by the scruff of his neck, pulling him into the canoe. Robin looked up at his dad and spluttered, "There goes Dulcie." Poor Dulcie had just gone under for the third time. Almost too late, Charlie managed to grab her and deposit her into the canoe, too. "Dulcie, what happened?" he yelled. "I don't know, Dr. Houston. I just sank and sank and sank. And when I hit bottom, I just pushed and pushed," she wailed. The children were gasping and crying and Charlie was in shock. He had almost lost them.

The Houston family grew again with the birth of their third child, David, in 1952. He was a seemingly contented child: Charlie insisted that he cried only nine times in the first five months, the most noteworthy being when Tenki gave him a bottle of milk directly from the icebox, mistakenly thinking that all Americans preferred their drinks cold. Charlie also admitted that, as a counterpoint to David's angelic behavior, he was the "wettest one we have ever had." The child that most worried Charlie was Robin, probably because he saw in Robin aspects of his own personality that he disliked most. He worried about Robin's volatile temper and his irritable nature. He forbade him to play with the Tibetan knife, or *kukri,* that Tenki had gifted him, for fear that Robin might do serious damage in a fit of rage. In contrast, Penny was supremely feminine, taken up with dolls, dresses, and playing house.

Family life was balanced, of course, with the continuing demands of Charlie's small-town practice, which sometimes revealed the darker side of the community. During a quiet family dinner, Charlie received a call from a man who purported that his child was having trouble breathing. Charlie rushed off immediately to the small, neat bungalow just off the main road and burst in to find a man and woman standing over a five-year-old girl, obviously dead. And dead for several hours. Charlie was puzzled by the pale, cold, emaciated child, and by the awful, unemotional silence of the parents. Despite persistent questioning, he couldn't obtain a satisfactory explanation. Suddenly he heard a feeble cry from upstairs. He rushed up and found another, even younger child, so weak and pale she was obviously near death. Without a moment's hesitation he picked her up, took her to the car, and drove her to the hospital, where medical staff nursed her back to life. She was dreadfully malnourished; her tissues were wasting from severe malnutrition, and her vitamin deficiencies were severe. The parents were arrested shortly after, went to trial, were jailed for their mistreatment, and were successfully charged with manslaughter. Charlie was the key witness in the trial. After his damaging testimony, the man turned to Charlie and threatened: "I'll get you. I'll get you when I'm out of jail if it's the last thing I do. I'll kill you, doctor. You hear that?" It was Charlie's first case of child abuse and it shocked him to the core.

Another time, on a quiet morning in his office, the local pharmacist called with, "Doc, there's a problem in the apartment over my store." There, in a disorderly room, Charlie found a naked woman, nearly dead, covered with blood. There was also blood spattered from floor to ceiling. He placed her in an ambulance and rushed her to the hospital, where she barely survived. Months later her attempted murderer was caught, tried, and convicted. He escaped for a time, and rumor had it that he was hiding in the woods behind the Houston residence, waiting to kill Charlie.

There were many tragedies, but Charlie retained one particularly dreadful memory. The owner of the local hardware store suffered bad attacks of asthma because of severe allergies, especially to house dust. Charlie had managed to control his condition quite effectively, but one day the man went into his basement and developed a terrible attack. "I put him into the hospital right away and did all the things we did in those days—oxygen tent, lots of fluids, etc., but it was before steroids." He didn't improve, so Charlie lay down in the next room and tried to soothe him. But the man gradually filled up, couldn't breathe, and died, choking on his lung fluids and spasms. "I didn't have the adequate knowledge or skills to save him; he shouldn't have died, and I have had him on my conscience ever since. He'd been a good friend."

Charlie's favorite patient was Elsie Allen, the widow of a prominent Boston doctor. Her humor, courage, and charm captivated him at once. She had suffered twenty years from asthma and was now confined to her home thirty miles from Exeter in southern Maine. She spent her days in bed, in an oxygen tent. Charlie had just returned from a medical meeting in Atlantic City, where Dr. Philip Hench had explained the use of cortisone. Hench had also casually suggested that the hormone ACTH, which naturally stimulates the body to make its own cortisone, might help a variety of allergic problems. Charlie called Dr. Kendall in Boston and asked if he could get a small supply of the scarce ACTH for Elsie. Kendall reluctantly agreed, pointing out that it was worth $900. Charlie picked up the drug at the train station, admitted Elsie into the hospital, and began to monitor the effects of this new, powerful, and little-known medication. After just one day she was well enough to emerge from the oxygen tent. She soon returned home and Charlie continued the treatment of ACTH, later changing it to cortisone. The entire family eventually befriended her as they accompanied Charlie on his periodic calls to check up on her. "Elsie Allen will remain in my pantheon of wonderful people."

Occasionally, people came to Charlie with their personal—sometimes marital—problems. Charlie referred the really serious ones to a city psychiatrist, but he inevitably became embroiled in the lives of many Exeter residents. In private he referred to it as "Peyton Place—but with curtains." As a doctor, he sometimes knew more than he felt comfortable with. "I soon learned that once a person has confided deeply his secrets in you, it's more likely than not that you'll lose that person as a friend," he explained. "I knew a lot, almost too much sometimes, about most of the prominent people in town."

Despite Charlie's efforts to fully immerse himself in his family, his practice, and his community, something fundamental was missing from his life. The Everest trip had changed him, as each of his big Himalayan journeys

SAVAGE SUMMIT

We entered the mountains as strangers, but we left as brothers.
—Charles Houston

It was morning—early—at Camp VI, high on the slopes of K2. Charlie had gone out of the tent to get fresh snow to melt for morning tea. "Gone out is totally inadequate to describe the process," he explained. "One must wriggle out from a warm and snug sleeping bag, into clothes which feel like solid ice. One must find the socks, dried during the night on my warm belly in the sleeping bag. One must replace the spare warm pair which one sleeps in. I had to squirm over the resentful body which shared my tent and pretended to sleep. I must find and force my feet into boots crusted inside and out with frost. . . . I was breathless, my heart pounding. My eyes were stuck together, my nose caked and dry, and the skin of lips and nose was peeling from sun and windburn. Life was unbearable. Why in God's name had we ever come to this alien place?" But at last he was out, numb, half alive, boiling with self-pity and resentment. It was at that very moment that he looked out. The sky was a fresh new blue, merging gently with the pink dawn, yet jet black above. But it wasn't the color of the sky that startled him: "The air was filled with tiny crystals, shimmering in the sunlight, lazily drifting here and there." It was one of those curious situations where the air had exactly the right amount of moisture and the temperature was just low enough that each droplet of moisture was frozen into a minute crystal of ice. "All of my bodily woes were gone instantly. It was so quiet you could hear your heart beat. I looked and looked, afraid to move, as the shimmering swept about and above me. It was a new day, perhaps a new world. That kind of vision you hold in your heart and soul forever."

No one had been near K2 since the second American expedition, led by Fritz Wiessner in 1939; World War II had effectively closed most borders in Asia, and the partition of India into Pakistan and India had left both nations in chaos. The war in Kashmir prevented foreigners from entering that area. With a war in Korea and the Chinese invasion of Tibet, few Himalayan expeditions were actually taking place, save for a few, illegal, surreptitious and highly dangerous forays by a handful of adventurers. Charlie and Bob Bates had all but given up on returning to K2 and had successfully applied for permission to climb Makalu in Nepal.

But Charlie had become acquainted with Ambassador Avra Warren in Karachi in November of 1950, and in early 1952 Ambassador Warren was in New York visiting Charlie's parents. Charlie took the opportunity to join them. The ambassador was encouraging; Dorcas wasn't. Not only would Charlie be gone for weeks on end, but she knew very well that it would be a dangerous—and expensive—undertaking. Once again, Dorcas's reticence proved unconvincing to Charlie. Ambassador Warren succeeded in convincing the Pakistani government to grant Charlie permission for the climb; it was now a possibility. Charlie next spoke with his old climbing partner and neighbor in Exeter, Bob Bates, who was immediately enthusiastic. And so the plan was hatched.

First Charlie had to negotiate with his Exeter medical partners. He broached the subject in the summer of 1952 and they reluctantly agreed. His loss of income was going to be a hardship, though, because although the 1938 expedition had cost only $9,500, he felt sure that this one might be up to three times as much. And as expedition leader, he would be responsible for finding the money. Even more important than budget was personnel. Charlie had learned important lessons about team dynamics, both from his 1938 K2 expedition and from the 1939 trip led by Fritz Wiessner, an expedition that had left a questionable legacy for the American climbing community.

To begin with, Charlie had always been baffled that Wiessner had never contacted him about details of the 1938 reconnaissance trip. Wiessner hadn't asked about the route, the weather patterns, the camps, or the approach. Of course some of this information was in the public domain through slide shows and the book written by Bates and Charlie. However, the important details that were of no interest to the public but which could mean the world of difference to someone actually on the route, remained unshared. Contradictorily, Wiessner was allegedly disappointed that none of Charlie's team could join him on his attempt. Charlie's recollection was that only House had been asked and that House eventually said no.

There was no animosity between Charlie and Wiessner. In fact, they had climbed and skied together extensively and Charlie readily acknowledged Wiessner's superb skills, as both a climber and a skier. Wiessner was a natural leader; when the two of them went into the mountains together, Charlie was content to follow. But Wiessner disgusted Charlie with his seemingly shallow aspirations, one of which was to sell his ski business and marry a rich widow. He also confessed that if he made the summit of K2, he would be "set for life." Charlie was critical of Wiessner's choice of teammates in 1939; he felt they weren't terribly experienced and didn't appear to bond as a team. But his harshest criticism was saved for Wiessner himself who, he felt, had led from the front, had shown little flexibility or compassion for his team, and ultimately had caused the death of Dudley Wolfe and three Sherpas, one of whom was Charlie's good friend.

Following the tragic 1939 expedition led by Wiessner, many questions were asked by leading members of the American Alpine Club, particularly in connection with the death of Dudley Wolfe high—and alone—on the mountain. Charlie had been asked to be part of an American Alpine Club committee to inquire into the decisions leading up to the tragedy, but he refused.[12] "Bob and I knew very well it would be even more important to have the right people; Wiessner's flawed group had shown that." So with this history in the back of his mind, he went to great lengths in choosing the party, talking to at least twenty-five climbers, many already well-known, others who would later become celebrated. Both Charlie and Bates felt that personality and ability to get along well with others, as well as expedition experience, were more important than mountaineering brilliance. One amusing theory had Houston's golden retriever, Honey, making the final decision. Charlie admitted, "It's true that our dog didn't like the people we didn't like. But that's as far as it went." He also relied on Dorcas's response to the climbers as they filed through the Houston home. "She had a very good feel for quality people," he explained. But in the end, it was Bates and Charlie who made the decisions and when the choice was difficult, they relied on their intuition. "Looking back, I don't see how we could have done better," he concluded.

Bob Craig had an outstanding climbing record in the Pacific Northwest and was the humorist in the group. Seattle climber Dee Molenaar was a geologist and artist who had climbed successfully in the Yukon Territory of Canada. He was steady and dependable as a climber and a companion, and was admitted onto the team based solely on Craig's strong recommendation. George Bell was an atomic scientist from Los Alamos with an impressive climbing record and a quiet personality; some called him unflappable. Art Gilkey was a graduate student in geology in New York and had directed the Juneau Icefield Research Project in 1952. Charlie and Bates agreed that Gilkey's intense drive, combined with a generous and self-effacing personality, made him an ideal companion, particularly in times of stress, of which there were sure to be a few. Pete Schoening, at twenty-seven the youngest, was a strong Seattle mountaineer. Although quite shy, he turned out to be the workhorse of the team. Of the group, only Bates and Charlie had previously climbed in the Himalayas. They needed a transport officer and found an excellent one in the Briton Tony Streather. Although Streather was only expected to function as a transport officer, he went on to surprise everyone with his strength and skill as a climber, all the while providing them with endless tales of adventures from around the world. Their permit required a Pakistani liaison officer, and here they were particularly fortunate in finding Mohammad Ata-Ullah, who later proved himself high up on the mountain. The big disappointment was that Bill House, who had been an important member of the 1938 expedition, was unable to come this time. He nevertheless served as expedition treasurer.

The selection process was not without its critics. Some climbers had lobbied aggressively for Charlie to choose them; rejecting them was difficult. Although he didn't show his anger at the time, Barry Bishop later told Charlie that his rejection was a shock. Because of the unsavory record that had built up around Paul Petzoldt, he too was declined. The experienced Willi Unsoeld was voted down, and Fritz Wiessner was not even considered. Of the other climbers interested, some were too young, others too religious, and a few were too self-absorbed.

Thinking about that small group, Charlie reflected a long time: "You know, being with the right people makes the difference between a happy

and a bad expedition and, sometimes, as in our case, it means the difference between life and death." It was ironic that, although Charlie had frequently experienced difficulty getting along with people, he felt that, for his
team, getting along was the most important element. Each member had his
strength, but none was a prima donna. None were stars. All accepted Charlie's leadership, and nobody challenged his decision to attempt the mountain
without bottled oxygen, something he was convinced was possible from his
high-altitude research during the war. They brought only two bottles—to
use in emergencies or in the case of frostbite.

The closing months of 1952 and early 1953 were frantically busy, as
Charlie had to secure funding for the expedition, choose and pack food and
equipment, work at his medical practice, and be a husband to Dorcas and
a father to his three children. But it wasn't only Charlie who was busy, for
Dorcas was preparing herself for the months ahead when she would have
sole responsibility for their family. That, combined with the worries of lost
income from the medical practice for the duration of the expedition, makes
it surprising that Dorcas agreed to Charlie's climb. But unlike Angel Bunny,
who years before had turned down Oscar's career advancement opportunity, Dorcas didn't say no. Unlike in Angel Bunny's case, perhaps it wouldn't
have made a difference if she had.

The entire expedition budget was $32,000. They received no govern-
ment grants, no foundation money, a few gifts from generous individuals,
seed money from each member of the team, and some significant loans. They
also had corporate support: Eddie Bauer donated fifty down jackets called the
Karakoram Parka. It was this very parka that Charlie was testing early one
morning, skating along the frozen Exeter River, when the ice unexpectedly
broke, plunging him into the frigid waters. He was pleasantly surprised to
discover that the jacket had flotation qualities as well. Dorcas unexpectedly
got involved in the corporate support when she discovered a new kind of
chocolate, manufactured by the Chunky Chocolate Company. Charlie tasted
it, liked it, and wrote the company about getting a bulk order. After some
back and forth, they donated sixty pounds of chocolate and thirty pounds of
sugar-coated peanuts to the expedition—plus a check for $50. And finally, the
Empress Manufacturing Company in Vancouver gave them a large quantity of
what Charlie remembered as "the finest jam in the world"!

Charlie had written to the National Broadcasting Company in New York
asking them for support in return for a film. They responded with some
enthusiasm and invited him to New York. At Radio City he was ushered into

the president's massive office. It was all rather intimidating. The president rose from his desk at the far end of the room, shook Charlie's hand and handed him a contract for his consideration. Charlie had already seen a draft of the contract and responded: "Thank you very much. This is a very generous contract and I can see that you have already signed it. $50,000 will be more than enough to cover the costs of this expedition." The man seemed somewhat surprised. He looked at the contract and shook his head. "This is not meant to be $50,000. It's meant to be $5,000," he said. He walked back to his desk, picked up the phone and dialed a number. Although Charlie could hear only one end of the conversation, it was quite apparent that he was asking a lawyer on the other end of the phone how the number could have been so mistakenly represented. After some time he hung up and simply said, "We made a mistake. We shouldn't have signed that contract. If you hold us to it, we will of course pay it. But we didn't intend to pay that much." Without hesitation Charlie responded, "Well, of course if you only meant $5,000, we'll be happy with that, and we're very grateful." NBC awarded them a contract for a documentary film, providing them with film, camera, and tape recorder, as well as smaller recorders they could use while climbing. And then *The Saturday Evening Post* gave them an advance for an exclusive series of articles. With this growing media interest, a young New York journalist, Bill White, persuaded Charlie to let him join them at his expense as far as Pakistan.

Amazingly, five years after the expedition, their total income had exceeded their costs—by about $20,000. A large portion of that was given to the American Alpine Club as a rotating loan to help others do what they had done. The rest was divided among the climbers themselves.

By March the team was assembled in the Houston kitchen, weighing and packing each article of food into plastic bags. They used the same "two men for one day" bags, tripled up to form larger bags that would supply two men for three days, a system taught to Charlie by Brad Washburn twenty years earlier on the Crillon trip. Dorcas, absolute master of her kitchen, now assumed a leading role in this stage of the expedition menu planning. As Bob Bates described it: "Have you ever had sticky raisins, excelsior and dehydrated potatoes gumming the linoleum of your kitchen floor? Have you had handfuls of dry, flaky, baby food oatmeal ground into your only dining room rug? Have you tried to use your best bread knife after it has cut twenty-four cakes of Italian fruit cake (*pane forte*) into eight sections each?"[13]

They packaged over a ton of food. In one corner of the kitchen, a group cut and weighed dried apricots. In another, a group weighed dried tomato soup. And in yet another, they packaged baby food, which they later found to be almost inedible. Bates's description was vivid: "How American babies can eat such stuff regularly I can't understand!"[14] As the group worked at a frenzied pace for two solid days, they developed an incredible hunger. After one particularly hard day of packaging, they effortlessly consumed a delicious twenty-four pound turkey, roasted on a spit in the fireplace.

Bates and Charlie crated everything and had it trucked to New York and loaded on the freighter *City of Carlisle* to Karachi, Pakistan, where Bates would receive it in advance of the party. Despite their attempts at keeping things "light," the supplies weighed a full 4,500 pounds. Charlie received a surprise present on that last day: a pair of hand-knitted socks from Tenki. Unfortunately for Charlie, Tenki wasn't a very experienced knitter and the socks were several sizes too large. Schoening arrived in New York after five days on a $94 bus journey from Seattle. Molenaar spent his last night in New York in Art Gilkey's tiny apartment—not a happy evening as it turned out, since Gilkey's girlfriend had just broken up with him. Nevertheless, the entire team was given a great send-off party in New York, where Christine Reid, a climbing member of the American Alpine Club and "sister" of the Harvard Five, presented them with a red and white silk umbrella upon which she had sewn the expedition name. Charlie's job was to carry the umbrella to the summit.

Upon arrival at the airport, they were informed that their baggage weighed 900 pounds more than their allowance. Pan American was sympathetic, though, and allowed them to don several layers of heavy clothing, wear their climbing boots, and even carry packs and ice axes on board! The NBC camera crews insisted on a number of parting shots, delaying the takeoff by twenty minutes.

Earlier that year, on January 27, Charlie had sent a letter to Colonel Ata-Ullah, inviting him to be on the expedition. He had been recommended to Charlie by the Colonel's good friend Mr. Aftab, of the Pakistan Ministry of Kashmir Affairs. Ata-Ullah was dumbfounded, convinced that his friend was playing a practical joke on him. Not only was K2 the second-highest mountain in the world, he was fifty years old and thirty pounds overweight. He knew he should explain these shortcomings to the unsuspecting Houston across the sea, but something held him back. It was excitement.

Nevertheless, he did write a truthful letter—of sorts. "Dear Doctor Houston, I am grateful for your invitation . . . although the spirit is willing, almost anxious to join you, my age and physique would not permit me to do much. Of technical mountaineering, I have no experience or knowledge whatsoever." Then to confuse Charlie completely, he added: "Having made quite clear that it will be entirely under false pretenses, I accept your gracious invitation to become a member of your party." [15] Now it was Charlie's problem, and he accepted the challenge.

What Charlie couldn't imagine was the level of excitement in the colonel's home. Not only was Ata-Ullah excited, his wife was in a heightened state of nervousness, and even his children had taken it upon themselves to provide him with research materials: everything from *Annapurna* to *Five Miles High* to the entire fifteen-volume series of *The Himalayan Journals* were now at his fingertips. But of course Ata-Ullah was well aware that studying alone would not get him even partway up K2. He needed to lose some weight. To help him monitor his progress, a neighbor loaned him a gigantic set of bathroom scales. Unfortunately, the bathroom was much too small to house the professional weighing machine, so it was installed in the dining room, right next to the deep-freeze. Ata-Ullah made good use of it, weighing himself before and after every meal, in addition to dozens of times throughout the day. By the appointed day—May 28—he had shed those extra pounds.

The newly svelte Ata-Ullah and Streather met the rest in Rawalpindi, sensing immediately that they would work well together as a team. Ata-Ullah was worried. He knew that for most of the team, it was their first visit to the East and they were likely filled with visions of romance and glamour and mystery. He well knew what they would find if they probed even slightly beneath the surface: poverty, disease, and dirt. But explore they did, simply choosing to ignore what did not please them. One memorable evening, as the sun was setting, they were partaking in a spectacular high tea on the lawn of General Shahid Hamid's home. Charlie was homesick, worrying aloud about Dorcas and the children. The general's wife, Tahirah, one of the most beautiful women Charlie had ever seen, responded with a warm and sincere invitation to have them come and stay with her for as long as they liked. Charlie couldn't believe it, but he acted quickly and extended the invitation to Dorcas the very next morning.

As they finished their last-minute arrangements over an early-morning breakfast in Ata-Ullah's home, the radio carried news that rocked them: Edmund Hillary and Tenzing Norgay had climbed Everest on the queen's birthday, and were safely down. Charlie recalled the effect the news had on him: "It was thrilling news, but, I must confess, I had a secret unworthy thought that this would upstage any triumph we might have in a few more months." Regardless, both Bates and Charlie wanted K2 instead. So they put any envy aside and sent a congratulatory cable to London. Now they had to match the accomplishment.

In 1938, Charlie's team had traveled overland from Srinagar, but now, fifteen years later, the ceasefire line between India and Pakistan cut their original approach route in half, and much of the Indus Valley in Pakistan was closed to all but the military. This time they would go directly from Rawalpindi to Skardu. Finally they were off, flying over the mountains in a rickety DC-3 so heavily laden that Charlie was doubtful it would get over the high mountain passes. But it did, flying near Nanga Parbat and finally dipping down to a crude landing strip in Skardu.

The spectacular flight to Skardu took only a few hours rather than the two weeks it had taken to walk the 241 miles in 1938. Not only had the mode of transportation changed: Skardu was a transformed place. In 1938 there had been 2,000 inhabitants living in isolation from the rest of the world. Now the population had almost quadrupled and the city itself was a bustling, hustling, growing community with a hospital, an electric light plant, and a multitude of military personnel and equipment thronging the streets. They were met by a huge welcoming party carrying banners that said: "Ask the United States for justice to Pakistan. Thank the Americans for their generosity." They rode in like conquerors, all rather embarrassing for the team. Pakistan was arguing strongly that the predominantly Muslim Kashmir belonged to them, not to India; they were taking advantage of the situation to bring home their point to this group of visiting Americans.

In Skardu, Streather was in charge of reviewing, choosing and hiring 200 porters for the journey to Askole. And here they met the Hunza men who had been selected by the Mir of Hunza to serve as mountain porters. Sherpas were not available in Baltistan because of bitterness against India. The Hunzas appeared a strong, handsome, independent lot, although lacking in mountaineering experience. Finally, on June 5th, they were off. One final poignant memory of that inaugural day was the "first day's lunch" that Dorcas had thoughtfully provided the team, something they would never have thought of themselves. It was a loving touch that Charlie never forgot.

The march in was exciting, in a familiar kind of way: "We crossed the Indus in the same wooden barge we used in 1938, allegedly the same that Alexander the Great was wrongly said to have used centuries before—wrong because he never came near Skardu. The days were long and hot and tiring, and we camped pretty much in the same places as in 1938." Many of the landmarks were familiar to him: the goatskin rafts, the rope bridges, the hot spring near Askole, and the village itself. As in 1938, Charlie marveled at the ingenuity of the villagers, who managed, through vertiginous irrigation schemes, to create startlingly green oases in the magnificent harshness of the Baltistan Karakoram. But despite their advanced engineering abilities, they seemed incapable of creating simple, clean living conditions for themselves. This bothered Charlie immensely as he observed almost non-existent sanitation and widespread illness. Being a doctor, he couldn't help imagine how greatly their lives would be improved with some simple principles of cleanliness.

As on any good approach march, the team bonded and got to know each other. Dee Molenaar recalled twenty-five years later that they became "a band of brothers." Ata-Ullah observed that at the beginning of the walk in, the Americans were "all for equality," pitching their own tents, washing their dishes, first ones up and last ones to bed. But he watched with amusement as this changed: "It is difficult to recollect when, and by what stages, they slipped from this high resolve . . . before long, the Hunzas had taken charge of the Americans and relegated them to the role of indolent Grand Moghuls."[16]

After reaching camp each afternoon, Charlie would hold "sick call," tending to a long line of complaints, from cuts, blisters and bruises to sprains and joint problems. He was liberal with his use of wintergreen ointment, the aroma being magnificently effective. Internal problems were most often treated with aspirin, often combined with Alka-Seltzer, which he quickly learned produced a wonderful psychological effect with its magnificent foam. Finally, on June 20th they walked the last twenty miles to the base of their mountain, which, on that day, was veiled in cloud. "We paid off the porters and settled in, as near as we could tell, to where we had camped fifteen years before. It had begun."

They had supplies for seventy days. Their strategy was to move up the mountain fast enough so as not to run out of food, but slowly enough to acclimatize to the altitude, a lesson they and others had learned in the previous few decades. They would go straight for the route they had found in 1938, the one they had called the Abruzzi Ridge. Charlie remembered: "It was immensely exciting. The setting is magnificent—a long view down the Godwin-Austen Glacier to the white magnificence of Chogolisa, so aptly named Bride Peak. Broad Peak towered above us to the south, and the great southern wall of K2 was so high and so steep above camp that we could not grasp its complex systems of icefalls, cliffs and avalanche debris."

Their plan was to keep one team of two up ahead, scouting the route and identifying the campsites, while the rest carried loads to stock each camp. Then another pair would take over the lead, always moving loads higher. They felt the Hunzas would go as high as 19,000 feet, but no higher. They had learned from past tragedies on Nanga Parbat in 1934 and on K2 in 1939 that it was essential to keep an open line of retreat in case they were caught in a storm. It meant a lot of hauling, as each camp had to be fully stocked. "It's old-fashioned today, but in 1953 it saved our lives," Charlie explained.

As they inched their way up the mountain, rediscovering old camps, reconstructing them and restocking them, they came across some interesting relics. At Camp II they found jam, Ovaltine, and an almost perfect four-man Logan tent left over from the Wiessner 1939 expedition. Higher up, they found even more remnants of that tragic attempt. But it was at Camp VI that the haunting traces of 1939 truly assaulted their sensibilities.

Along the way, expedition leader—and doctor—Charlie did more than climb. Bates had overzealously chomped into an extremely tough chicken leg at a dinner given them at Askole and as a result had loosened one of his teeth. It began to abscess, causing considerable pain, so it had to come out. Charlie arranged for his forceps to be brought up to Camp II and for Bates to descend from Camp III. Charlie then routinely removed his friend's tooth. One of the observing Hunzas, a practicing dentist at home, was fascinated and impressed by the forceps in particular, so Charlie later gave them to him, after he was sure they would no longer be needed on the trip.

Toward the end of July they came to House's Chimney, a vertical crack in a great cliff, about 150 feet high. At 22,000 feet, it was one of the most difficult parts of the climb. Charlie had secretly doubted his ability to climb it for days. There were still ropes remaining from 1938 and 1939, but these were not to be trusted, so the chimney had to be climbed afresh. "Though it wasn't my turn to lead, I asked the others if I might go first. I was afraid of that place, afraid of being unable to do it, and even more afraid that we might be caught above it in bad weather. . . . Well, they agreed, and to my great relief, I made it up not easily, but well enough." Schoening then made a simple pulley system to haul up the loads and Molenaar did most of the pulley work. As well, they fixed new ropes in the chimney to replace the old ones. In two days they were up at Camp V where they were delighted to consume the powdered milk and cocoa they found in a tent left from 1939.

Then it was on to the Black Pyramid, laced with loose snow. As they climbed higher, the good high-pressure weather system progressively broke down. The days were grey and cloudy now, with wind-driven snow crystals stinging their faces. This steep, polished, dangerous stretch had few good belay spots, but they managed to gain the broken rock ridge to establish their Camp VI. The three narrow platforms they had painfully built in 1938 were still there, and on one they found a battered tent from the 1939 effort.

This was the tent from which the three Sherpas had departed on July 29, 1939, on their unsuccessful attempt to rescue Dudley Wolfe, who was trapped at Camp VII. In the remains of the tent, Charlie's team found three rolled Sherpa sleeping bags, one Primus stove, some Ovaltine, and, meticulously wrapped in a handkerchief inside a Primus stove box, an aromatic bundle of Darjeeling tea. These items had been carefully stored and left to be picked up on their way down the mountain. But the three Sherpas never made it back and there was no further trace of any of them until the remains of Pasang Kikuli were found in 1993 and those of Dudley Wolfe were discovered in 2002 on a remote stretch of the Godwin-Austen Glacier, at the base of the mountain.

At the end of July Charlie and his teammates were trapped in Camp VI by more stormy days. They were nearing the summit, but they were also feeling the strain. The tent banter became more serious. Needing only a few days of good weather, they continued crawling upward.

Each climber carried loads to where they thought the next camp should be, near the steep ice slope across which Petzoldt and Charlie had cut steps in 1938. But they could not find the site of Camp VII from either 1938 or 1939. To Charlie it seemed that the topography had changed somewhat from 1938. Perhaps the result of an avalanche.

On July 30th they carried more loads and then left Schoening and Gilkey to pitch a tent on a narrow ledge where they had decided to site the camp. The next day they looked for a route higher up. With the change in topography Charlie decided to try a different approach from that used in 1938. "The ice slope wasn't as defined, and the slope above our little campsite seemed a better route." So Gilkey and Schoening labored up the deep snow and by late afternoon came out on the wide, gently sloping snow shoulder that Petzoldt and Charlie had crossed in 1938—an ideal spot, they thought, for the final camp.

Storms continued to batter them, and they were now forced to climb and carry loads in unsettled weather, taking an extra day at almost every camp. The terrain was relentlessly steep, and they were careful and conservative in their approach for, as Charlie stated: "We believed that climbing was a sport and not a life and death challenge." Having used short stretches of fixed rope, they now had all the camps stocked with tents, food and fuel, and, by August 1, they were established in their highest camp—Camp VIII. They were climbing as a team, and the mood was optimistic: "Even more important was the spirit which made us a real team. We changed partners every few days, so that everyone had a chance to pioneer and to share a tent with another person. We were getting very closely knit. Maybe I'm naïve but I really believe that no one of us was so ambitious for the top as to push another back. We took turns, and when the final summit decision had to be made we voted for the summit team. By then we were in trouble, though we didn't realize how bad, and without this togetherness we probably would not have survived."

Throughout the expedition Charlie had exhibited an understated style of leadership. He indicated that he wanted all members of the trip to experience leadership at some point, and they did. But ultimately, it came down to Charlie. Schoening recalled: "Any significant or worthwhile venture needs a strong leader . . . all members of a team need to know the goal and leader and agree to both."[17] In Schoening's opinion, Charlie was that leader. And as the leader, he bore the brunt of any post-expedition criticism.

About their strategy, Charlie later stated, "Looking back, knowing all we know today, I still believe, and the others agree, that we had done the right thing. After the fact, some criticized us for keeping the whole party together in that one high camp. Some said we should have kept a back-up one or two camps lower down. All we had for support was Ata-Ullah and the Hunzas at base camp and they would not, could not, help if we had trouble. We don't agree." Instead, their plan was to have the carrying capacity of all eight men up high in order to establish an even higher camp, from which two men would attempt the summit. On their summit attempt day, another pair would move up to either support the first summit team on their descent, or try for the summit themselves the following day. Rightly or wrongly, for better or worse, they were all there in four tents with plenty of food and fuel, three thousand feet from the top. They were elated.

There was a slight setback on the morning of August 2nd, when both Gilkey and Schoening were found semi-conscious. This frightening experience occurred because they had sealed off their tent from blowing snow, inadvertently cutting off the fresh-air supply. At some point during the night, Schoening must have realized the problem, as he slid over to the door and stuck his head out. It was a close call for both of them.

The weather had been slowly deteriorating over the past weeks. Charlie radioed down to Ata-Ullah for a weather forecast, and although the news wasn't good, Charlie closed with: "Three days of good weather is all we want." Those three consecutive days never came.

Now it was the night of August 2nd, and they had ten days' worth of food left. The storm struck so violently that they couldn't even communicate with the next tent a mere few feet away. They could do nothing but lie in their sleeping bags and listen to the battering of the tent. One tent developed a tear and disintegrated, forcing Charlie and Bell to crowd in with the others. It was almost impossible to keep the stoves lit because of the winds. They tried to absorb liquid by mixing snow and jam to make a kind of high-altitude sherbet, but it left them simply parched. As each day passed, they became more dehydrated, more exhausted. The tents' survival was constantly in question. The storm howled. The outlook worsened. They fought to stay alive.

Back in base camp, Ata-Ullah despaired, but could do nothing other than keep communicating. He could only imagine how fierce the storm must be ten thousand feet higher than his camp, and yet he heard from Charlie each day, and the morale remained high. "It was a privilege to be with such men," he said. "I never knew till then that even pride could bring tears to the eyes."[18]

Though etched in Charlie's memory, and confirmed by the tape recording the team made on the night they finally reached base camp again, the bare facts of what happened next are blurred by the fog of high altitude and the lapse of time. The facts recorded on the tape convey only weakly the emotions that went through the climbers at the time. Charlie recounted as best he could what happened next: "Despite the storm, we had a secret ballot to choose the summit teams and chose Bell and Craig for the first team, Gilkey and Schoening for the second." [The official newsletter said otherwise, reversing the order of Craig and Gilkey.] He added that, if they reached the summit, they planned to keep the names of the actual summit climbers secret in order to emphasize the team spirit of equality. More than fifty years later, Bates still marveled at what must surely have been the highest secret ballot ever taken, as well as the fairness of it all and the democratic leadership style that Charlie demonstrated.

Charlie continued: "It was hard to move from one tent to the next against the furious wind, so mostly we lay in bed, reading, talking, writing in diaries, or just dozing fitfully. Days passed slowly." The eight of them were up against a wild Karakoram storm, removed from all help, cut off from the rest of the world, literally fighting for their lives.

It was at this moment that the disastrous discovery of Gilkey's thrombophlebitis occurred, triggering a series of events that would test them to the limit. Realizing that Gilkey was in grave danger if he remained at that altitude, they sprang into action, initiating their rescue attempt. Their first effort at descending was quickly curtailed as they discovered that the avalanche hazard on the slope had increased to a dangerous level. Back in their tents, with the wind howling anew, they reviewed their options. "You don't think clearly at this great altitude," Charlie explained. "You are dull and your physical and mental reactions are slow." Ata-Ullah continued to relay the grim weather forecasts, further deepening their despair. One of the expedition tapes captured the feeling: "And you lie there in your sleeping bag, warm, with snow blowing in on you, the tent buffeting over your head, unable to cook, can't light the stove, can't melt snow for water, can't cook. It seems impossible to endure it, and it goes on and on and on and on."[19]

When a clot appeared in Gilkey's other leg, their options narrowed. They would have to descend, regardless of the weather—or the avalanche conditions. And so the iconic rescue commenced: "Wrapping Art again in his sleeping bag and the smashed tent, we started down the rock rib. The weather worsened. Blown snow fogged our glasses. Fingers and toes were quickly numb. Looking back, I don't see how we did what we did. Much of the force came from Pete and Bob [Craig], who had helped on a number of tough mountain rescues. We struggled for hours. Then we came to a steeper place."

Precisely what happened in the next hour is not entirely clear; each climber remembers the event differently. What is certain is that Gilkey was lowered down the little cliff, and he and Craig were almost carried away by a small avalanche. Schoening went across to a large rock perhaps thirty feet away, and anchored Gilkey while the others started down. Craig, exhausted by the avalanche, unroped and made his way to the traces of Camp VII. Then Bell slipped, and in moments four others were pulled off and falling. Streather, roped to Bell, was immediately ripped off the slope, slamming into the rope between Charlie and Bates. Charlie was thrown down and Bates desperately attempted an ice-ax belay but was thrown violently backward. They bounced and skidded and then suddenly stopped. Somehow the ropes had tangled with those between Molenaar and the immobile Gilkey, who was still firmly belayed by Schoening. After falls of from 150 to 300 feet, the entire group was stopped short by Schoening's ice-ax belay.

As Schoening described it: "I was in a belay position facing the ice slope . . . Out of the corner of my eye I saw George slip, and thus knew I needed to brace against the impending impact. From this point on I concentrated solely on executing the belay; there was no looking around. I felt considerable force on the rope in stopping the fall. It was a long time before Art was anchored and the others secure so I could go off belay."[20] It was his finest hour. With one ice-ax, he had saved the lives of six climbers helplessly entangled in their snared ropes—surely the greatest belay of all time.

Molenaar was bleeding from his nose; Streather was trying wildly to right himself; Bell had lost his mitts, and his hands were frozen into what looked like clubs; and Charlie was unconscious. Bates carefully unroped, went down to Charlie, and moved him into an upright position. "I don't remember any of this," Charlie said much later. Apparently, Bates shouted at him: "Charlie, if you ever want to see Dorcas and your children again, get up and climb." Charlie was concussed, but this roused him. "Slowly, painfully, all of us got across to the pitifully small ledge on which Craig was slowly putting up a tent," he recalled. While the team hacked platforms out of the ice, pitched the tents, and cared for the injured, Gilkey remained on the slope, securely anchored to two ice axes. About half an hour later, when Streather and Bates went over to him, hoping somehow to move him to the camp, Gilkey—and the two ice axes—were gone.

Initially, when they found the slope to be bare, they wondered if they were going snow-blind. Their next thought: avalanche. They were horrified. Their dear friend who had been in grave medical danger, and whom they had all risked their lives to rescue, had simply disappeared. They had heard Gilkey calling out to them not more than ten minutes before—and now he was gone. Fifty years later, Molenaar described it as "the most miserable day of my life." They concluded that he must have been carried away by a larger avalanche. But even then, they harbored doubts about what had happened to Gilkey. Could he have released himself from the rope, knowing how hopeless further rescue would be? They acknowledged that it was the kind of sacrifice he would have made, but Gilkey was barely conscious, since Charlie had given him a shot of morphine just before reaching the cliff. It seemed unlikely that he would have even had the strength to cut himself loose.

Much later, Charlie—and others—revised their view. It may have been Charlie's friend and Everest climber Tom Hornbein who first went public with the hypothesis, in his essay for *Voices From the Summit*. He asked simply: "Might Gilkey . . . have taken the opportunity to disconnect himself from the mountainside to which he had been secured?"[21] In 2003, while Charlie was working on his K2 film *Brotherhood of the Rope*, he listened again to the audiotapes made by the team immediately upon returning from the mountain in August 1953. He then finally became convinced of what Gilkey had actually done. "I've listened to the tapes over and over. I believe that Art, knowing we were hurt, knowing we wouldn't abandon him, wiggled himself loose to save our lives. He couldn't take the ice ax out as he was too weak. . . . I never took it seriously. I believe it now." Charlie was quite clear about this in a television interview with Bill Moyers in 2004. In contrast, Bates never accepted that theory, convinced it was an accident—not suicide—that defined Gilkey's death. As for Schoening—the man who actually held him and all the others with his miraculous belay—he remained convinced that they could have succeeded with the entire rescue: "I felt, and still feel [in 2004], we could have gotten Art down. It would have taken longer than descending by ourselves and frostbite would have been more severe. But based on experience doing rescues on steep terrain, I believe we could have done it."[22]

The rest of the team huddled together that dreadful night in two cramped tents. Luckily, the wind had stopped and they were able to make, and drink, gallons of tea. But Charlie was in a bad state, hallucinating and trying to cut a hole in the tent so that they could "get more oxygen."

The next few days are blurred in Charlie's memory: "Though I am proud of what we did and tried to do during the terrible days at Camp VIII, I think the descent from Camp VII to base was almost an even greater accomplishment." It certainly was, for the team was in pretty rough shape. Charlie's head injury had left him confused and weak. The others were suffering from debilitating injuries that severely impaired their abilities to downclimb the steep and treacherous slopes. There wasn't much belaying being done; Craig recalled that they short-roped most of the descent and that Charlie, although not completely lucid, remained "persistent and steady." Bates confirmed Charlie's condition, saying that, "Charlie probably saved my life at least two times."

House's Chimney was particularly difficult. It was dark when they reached it, and Charlie insisted on being the last one down, belaying Bates before he began to downclimb it himself. Others remember that it was not Charlie who was last down through the chimney and that his memory is clouded due to the concussion he had sustained. But Charlie was adamant: "I was last down because I felt responsible for the team; I felt guilty for having failed them, and it was my job to go last."

The Hunzas rushed up, and late in the afternoon of August 14th welcomed them to Camp II. Craig's account of their reunion with the Hunzas movingly revealed the depth of emotion, and the bond, between the climbing team and the Hunzas: "It was truly a never to be forgotten hour." The porters fed them, massaged their legs, wept with them, and prayed for them. Bates remembered: "Our own feelings were too deep for words. Somehow all but one of us had been saved to live again and climb again and savor the joys of friendlier mountains." From there it was to base camp, where they first took stock of their injuries. Bell's toes were black and he couldn't walk. Craig's feet weren't much better, but at least he could hobble. The rest were bruised and battered, but on their feet.

They were a defeated yet victorious band of men. Ata-Ullah wrote that they appeared to have acquired a maturity well beyond their years. Bates recalled the experience: "Seventeen days of monsoon storm, in an area where no monsoon had ever been reported before, had defeated us. Phlebitis, a disease never encountered on any mountain expedition before, had caused the death of one of us. . . . But in a small way we triumphed. We were above 25,000 feet longer than anyone has ever been before. Though denied the summit of the world's second highest peak, we withstood one of the most vicious storms climbers have ever recorded."[23] Their performance at altitude was indeed impressive: sixty days at or above 16,500 feet, twenty-five days above 20,000 feet, and an astonishing ten days at 25,500 feet. They were all in superb physical condition, having carried loads varying from twenty-five pounds to fifty-five pounds. And they had successfully used the deliberate hyperventilation and controlled rhythmic breathing methods pioneered by Charlie in his research with World War II pilots.

They had triumphed at the human level too. Somehow they had learned early to work together, to share the trials and the joys of their mountain. Some kind of magic was created in that motley crew of men as they struggled for their lives. That magic remained with each of them—a gift of friendship that perhaps could only be formed in the intensity of their grief, their efforts, and, ultimately, in their survival. In 1978 the American climber and K2 summiter Jim Wickwire wrote in his foreword to *K2: The Savage Mountain*: "As [Louis] Reichardt and I walked those last few steps to the summit, I could feel the presence of Houston, Bates, Schoening, and the others who, but for the vagaries of storm and circumstance, would have been there a quarter-century ahead of us. Their struggle and character is one of the great stories of modern mountaineering."[24]

The Hunzas built a cairn on a small ridge above camp and held a brief, solemn memorial service for Gilkey. It became a memorial for many others who subsequently died on that beautiful and dangerous mountain. The porters arrived, and the team began their slow and painful return march, arriving in Skardu on August 25th. From there they flew to Rawalpindi, where a surprise awaited them.

While the team was on the mountain, Charlie's father had brought Dorcas to Pakistan and, as promised, Tahirah Hamid had welcomed her as a cherished guest. Although General Hamid had received a radio message about the accident, this information had not been passed on to Dorcas. Charlie's father persuaded Dorcas to meet the team in Rawalpindi; for Charlie, their meeting remained burned in his memory: "When we met Dorcas at the airport, it may have been the first time that I really, fully grasped the implications of my accident for my family. Though I didn't know it then, this ended my mountaineering days." He was physically and emotionally exhausted, and at that moment felt an enormous sense of failure. This "failure" resonated quite differently for others. Messner's all-time hero was Ernest Shackleton, a man who always failed, but who "got his people back." Messner referred to Charlie as a non-traditional leader and a hero whose greatest contribution was that, with the sad exception of Gilkey, "he too got his people down."

Charlie had been the doctor and the leader of the expedition, and Gilkey's death affected him deeply. Although he later admitted that Gilkey's death turned out to be a "miraculous deliverance from an intolerable and fatal situation," he carried an enormous sense of responsibility and guilt. But he never discussed it with anyone. He knew that others had seen their climbing companions die and they had carried on climbing. Charlie could not.

Though Charlie consistently cited the two reasons he gave up climbing as failing his team and his need to be there for his family, physician/climber Tom Hornbein challenged him. Hornbein thought a lot about his friend's statements, and didn't accept that Charlie—or anyone—could take complete responsibility for what happened on the mountain. He suspected that Charlie may have been afflicted with something he refers to as "medical omniscience"—that all-knowing, all-powerful state of mind that Hornbein frankly dismissed as a "hand up." And on the family commitment, he pointed out that, although Charlie didn't do any more major climbing expeditions, he continued to spend long periods away from home on various missions and research projects. But, he added, "It's harder for a family to complain if your obsession has some societal value!"

For Charlie, the K2 ordeal wasn't quite over. On August 4th, 1954, Ardito

Desio's Italian team reached the summit. Back in New Hampshire, Charlie took it stoically at first, but it hurt his spirit. In fact he had already obtained permission to try again in 1955, and Desio's triumph "seemed a violation of [my] mountain." Hornbein believed that part of Charlie's decision to stop climbing was driven by the Italian victory on K2. Though Charlie denied it, the victory obviously affected him deeply, for the day after he learned of the Italian triumph, he wandered into the local hospital in Nashua, forty miles from Exeter, with no idea of who or where he was and with absolutely no identification on him. A nurse comforted him and called the police, who recognized the Exeter label on Charlie's tie. The police officer called the store in Exeter, described the man, and Dorcas and Henry Saltonstall came to rescue him. They immediately put him in a hospital and called his good friend Hal Babcock, who came from his psychiatric practice to examine him. Although Charlie was weeping inconsolably and his short-term memory was gone, it was clear that he wasn't suicidal, so his wife and good friend took him home. He was diagnosed with global amnesia. "The whole thing was devastating," Charlie remembered. "I had been working hard, looking after a few very difficult and demanding patients, and Desio's climb must have pushed me over."

But there was still more. In an effort to recover, Charlie retreated to the healing waters of Honnedaga Lake. During that drive, he had a gruesome experience. "I saw blood on the highway ahead of me. Large splotches here and there, like the blood down through which we had climbed after the accident—Gilkey's blood. I hadn't ever spoken of it."

Ten days at Honnedaga Lake were therapeutic for Charlie, and he returned to work. But much had changed for him. For many years after, he became tense, quiet, and unusually depressed during the first ten days of August. Years later he wrote in an afterword for the third printing of the book he and Bates had written following the 1953 climb:

> For me K2 1938 [should be 1953] remains a glorious bitter-sweet memory of a great adventure. Physically my injuries healed rapidly; the emotional wounds left scars. I remember only sharp, vivid fragments of those ten days in August, but the rest of our odyssey is clear and unforgettably etched in my mind. . . . As I lay unconscious after the fall Bob had roused me with memory of my wife and children. Once home again, I slowly recognized that they were and remain the center of my world. To risk losing them became unthinkable.

In Rawalpindi on the way home we had met Ardito Desio who was planning a huge Italian expedition in 1954. I sought and obtained permission for an attempt in 1955. After Desio's team reached the summit, I took brief refuge in amnesia, and returned my permit for 1955 . . .

Over the years the ties which held our little band together in August 1953 have strengthened. Before the expedition Bob and I had selected our companions for what we perceived their character and personality rather than for their climbing brilliance. They were all good climbers of course, but even more—they were people we liked, people we felt intuitively we could rely on, men of character. We had not been mistaken. Those characteristics had saved our lives.

Those first ten days in August 1953 inexorably changed my life. After 1954 I quit climbing. I had lost interest in attempting the great mountains perhaps because the guilt I felt had soured them for me. As the prime mover for the expedition and the doctor I had failed: we did not reach the summit, and I had been unable to save our friend's life. That our peers praise us for actions we saw implicit in the mountain spirit is irrelevant. I turned to teaching and practicing medicine, and to research and writing about high altitude. To me, K2, though a failure, was a glorious epiphany. [25]

Their account of the climb, *K2: The Savage Mountain*, became a mountaineering classic, but the process was not without strain, particularly between Charlie and Bates. Charlie wanted the account to be a group effort, while Bates wanted to write it himself. In the end, the book did have multiple authors, but Bates maintained control of the process. Finally, the book was published to great acclaim. The series of exquisite watercolors by Molenaar, painted high atop the mountain, became another legacy of the expedition.

Twenty-five years after the event, the remaining members of the climbing party spent a few days together in the Wind River Range in Wyoming, reliving those four days of nightmarish descent. For the first time since 1953, they spoke with great emotion of the blood splotches on the rocks, and the tangled rope and fragments of cloth down through which they climbed. With hindsight and perspective, Charlie summed it up a little differently: " . . . our expedition succeeded despite the death and defeat . . . because we went for the joy of a great venture, for excitement tempered by the prevailing codes of safety." Bates added: "The Brotherhood of the Rope established on K2 outlasted the expedition by decades and was based on a shared sense of values, interest and mutual respect and affection."

Another K2 climber, Jim Wickwire, one of the first two Americans to summit K2 in a strife-ridden—yet successful—expedition in 1978, wrote in a letter to Charlie that, "Even better, I think, than having climbed K2 in 1978 would have been to have been with you 25 years before." Messner stated, years after the Italian victory on K2: "I have great respect for the Italians who summitted K2 for the first time in 1954, but even greater respect for the Americans and the way they failed in 1953. They were decent. They were strong. And they failed in the most beautiful way you can imagine. This is the inspiration for a lifetime." Such was the power and influence of the spirit of the 1953 K2 expedition.

DARK DAYS IN EXETER

Is it not better to take risks . . . than to die within from rot?
—Charles Houston

Back in Exeter, within the little clinic, trouble was brewing. Having founded it with idealism, both Saltonstall and Charlie believed they could expand the clinic and add more specialists. They were confident that group practice was the wave of the future; the focus would be on sharing rather than competing. In place of the traditional index cards that individual doctors tended to keep on each patient, they had developed a file system where every piece of information about that patient, including hospital and consultant notes and letters, was contained in one place, available to all the partners.

They tried to encourage a sense of teamwork, meeting for lunch once a week in their tiny "library" in the clinic. And once a month they would all get together for dinner with their families. They tried to cultivate a shared vision of the future. But not all of the partners embraced the idealism as wholeheartedly as Charlie and Saltonstall. Charlie was not tolerant of others' shortcomings, nor even of their opinions and advice if they differed from his own. He needed to be right, and he wanted others to know that he was right. Slowly, his alienation from the group began. In addition, he began to feel that Exeter was too small a stage: "I wanted a bigger world," he admitted.

He became ill-tempered and impatient. He was insecure of his stature in the community and within his group of colleagues, feeling less popular, more isolated, and underappreciated. Logically he knew this wasn't true, but his emotions overruled logic and he became despondent and increasingly, illogically critical of himself: "Certainly I talk too much and concentrate on my own affairs too much—which does not make me a welcome conversationalist." The self-analysis was painful. In his private journal Charlie confided that he was truly unhappy, not from any specific misfortune but for emotional and personal reasons. The "phantom of K2" continued to plague him. But it wasn't just that. He had grown sick of what he perceived as pettiness and hypocrisy among his friends, and he was jealous of the Exeter Academy circle, which he was convinced was pointedly ignoring him.

Within the clinic itself he felt that his leadership was unfairly challenged, and after some time he concluded that he could not continue working with those who were unwilling to follow his dream. In one of his cruelest moments he categorized his colleagues as "people with little vision, small ambitions, and only average intelligence," though admitting that their "good will, integrity, and desire to serve were beyond question." He and his colleagues rarely communicated with each other any more, and he felt as though he was living in a medical vacuum. He accepted at least some of the fault as his own, realizing that he was nostalgic for the more exciting days of his past: the thrill of hospital training, the intoxicating work in the research laboratory, and Operation Everest in Pensacola. They had given Charlie glimpses into the academic world, and certainly the publication of Charlie's Operation Everest reports had attracted wide attention.

But it wasn't just the professional "great days" that he was missing. During his time in Exeter he had experienced two exciting expeditions: Everest in 1950 and K2 in 1953. Particularly after the K2 expedition, there were extra demands of writing and lecturing, and finally the shattering amnesia incident in August of 1954. And despite their close bond during the K2 ordeal, Charlie and Bates were going through a difficult period. Charlie hated this; he hated their discomfort with each other, the awkward pauses, the gamesmanship, and seeming competitiveness. Although he didn't know how to "fix" it, this cooling of their friendship hurt him deeply.

Charlie had been exposed to a larger world, more important people, and

March in to K2 in 1938

Charlie Houston at 20,000 feet on Savoia Pass during the K2 1938 expedition

Paul Petzoldt, Norman Streatfield, Charlie Houston, Dick Burdsall and Bob Bates on lunch break on the way to K2 in 1938

Charlie Houston and Bob Bates on the K2
1938 expedition

Bob Bates, Charlie Houston and George Bell with the Harvard Mountaineering Club
pendant on K2, 1938

Charlie Houston bathing at base camp (K2 1938)

Charlie Houston at the high point on K2, 1938

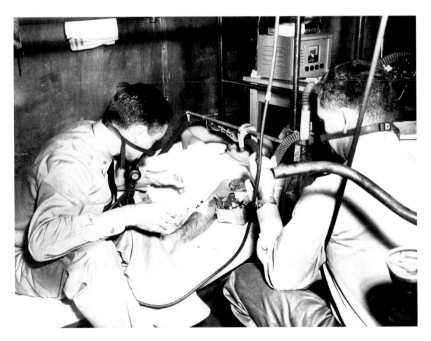

Monitoring a subject inside the chamber of Operation Everest I (1944)

Everest team photo: Andy Bakewell, Oscar Houston, Betsy Cowles, Bill Tilman, Charlie Houston (1950)

Namche Bazaar and Everest (1950)

Thyangboche Monastary in the snow (1950)

Betsy Cowles preparing Thanksgiving on the way into Everest (1950)

greater issues. Indeed, the Exeter stage had become too small for him. He slipped into a deeper and deeper depression. Because the first and last week of each month presented the toughest times, he wondered, could it be the phases of the moon? He considered that possibility, and then berated himself for being "faddist or cultist." He began to examine every aspect of his life with an unforgiving microscope. His temper spells precipitated violent arguments with Dorcas that caused him to despise himself even more.

Charlie began to question his very commitment to medicine. He complained about the humdrum routine of his practice, the physical demands, the impaired freedom imposed by night calls, and the lack of intelligence he found in most of his patients. He craved serious medical problems, those that would challenge his mind.

This led to his inevitable conclusion that he was fatally flawed: "I am intrinsically very lazy . . . I can't stand routine, I hate to be interfered with." He berated himself for his own sense of self-importance: "I have an exalted sense of my own abilities . . . but a surprising lack of confidence in others. I feel that 'I am too good' . . . that I 'am too well educated' . . . that 'I haven't time for the stupid' person." He recognized his need to be stimulated and challenged by other sharp minds, yet hated the fact that he appeared unable to motivate himself in this regard.

Then Charlie became convinced that he needed another major expedition. He realized the importance he placed on retaining a position of prominence in the climbing fraternity, and he felt sure that this position was slipping. Although he rebuked himself for being motivated by such recognition, he admitted it in his private journal: "but to deny the feeling exists would be a lie." To be fair, it was more than just the recognition that he craved. He truly loved the expedition life, the feeling of high adventure, the village crowds, the deep friendships formed on expeditions, and the sense of overcoming fear. He wrote: "It is the chance to be briefly free of the small concerns of our common lives, to strip off nonessentials, to come down to the core of life itself."[26] Perhaps that was precisely what Charlie needed, to strip his life down to the core.

He acknowledged that one of the reasons he had quit climbing was his sense of responsibility to his family, and he thoughtfully considered other climbing families whose lives had been shattered by injury or death. But even here, he questioned his decision to abandon climbing, citing Mallory's family, whom he felt sure had suffered by Mallory's disappearance but who had attained something bigger: "Mallory's family certainly suffered by his death, yet there is an immortality about him and his life which has always shrouded them in a special atmosphere." Even a death caused by adventure became acceptable: "Is it not better to die that way than to live, nibbled to death by eiderdown ducks? I think it is." Increasingly he felt that his life was taking on a sameness and predictability that were simply unacceptable, and in his most private moments, he railed: "Is it not better to take risks . . . than die within from rot? Is it not better to change one's life completely than to wait for the brain to set firmly and irreversibly in one way of life and one environment? I think it is . . . taking risks, not for the sake of danger alone, but for the sake of growth, is more important than any security one can buy or inherit." These feelings he kept to himself.

Charlie would not confide his deepest depressions to Dorcas, even though her judgment was solid and sound. He loved her deeply, and increasingly relied on her for his own limited stability, but he also felt that Dorcas was not the profound thinker he could have wished for in a partner, and he realized that they were drifting apart. To Charlie, she seemed now to function more as a housekeeper than as a friend, lover, and companion, obsessed as she was with keeping a perfect house and raising a perfect family. Although she had excellent taste, a vivid imagination, and creative talents, he felt that she tended to bury them. Of course she buried them: she was overwhelmed with the logistical responsibilities of holding their family together. Charlie instinctively knew that, and appreciated her sacrifice, but still wanted more. He wanted a partner who could share his love of the outdoors, who could spar equally with his probing mind, and who could enthusiastically embrace his soaring imagination. He felt completely alone.

He worried incessantly about his role as a father, feeling that, here too, he was barely making do. He was most concerned about Robin, in whom he saw himself so clearly reflected, especially his impatience and restlessness: "He is so like me, I could cry," Charlie wrote in his private journal. Robin was a quick and agile boy with deep feelings and strong passions—but seemingly little direction. Charlie saw immense potential in him, but had no idea how to direct or mentor him. He worried that Robin would follow the path he had taken: "getting things too easily because of his charm and his quick mind, and never exploring anything deeply or becoming master of one field." Penny, however, possessed innate social skills and an ability to love and be loved. And David, his youngest, presented no worries at all. With all of his children, there was the added financial pressure of giving them the best education he could afford, which in Charlie's mind meant a good private prep school and one of the very best universities in the country. At the same time, he knew that he must allow them to live their own lives and not use gifts or privileges as bribes or leverage to influence their decisions. Above all, he vowed to not dominate their lives.

Developments within the clinic reinforced Charlie's need to change. Even though by 1955 the group was prospering, there was unsettling turnover in the partners. As the clinic grew, Charlie pushed for a larger building, closer to the hospital. He wanted to have the flexibility to invite specialists from the city to their practice once a month. "I really pushed very hard, too hard. I suspect that the others found me difficult to bear. My vision of the future extended beyond theirs, even beyond what Henry saw." At times, Charlie was sure that it was his own arrogance that failed to convince his partners to expand their vision. Saltonstall finally confronted Charlie with the shocking statement that it would be better for the clinic if Charlie left, at least if he continued in his current state of mind. Saltonstall further suggested that Charlie see a psychiatrist, an idea that Charlie firmly rejected.

In the summer of 1956, while Charlie's Exeter years were grinding down to their inevitable and somewhat miserable end, an unexpected call came from Walter Paepke, a wealthy Chicago executive and president of the Container Corporation of America. He invited Charlie to be part of something radically new—the Aspen Institute for Humanistic Studies in Aspen, Colorado. This was to be an innovative, holistic institute that would link music, arts, physical health, and intellectual excellence. Married to the beautiful and talented daughter of an academic at Stanford, Paepke was motivated to prove to his in-laws that he was more than a man of money. His dream was ambitious: take the leaders of the United States and influence their intellectual and physical lives by showing them ways to good health of body—and mind. Half their days would focus on physical training, nutrition and medicine; the other half would be devoted to intellectual exercise.

The institute's director was Bob Craig, from the K2 expedition team; he had instigated the invitation to Charlie. When Craig had returned to Aspen from K2 back in 1953, Paepke had recruited him for the institute and appointed him the first director. Craig had been impressed with Charlie the very first time they met in Exeter, finding him to be a person of incredible charm and intensity, and he felt that he needed to get Paepke and Charlie together. He knew that Charlie was also interested in the concept of a sound body and mind combined with spiritual health. Craig also admired Charlie's attitude toward science, which mirrored his own credo: "I have enormous respect for people who live by the rules of science and seek truth to the extent that we can know it." He had also seen Charlie's enormous compassion for his patients, and he felt sure that he and Paepke would hit it off.

Charlie was intrigued. He left his family vacationing in Honnedaga, flew to Denver, and then transferred to Paepke's private plane for the final turbulent leg of the journey. They landed at dusk on a meadow, the unofficial landing pad for the small alpine village of Aspen. He was immediately thrust into a festive round of cocktail parties, fabulous dinners, stimulating conversations with distinguished doctors, and extraordinary fishing in Aspen's mountain streams. The entire experience was intensified by the clear, alpine air. He watched ground being broken for the new health center, he absorbed the inspiring landscape, and he experienced the full force of Paepke's dynamism for the first time. It was a short, intoxicating visit, and for Charlie's deeply unhappy, restless soul, it was an exciting contrast.

Back home again, Charlie discussed the possibilities with Dorcas, but it was still too vague an offer to be taken seriously. He couldn't adequately translate the excitement he had felt in Aspen, and so settled back into the drudgery that his Exeter private practice had become. The courtship continued as Paepke called on a regular basis. The next summer, the entire family was invited to spend a week in Aspen. From Denver they drove to Aspen on the rough dirt road through Independence Pass. The air was sweet; the sky was blue; the mountains were wild and inviting. It was all quite seductive.

Paepke wooed both Charlie and Dorcas throughout that week, revealing his dreams for the future and introducing them to those in the community who would assist him in that dream. Paepke's vision was risky, though, and Charlie was nervous about committing. Paepke finally made a firm proposal, offering them a house and a reasonable salary but no contract. "Men who need a contract shouldn't be given one; those we want don't need one," was how he put it.

Charlie accepted the offer in September and, as expected, subsequently agonized over the decision. On the one hand, it seemed that he needed the adventure, to explore, to broaden his world. He needed to grow—or die. On the other hand, it seemed a cruel and selfish idea to needlessly move his family. Dorcas was clear about her feelings of fear and regret; as always, Charlie played the role of the dreamer, Dorcas that of the pragmatist. In the end, the dreamer won out. Charlie, in his mid-forties, full of vigor and imagination, became determined to live up to the challenge posed by Paepke's vision.

Charlie announced his plan to leave Exeter after Labor Day. Word spread quickly. When he finally left, his partners appeared neither saddened nor relieved to see him go; the clinical staff simply withdrew. It left him feeling terribly alone. But Charlie's time was over. After ten years, it was time to move on.

Even more shocking to Charlie and his family was the community's response to their leaving—virtual isolation. They had expected some small increase in invitations, some words of regret, a little extra warmth. But there was nothing. He felt anger, betrayal, and hurt, but he was also forced into even more painful self-examination, realizing that it could have been his role as a community doctor, not his value as a human being, that had made him "acceptable" to their supposed friends. Yet some of their isolation was self-imposed. Charlie and Dorcas had systematically withdrawn from academy affairs, claiming to be annoyed by the insularity of the faculty. They had also withdrawn from other community affairs such as the PTA, and the League of Women Voters, feeling that these were time-consuming and unimportant. The couple had become more critical and more demanding of their friendships each year in Exeter. Now they were being repaid for their perceived, and actual, elitism.

The moving van arrived on a gray and foggy night, the 22nd of December. After everything was packed, and just as they were about to leave, the van became horribly mired in the mud. It was now 10:00 PM. Charlie called one of his patients, who rescued them with a giant forklift, lifting the rear of the moving van and liberating it from its muddy prison. Feeling suddenly free, Charlie gathered his little family and trundled off to the Exeter Inn for the deep relief of sleep.

SOPHISTICATED FRONTIER

*The world is a better place to live in because it contains human
beings who will give up ease and security in order to do what they
themselves think worth doing.*
    —Walter Lippman

Six months after the despondency of Exeter, Charlie and his family
were on a high—literally and figuratively. They had settled into their
new life in the alpine village of Aspen, Colorado. In his private journals Charlie reflected on his new attitude. The entries are poignant, self-
conscious, and somewhat amusing: "Perhaps the biggest thing . . . has been
the self-discipline and control which I have acquired . . . I haven't lost my
temper at all—or at most three times and then mildly. I haven't sulked (except twice) . . . I haven't been depressed severely . . . this experience has
been invaluable." What had happened to so dramatically change Charlie's
frame of mind?

Aspen was a small town with only a few hundred permanent residents,
most of whom were direct descendents of the original mining settlers. The
remaining inhabitants were an unusual collection of artists, storekeepers,
writers, and poets, who had chosen to live in that remote, wild place. It
had a frontier atmosphere—physically primitive, but sophisticated both

intellectually and artistically. The roads were dirt, dusty in the summer but blanketed in snow in winter. Most of the houses were old and shabby. The town had a few shops for tourists, a good market, a great hardware store, a few motels, and one very good hotel. The Hotel Jerome was the centerpiece of Main Street and a relic of the roaring Victorian days when silver was king and Aspen had over 15,000 residents.

Paepke had bought several hundred acres of meadow situated between two streams flowing into the valley from two subsidiary valleys. At their confluence sat the health center, where beautifully designed lodgings over-looked the pool and garden, in readiness for some of the most influential patients in the country. It was a grand dream, one that not all the town residents embraced.

Charlie and his family arrived in Aspen on New Year's Eve, 1956, physically and mentally depleted, both excited and frightened. For the first weeks it snowed every night—quiet snowfalls that dawned each morning with fresh, soft powder. They marveled at "crystal clear days so beautiful they hurt." There was so much snow in Aspen that cars wore red pennants on their radio antennae in order to be seen at the deeply buried intersections. Charlie would trudge off to the health center a mile away and the children would walk to school—unforgettable days in a new environment where the snowbound streets were not plowed, merely packed. The small house Paepke had given them looked eastward across Hallam Lake toward the mountains leading up to Independence Pass. In the early morning, without leaving their bed, Charlie and Dorcas could watch the sunrise stain the snowy peaks shades of pink and gold.

Naturally, the family took up skiing. Learning initially on a small hill near their house, they soon began skiing on the big mountain. On most days the powder remained untouched until late morning. It was a soft, forgiving snowpack that was a joy to ski. Bob Craig skied often with them, and observed that Charlie was very good at it. But Charlie's greatest passion was fly fishing, and within a year he had discovered all kinds of secret fishing holes around Aspen, some—but not all—of which he shared with Craig.

The health center staff was small. Bruno was an Austrian ski instructor and masseur who was not easy to work with, perhaps due to some frustration about Charlie having been brought in to run the center. In contrast, Bruno's wife, Erna, was excited about the program and was happy to cooperate. Charlie had not been given much direction by Paepke, so he worked independently, using his imagination and talents to make the program work. His usual practice was to take a complete medical history of his patients, give them a thorough physical examination, and then listen extensively to a wide array of emotional problems. The patients were predominantly men and the lineup was impressive: chief executives in successful businesses, bank presidents, lawyers, judges, writers, artists, and musicians.

The daily régime devoted the mornings to health and fitness and the afternoons and evenings to reading, discussion, and intellectual activity. Charlie occasionally took groups out for an early-morning walk in the bracing mountain air, followed by a sumptuous breakfast—usually prepared by Dorcas. Then came gymnastics, a sauna, a roll in the snow, and a massage. At first Charlie felt some small twinges of embarrassment at being involved in this venture, doubting its soundness. But over time he felt confident that the philosophy of overall wellness was good and that it made a difference in his patients.

Gradually the townspeople began asking Charlie for medical services, and so he began a small, private medical practice. Since there were only two other doctors in town, his presence was welcomed. But medical care in this remote community was still relatively primitive. The hospital was sixty years old, and anesthesia took the form of open-drop ether, administered by the caretaker-janitor who had learned the craft over thirty years previously from a general practitioner. The operating room was cooled in summer by simply opening the windows, and the X-ray machine tended to spark when used. The eighteen beds were old and uncomfortable, but the food was excellent and the nursing staff was top notch, attracted to the area not because of the medical facilities but because of the skiing.

Although Charlie was encouraged to do general medicine, the two local doctors jealously guarded their trauma and obstetrical services, since this was where the bulk of their income originated. As a result, Charlie's income settled at $17,000 a year, plus housing and ski passes for his family. He had no health insurance and no other benefits.

Whenever Paepke was in town with his wife, Elizabeth (nicknamed Pussy), they visited together, frequently enjoying Dorcas's fine dinners. And so it was that on New Year's Day, 1959, the Paepkes were at the Houstons, gazing out onto the mostly frozen Hallam Lake just below the house. They were shocked to see that a massive bull elk had broken through the ice and was struggling for his life. Charlie leapt into action and announced that he would attempt a rescue with his canoe. He later admitted that he had no idea how he was going to accomplish this rescue, but he nevertheless placed the canoe into the remaining open water and paddled as close to the elk as possible. Unfortunately, this only caused the animal to become even more alarmed. Charlie slowly and methodically began breaking the ice with his paddle, and finally opened a passage through the ice for the elk to wade ashore—whereupon it promptly charged Charlie. To the admiring eyes of his family and colleagues, Charlie managed to defend himself with his paddle, and the elk trundled off into the bush.

When he wasn't having wildlife adventures or running the health center in Aspen, Charlie was expected to travel to Chicago and other major cities to sell the program. "I didn't like this, in fact I really hated it; I wasn't a good salesman . . . I did rather enjoy meeting these important men and women and I confess to a certain snobbery!" Paepke opened doors for him, but it was Charlie who had to go through them—and sell the program. His job was to influence people and convince them that the program would help them find, and keep, good health. For the most part he found that people weren't interested: Charlie blamed himself for that, feeling that he just didn't have what it took to sell the concept. Paepke had patterned it after the very successful European health spas: realistically, however, it was probably twenty years too soon to be completely accepted in the United States.

After only a year and a half, Paepke was forced to break the bad news: the institute was struggling for survival, and the health program would have to close and become a fee-for-service exercise center. Charlie's salary would end in two months. Although terribly disappointed, Charlie didn't blame him. Paepke was a successful businessman because he had never avoided tough decisions. This was a tough one, but it had to be made. "Now we were in real trouble," Charlie recalled. He couldn't go back to Exeter, and he had no other plan in mind. The only real option was to stay in Aspen and try to make a living practicing private medicine. But it was a serious situation: the children were approaching college age, and the house that Paepke had provided would no longer be available.

The situation worsened. Charlie's youngest sister, Janet, had grown up beautiful, talented, and charming. She had been a bit wild in her teens, staying out all night, going off to New York, and charging up huge amounts on her mother's store accounts. She was finally forced into psychological counseling, which, according to Charlie, did her no good at all. Many of the sailors visiting the family home during the war were infatuated with the wildly beautiful Janet. She in turn became captivated by one of them, and promptly married him. Michael was a charming man, reminding Charlie of Ashley Wilkes in *Gone with the Wind*. They had five children in quick succession and lived for a while in England, and then back in the United States. Despite his charm, Michael was ineffective as a family man and their marriage began to wobble. Their finances deteriorated and both began getting counseling. Janet ran away several times, made an apparent attempt at suicide, and was sent to a "rest farm" to recover. She eventually left that institution, but ran away from her responsibilities again, ending up at the old family home at Great Neck.

Tragedy struck when Janet had the horrifying experience of discovering Michael hanging from a rafter in the cellar. She cut him down and, to her shocked surprise, found that he was still alive. But instead of calling for help, she fled; for some time, Janet and the children were nowhere to be found. Michael lived about six weeks but finally perished, as he had planned. Janet eventually showed up and was subsequently hospitalized for mental illness, leaving the problem of caring for her children. Charlie's mother called and asked Charlie and Dorcas to help with the family crisis, and as a result two of the children, Diana and Johnny, came to live with Charlie and his family. The remaining three went to Charlie's parents.

Diana was the oldest, a little "willful—very much like her mother," Charlie recalled. She was not terribly happy with her new living arrangement. She ate and slept with the family, but didn't engage with them in any way; she kept mostly silent. She also frequently ran away, and the Houstons would have to send out a search party, usually to find her in one of the local bars. Within six months Diana opted to return to England and live with an aunt. Charlie and Dorcas were relieved that this alien presence was gone, but were ashamed of their feelings and said nothing. Johnny, the younger boy, appeared confused, clumsy, and slow. His living, eating, and washing habits were poor, even disgusting to Charlie and Dorcas. But he was a warm and loving child. Johnny remembered that time: "I went to Aspen when my father hung himself. I was a wreck. I had serious behavioral problems. I was wild—even criminal. Dorcas straightened my little ass out." In fact, Johnny recalled quite clearly that Dorcas was the tougher of the two, Charlie the soft one.

Little Johnny needed constant prodding, but he stayed on and eventually became a surrogate son. "He was wonderful . . . I am very close to him," Charlie admitted. It wasn't always easy for the other three Houston children, though, and there was a certain amount of bickering. Charlie finally gave boxing gloves to Johnny and Penny and instructed them to "fight it out," which they did. "I remember the driveway on a cold November evening . . .

tears running down their cheeks, weeping and wailing while they slugged it out." In fact their fists seldom connected, but they managed to work out their differences with their misguided punches and eventually laughed about the incident. With a small monthly allowance from Charlie's father for the children, and a small but steady medical practice in Aspen, the family stayed on.

At the same time, Bob Oden, a well-known orthopedist from Chicago, flew in and told Charlie that he was fed up with the pace and politics of the big city and wanted to move to Aspen—provided that Charlie would become his medical consultant. Oden seemed like a good potential partner, so Charlie said yes, and they moved into the new Aspen Clinic. They were dreamers, and they dreamed no small dreams. "We thought we could create the Mayo Clinic here in Aspen," Oden admitted. But they were also practical. As a specialist, Oden attracted much of the fracture work (important in a ski town), and so the business grew. They were a good team. As Oden described it, "I did the surgery and Charlie kept the patient alive."

With their increased financial stability, Charlie and Dorcas began looking for a place to call their own. They found a beautiful green meadow on Red Mountain, across the river from the health center, and, with some trepidation, purchased two acres of land for what seemed an astonishingly high sum: $5,000 an acre. Now they needed a home. So they hired an architect, described their needs, and began plans to build. Yet before this new phase of their Aspen life could take shape, and midway through construction, Charlie became involved in a research project in Cleveland. Once again, Dorcas was left to pick up the pieces. She was responsible for five young people in a town she had lived in for only two years. Fired up with a new idea—this time about artificial hearts—Charlie was off.

〰

In fact, it had been back in Exeter that Charlie first began thinking about the practicality of an artificial heart. While caring for a man who was dying of heart failure, Charlie had become frustrated by his inability to truly help. The man's heart had simply worn out. He had had mild rheumatic fever as a child, and over the years the badly damaged mitral valve had ceased functioning. This was a typical case of childhood rheumatic fever "licking the joints but biting the heart," in the words of the famous pathologist George McCallum. As the patient aged, his heart function deteriorated to congestive heart failure and exhaustion. One day he finally said to Charlie that he would rather be dead than continue as he was. Charlie admitted him to a

Boston hospital and then assisted a surgeon who tried in vain to correct the dilated valve in the man's tremendously enlarged heart. The patient died on the operating table, and both doctors wept in frustration.

Although the heart was traditionally assigned emotional, spiritual, and physical connotations far beyond what could be proved, Charlie knew it was nothing more than a pump, a mechanical organ designed to propel blood. It logically followed that heart failure was nothing more than a mechanical failure. Why not build an artificial pump and replace the dead or dying one?

There were certainly plenty of precedents with other vital organs. Artificial kidneys were used in hundreds of hospitals throughout the world, and heart-lung machines provided successful temporary bypasses during open-heart surgery. It seemed logical to Charlie that a mechanical pump might permanently replace an incompetent heart, even though knowledge of heart bypass or transplantation was very primitive in 1956. Shortly after World War I, Alexis Carrel and Charles Lindberg had done some experimental work on a device that kept living hearts alive, and John Gibbon had developed the temporary heart-lung bypass that laid the groundwork for open-heart surgery. But only a handful of laboratories were actually starting to "build" hearts, and little was published on the subject.

Charlie, interested in the possibility of an artificial heart, began making crude designs and building models in the open garage attached to his house in Aspen; he later moved his work to the basement. "By then I had begun my primitive, naïve and really ludicrous efforts. In an unheated garage, with primitive tools I designed and built a number of crude pumps—one of which years later would be the basis for a better model which actually sustained life in an experimental animal." He was at a disadvantage, though, because he knew almost nothing of the problems of clotting and the breakdown of red cells—knowledge that was absolutely critical to the design. Even his knowledge of hydraulic systems was rudimentary: "In fact I had no business in this venture at all. Yet it was too fascinating to give up."

On the spur of the moment, he decided to describe his ideas in a letter to the director of the National Heart Institute. Amazingly, he received a letter back asking for more details. Charlie wrote back, delighted at their interest in his project. In retrospect, Charlie thought it must have been the novelty of a small-town doctor working on such an unusual and ambitious project that caught the attention of Washington. After much back and forth, Charlie asked for a research grant of $2,000 to expand on what he had done. They pressed him to accept $3,000.

He learned that Dr. Willem Kolff was doing pioneering research in heart valve development as a logical follow-up to the artificial kidney he had developed during World War II. So Charlie used part of his grant money to visit Kolff in Cleveland. Kolff was a dynamic and fascinating man. During the occupation of Holland in World War II, directly under the noses of the Nazis, he had produced out of mere scraps of plastic the first machines capable of human dialysis. Charlie rather simplistically concluded, "Surely . . . if Kolff could do the kidney in the cellar of his house, I ought to be able to finish the heart in mine." So in February of 1959, Charlie packed up and went to Cleveland.

※

Kolff put him up in a boarding house within walking distance of the Cleveland Clinic, and Charlie worked feverishly for three months, learning from Kolff, building heart valves and hearts. "I worked my butt off," Charlie recalled. He learned how to operate a precision lathe and how to make and use mock circulations on which the various heart valves and heart pumps were tested and studied. First they made molds, then castings, then negative molds, which they dipped into a solution of polyurethane, then slowly dried by rotating in an ice bath. Once dried, the very thin and delicate valves were peeled from the mold and tested on the mock circulation. Only one in five functioned.

There were plenty of problems to solve. Blood had to be handled with great care in order to avoid clotting, red cell destruction, and platelet destruction. Trauma had to be kept to a minimum. They discovered that blood clots formed on almost any surface, so they spent hours trying to design valve and heart surfaces that would not attract clots. Clots were often lethal, breaking off and lodging in the brain or lung. Charlie learned that the choice of materials used to build the valves and vessels of a mechanical heart was vital, and Teflon, polyurethane, and polyvinyl appeared to be the best to avoid the deposition of any foreign materials into the bloodstream.

Charlie worked twelve hours every day, as well as weekends—and he loved it. "The months in Cleveland were marvelous! About six in the morning I trudged through the windy icy darkness to the laboratory, and about ten at night I trudged home, sometimes forgetting to eat, totally engrossed in work." Under the tutelage of a young Japanese doctor, Tetsuzo Akutsu, he learned how to use polyurethane and to make exquisitely delicate heart valves. He experimented with pumps, trying out various methods of compressing ventricles: air, hydraulic fluid, mechanical compression by pistons, plates, rollers or even mechanical fingers. He discovered that, regardless of design, the pump needed to be pliable and non-traumatic to the circulating red blood cells, easily adjusting to heart rate changes and volume. He learned that there were a number of options for the location of the pump; it could be placed in the cavity left by the removal of the living heart or even within the abdomen. He experimented with magnetic and motor-driven electric power, but predicted that the future lay with pumps driven by atomic energy. Either way, it seemed imperative to have wires passing through the chest wall to power the pump. A particularly puzzling problem was that of regulating the stroke volume between the two ventricles. It seemed impossible to make them exactly equal, but after some experimentation he concluded that it wasn't necessary, at least on a stroke-by-stroke basis: the output from each ventricle only needed to be equal over a longer period of time.

Within a short time he and Akutsu began implanting their hearts in "hound dogs obtained by the Clinic . . . I hated the dog days, but they were necessary." The first was on May 26, 1959, when a pump was placed within the thorax of an anesthetized fifty-seven-pound dog. The first step was to anesthetize the dog and draw all the blood, redirecting it to a machine to bypass the heart. The heart could then be removed, and arterial connections were made using the artificial atria. The entire connection was done in less than an hour, during which time circulation was maintained by a Bjork heart-lung machine. They operated on a couple of dogs each week, but it wasn't until the day before Charlie left that they achieved what they considered a true success: they closed up the chest and managed to maintain the life of a dog for almost six additional hours.

Something always seemed to go wrong with the equipment, resulting in no long-term survivors. And then one day the experiment took a strange turn. Charlie and his fellow researchers were ordered to have several valves of different sizes, mounted in their gold rings, ready for implantation. And in came a human patient. A middle-aged man with one damaged valve, he was considered an ideal candidate because he wasn't terribly ill. Charlie was shocked, but the senior surgeon insisted that this was the perfect candidate. Charlie protested to Kolff but he was overruled. The surgery went well, but a few hours later the patient died when the valve slipped out of place. Charlie felt personally responsible, even though he had protested the surgery in the first place.

Although Charlie missed his family, he was obsessed with making a heart that would work. As time ran out he became increasingly frantic, rushing production and producing many failures. Finally, he was forced to adjust his expectations to, not a "final" or even "near-final" design, but an implantation that would sustain normal respiration and circulation for a period of days or weeks—something that would lead to more advanced models. By June 20th he had the "perfect working heart." He and Akutsu carefully chose the most promising and strongest dog. They bled the dog donor and set up the operating room with extra care. The first incision was made at 10:00 AM, and the heart was removed shortly after. The pendulum pump was in place by 11:15 AM. Everything seemed to be going well. After about fifteen minutes it was clear that the pump was functioning, blood pressure was sustained, and there were no leaks or tears in the fragile arteries. Akutsu closed up the chest. The dog's reflexes returned, its pupils became active, and for the next ten hours they carefully monitored all of its vital signs, urine output, blood pressure and the content of free hemoglobin in its blood. Then they X-rayed its chest, revealing not only that the heart was in place but that there was no pulmonary edema in its lungs. They allowed the dog to recover partial consciousness, administering Demerol to spare it any pain. It became clear that the dog had a working heart. Finally, after fifteen hours, the dog was sacrificed, an autopsy was performed, and the heart was removed.

Charlie was thrilled with this accomplishment, but continued to miss his family, especially Dorcas. When Charlie enjoyed an innocent dinner out with a friend, Helen Poutasse, and mentioned it in a letter to Dorcas, he was shocked to receive a strongly worded protest from her. A week later, on a visit home, they both realized that this small event had rocked the very foundation of their marriage. Yet they reconnected, enjoying a rapturous weekend followed by frequent calls and letters, all expressing their new-found love for each other. It was like a second honeymoon for them. It changed Charlie's entire view of the world; he felt relaxed and gay, cheerful and generous. Of all the good things that happened in Cleveland, he felt this to be the most important. He vowed to take Dorcas's opinions and needs more seriously in the future.

After the three months of research were completed, Charlie left Cleveland in an exhilarated and exhausted stupor. He returned to Aspen, armed with another grant, and published several articles in medical journals, describing the research he and Akutsu had done. He continued working independently in Aspen and eventually developed a heart designed around a completely new and different principle based on compressed air or water pressure. To assist him, he recruited a talented machinist to build a part that would rest outside the body. This new heart they would implant in dogs—a total of twenty-one mongrels each weighing thirty-five to seventy-seven pounds. Charlie would leave Aspen at 4:00 AM and reach St. Francis Hospital in Denver at 8:00 AM, where the operating-room team and Denver surgeon Jerry Rainer were ready and waiting. Together with Rainer, he would go into surgery for several hours, implanting a new model into a dog.

Charlie's new design was radically different: it comprised two compressible ventricles contained in a tight sac into which air was pumped under pressure. Into, and from, each ventricle were plastic tubes connected to the appropriate veins and arteries. Each of those tubes lay within a rigid housing into which air could be pumped. The air came from three bellows driven by a motor, each bellow delivering timed pressure in relation to the valves. Once the heart was implanted, the incision was tightly closed and the monitoring began. The doctors checked blood samples, arterial and venous pressures and responsiveness throughout. The animal would be declared dead only once there were no outward signs of life and no attempts at respiratory movements. Charlie would then hurry back to Aspen for evening office hours in his own clinic. As the routine intensified, the dogs began living longer and longer: one to two hours, two to five hours, five to nine hours; by the spring of 1962 they had dogs surviving for twenty-two hours or longer.

The causes of failure were many. One had to do with the fixation of the valves, which was dependent on a polyurethane-Lucite bonding that Charlie described as only "moderately firm," and subject to a constant shearing force of air pressure for valve function. He predicted that future models would need some kind of "O" rings for a firmer mechanical seating. In three cases, failure was caused by the piston-loading spring breaking. Three of the dogs died of severe pulmonary edema and one died of a clot formation. He attributed the cause of three additional failures to "faulty surgical technique."

Charlie's model had a unique feature that allowed him to change how each of the valves worked without touching the heart. He could modify the rate and force of the contracting ventricles at will by changing the air pressure, therefore adjusting the circulation easily. It was a very useful model from which to study what happened when one or more of the four valves opened or closed badly, or when one of the ventricles weakened. Its greatest value was as a research tool.

With Wolff's consent, and with growing confidence, Charlie published two articles in the *American Heart Journal*, describing the models he had used in Cleveland, as well as the later Aspen model. He summarized the artificial heart designs, detailed the twenty-one implantations, including autopsy reports, and suggested several design improvements. His greatest excitement was directed toward the future, as he was convinced that the artificial heart was now at the same stage of development that artificial kidneys had been at twenty years previous, and the heart-lung machine just ten years before.

Then came a visit by some prominent surgery professors who, upon their arrival in Aspen, were perfectly furious at their difficulty in finding Charlie. They arrived at midnight, fuming, "What the hell are we doing up here?" Charlie calmed them down with a couple of drinks, put them to bed, and the next day showed them the work he had been doing. They were stunned at his progress. Later that day, they sat him down and explained that they couldn't support him any longer in Aspen, as he had done all that was possible in this location. But if he were willing to give up his practice and move to an academic center in Ohio, they agreed to give him ten years of full funding. Now it was Charlie's turn to be stunned. Just prior to their visit, Charlie had been approached by General Motors Defense Systems to move north with full funding to conduct research with them on space and physiology. Charlie thought long and hard about each of the offers and, surprisingly, concluded they weren't right for him: "I'm not a research minded person . . . I'm a doer—an innovator . . . an entrepreneur." Shortly after, Dr. Paul Dudley White came to visit. He too found Charlie's work interesting, but predicted that a *transplanted* human heart was the future—*not* an artificial heart. In fact, Dudley White was right, and Charlie's project died a natural death.

〰

The heart research finished, Charlie returned to his general practice with renewed energy. Because of the nature of the town and its recreational attractions, his patients represented some of the country's most powerful elite, a situation that appealed to Charlie. And so it was not unusual to find Robert McNamara celebrating New Year's Eve with the family. The phone rang with a message for McNamara from his hotel: President Kennedy had called. When McNamara returned the call, he learned that he had just been named secretary of defense. Tom Cabot, who was also at dinner that evening, immediately proposed a toast: "What's bad for Ford, is good for the country."[27] Little did anyone in the room know what lay ahead. Because Charlie knew and trusted McNamara, he supported the Vietnam war for a long time, but eventually he believed it was a tragic mistake and the war became a topic the two agreed to avoid in the many years of their friendship.

Charlie saw old friends too. Bob Craig was a frequent visitor, growing to know the entire family, not just Charlie, very well. He was particularly fond of Dorcas, whom he saw as the backbone of the family. Although Craig had the impression that she wasn't an outwardly happy person, she seemed extremely self-contained and at peace with herself. And although he didn't think Dorcas was beautiful in the classic sense, he saw a quality about her that was special. What most impressed him was her strength. And it was clear that she adored Charlie. Craig thought it couldn't have been easy for her, with Charlie heading off on one expedition after another, or one research project after the other. But she seemed to know what she was getting when she married him, and she accepted him for who he was. Craig was amused by Dorcas's tolerance of Charlie's appeal to women: "She knew that virtually every girl that he would run into . . . was knocked out by Charlie." Craig couldn't understand why. "He wasn't that good looking. He wasn't an operator. He was a little bit flirtatious but he wasn't what I would call a 'cad.'" And she was also tolerant of what Craig called "Charlie's snobbishness." Both Craig and Charlie had some secret sayings that reflected their attitudes. For example, NAC meant "not a chap." More revealingly, NOK meant "not one of our kind"! Craig laughed at Charlie's feeble attempts at distancing himself from his wealthy background. "He's a snob, and so to counteract his snobbism, he wants people to think he's a bit of a socialist . . . he is left of center, but basically, he's an elitist," Craig contended.

Left of center or right of center, socialist or elitist, Charlie was stimulated by the conversations he had with Craig and the McNamaras, the Steins, the Cabots, the Goldberts, the Stevensons and others—about religion, morality, science, politics, power, the past, and the future. But not all conversations were as rewarding. He began to notice an emerging pattern in Aspen that disturbed him. Increasingly he met residents who were enormously wealthy but whose ambitions were focused primarily on pleasure: "There are too many rich ne'er-do-wells, too many broken homes, too much sleeping around, too many people with little to contribute." Charlie was saddened by the sometimes corrosive power of inherited wealth and position.

Aspen was not simply an endless circle of social engagements. Charlie was frequently called to tend to dangerous and acute situations, with still relatively few drugs and equipment at his disposal. Perhaps the most dramatic example occurred one night when a call came in from a dinner party at midnight. The hostess was in a panic because one of her dinner guests was suffering a heart attack. Charlie grabbed his bag and hurried over. The EKG showed an acute infarction, and while the strip was running, the patient's heart stopped. This was years before CPR, so Charlie reacted immediately with the accepted practice of the time—injecting the heart with adrenaline. Nothing happened. Minutes passed. He realized that this man was going to die if he didn't do something drastic. He calmly asked the hostess to bring him a large knife and then asked her to send the guests away. There, on the sofa of her living room, he proceeded to open the man's chest with that kitchen knife. Once it was open, he began massaging the man's heart with his bare hands, hoping it would begin to beat. It trembled and Charlie felt a few faint beats, then a few stronger ones. Then—nothing. Again, a few beats. Then it stopped—for good. The ambulance arrived a few moments later, and the driver, a good friend of Charlie's, said, "What the hell have you done now, Charlie?"

Charlie's medical experiences in Aspen were nothing if not varied. He counted among his patients two bulls. He had recently been in Salt Lake City, where he had learned about brisket disease, a form of heart failure that affects some strains of cattle when taken from low to high altitude. Soon after he returned to Aspen, he was approached by a wealthy rancher friend, Wirk Cook, who asked him to look at two prize bulls he had just bought. A ranch hand tied the first one up while Charlie set his electrocardiogram to take a tracing of the bull's heart in action. Absolutely nothing came through. Finally the ranch hand drawled, "Doc, I think yo patient's daid." And so he was. The struggle had killed him. Charlie managed to treat the other bull without a struggle, and, thankfully, he survived. But for quite some time after, whenever Charlie would suggest an electrocardiogram to one of his Aspen patients, they would look at him warily and say, "I'd rather not, Doc. I heard what happened to Wirk Cook's bull."

Then, on New Year's Eve, 1958, Charlie became involved in an incident that would change his life. The phone rang and a young man named Pat informed Charlie that he and a friend, Alex Drummond, had been on a backcountry ski trip and his friend was very sick. They were camped up above Snowmass Lake at about 9,000 feet. The two had crossed the 12,000-foot Buckskin Pass a couple of days earlier, and Drummond had become short of breath and strangely irritable. He was moving so slowly that they hardly made it over the pass. The two made it down a short distance, and then Drummond collapsed. That night, he coughed constantly, and it was clear that his lungs were full of fluid. The next morning he was too weak to pack up, although he made an attempt to continue with the trip, leaning over his poles, gasping for air, helpless to his advancing condition. Strangely, he had experienced this before, a year earlier when skiing into the 12,000-foot Pearl Basin above Ashcroft. But Drummond continued on as best he could, skiing less than a mile that day. He raved throughout the night, mostly about grocery stores. Once again, the next morning, he set off, collapsing after not more than a hundred feet. It was then that his partner set up the tent, made Drummond as comfortable as he could, and began skiing the twenty miles down the wild valley to get help.

As Charlie listened to the story, it was clear that a rescue was required. He called the sheriff, who came up with the not-too-helpful suggestion that they get a posse together with a team of horses to go and pull the boy out. Charlie happened to know that the sheriff's posse was, at the moment, deep into New Year's Eve celebrations. Next was a call to the army, who assured him that a helicopter would arrive at first light, weather dependent. Taking the gloomy weather forecast into consideration, Charlie wisely began calling his friends and neighbors, putting together a ground-based rescue team—not an easy task on New Year's Eve. By midnight they had a group of seven organized to meet at dawn, when they would board a Weasel treaded snow vehicle to tow them partway up the valley.

It was a cold gray dawn and the Weasel operator was late; they finally found him in a compromising situation. Tousled, hung over and exhausted, the driver reluctantly appeared at 5:30 AM. Off they went, the Weasel carrying some of the rescuers on board and towing the rest. They went as far as they could in the snow cat by 9:00 AM, and then put on their skis and headed up the valley, reaching Drummond at about noon. Charlie half expected him to be dead, so he approached the tent alone. But Drummond was alive, although coughing terribly and much too weak to move. They bundled him up in his sleeping bag, tied him securely to Charlie's toboggan, and pulled him back to the Weasel, which they reached just after dusk. By nine that night he was safely tucked in at the Pitkin County Hospital.

Charlie assumed he had pneumonia, although there were many atypical features: he had almost no fever, his white blood count was not strikingly elevated, he did not appear toxic, and both his lungs were almost completely filled with fluid. But there were many rales and wheezes throughout both lungs, and the X-ray showed patchy densities that could have been bronchia-pneumonia. As well, his toes, nose and ears were blackened with frostbite. By the next morning his X-ray showed such improvement that Charlie began to have second thoughts about the diagnosis of pneumonia. How could he explain the considerable fluid in his lungs? This was more consistent with pulmonary edema, a condition usually caused by heart failure. This young man was otherwise perfectly healthy, with no history of heart disease. Charlie called several cardiologists, who thought it must just be an unusual example of heart failure, perhaps due to a combination of altitude, extreme cold, and exertion. He then called Drummond's mother, and something she suggested caught his attention. Intuitively, she wondered if what appeared to be heart failure might have been caused by the altitude. By the next morning Drummond seemed almost completely recovered.

An article appeared in the local paper, stating: "A medical discovery of real importance to mountain-climbers may have been made here last week . . . according to Dr. Charles Houston . . . it was first thought that Drummond was suffering from pneumonia . . . However he said that he thought further study would prove that Drummond . . . suffered from a peculiar heart trouble connected with the altitude . . . and that the case would receive much attention from the medical world."[28]

The case continued to intrigue Charlie, so he invited Drummond back to Aspen to ski hard for a few days at over 11,000 feet. Although Drummond said he felt fine and had no obvious symptoms, Charlie thought he heard a suggestion of a murmur, reinforcing the belief that he had a problem with a heart valve. Then he received a letter from Drummond's mother. In retrospect, Charlie felt she was the one who first put her finger on the correct diagnosis. She wrote: "Knowing how he has exerted for years, I can't help feeling the explanation must be in the sudden change from mild sea level climate to extreme cold at very high altitudes . . . " She referred to previous incidents where her son had experienced similar symptoms upon going to higher altitudes. Charlie was stunned, and decades later said: "What marvelous insight! There is not a great deal we have added in the ensuing years. Trust a mother to think the thing through in short order."

Charlie immediately felt compelled to alert climbers and ski mountaineers about the possible danger of going to high altitude, regardless of any previous heart disease history. In the summer of 1959, he submitted an account of the case to the mountaineering journal *Summit* and it appeared the following April, entitled "Pneumonia or Heart Failure."

A few weeks after the incident, prominent Boston cardiologist Paul Dudley White came to visit Charlie again. White told Charlie that he didn't believe the boy had heart disease, agreeing that his problem was probably related to high altitude. He urged Charlie to publish the details of Alex's case with four other stories Charlie had collected about climbing friends who had died of "pneumonia" on high mountains.

His short article "Acute Pulmonary Edema of High Altitude," now considered a classic, appeared in September 1960 in the *New England Journal
of Medicine*. It immediately attracted letters with similar stories from many
countries. At this time virtually all physicians in the United States faced
with a patient showing the symptoms of pulmonary edema would consider
only two possible diagnoses: left heart failure or pneumonia. Charlie's study
changed that. But Charlie, along with his American colleagues, was also unaware that medical reports similar to his own had been published a few years
earlier in South America. In fact, there were a number of papers published in
Spanish that described what eventually became known as high-altitude pulmonary edema (HAPE). But Charlie didn't have access to a medical library
at the time and didn't learn about these articles for many years.

For Charlie, Drummond's case renewed his interest in altitude problems,
spurring future research projects and continued work in that field. "I doubt
whether any of this would have happened if I had not been there on New
Year's Eve when Pat was seeking a doctor—any doctor—to rescue his sick
companion," Charlie says.

After his newly gained fame from the published article, two doctors from
the National Institutes of Health in Washington arrived in Aspen. After a
few days of observing Charlie, they finally met with him to ask him what
he would do if they gave him a grant of $100,000 a year for ten years to do
altitude research. Charlie could hardly believe his ears. They said, "Take your
time and get back to us with some ideas." Charlie did, but the proposal was
inadequate. "I didn't have the background even to outline where this could
go. So of course it came to nothing," he admitted.

Despite the heavy load of research and medicine, Charlie still found
time to explore the mountains with his family. He and Dorcas worked
hard to provide their children a deep appreciation for the outdoors; topo-
graphic maps were a big part of their education. They camped, canoed,
skied, and skated. Using USGS maps, they found remote lakes teeming
with delicious fish. In winter they hiked up to high, frozen ponds, skating
on the mirrored black ice. They sometimes skated down the frozen edges
of the river, even though the center was not solid. Dorcas would sit on the
edge, sipping sherry, perhaps in order to dull the apocalyptic vision of one
of her children sliding off into the rushing cold water. Charlie's nephew
Johnny described the time in Aspen as his "golden years": four years of
outdoor living and wildly interesting people coming through the doors,
plus two caring and intelligent surrogate parents.

Throughout this seemingly rewarding existence, Charlie still experienced periodic bouts of depression. He tried getting more sleep, reading more, going to the occasional movie, or walking more often. Nothing worked. He became convinced that his depression was cyclical and speculated that he might be manic depressive. He wondered how he could break the cycle. A technique that had always worked in the past was to tackle tasks that could be easily dealt with: paying bills, sorting papers, tidying up. But even this was too much for him now.

The depression continued unabated. January 1961 possibly marked the low point of Charlie's life. In his journal he lamented: "I am forty seven and a half years old and facing ruin—financial, emotional, and professional." But he quickly committed to paper that he would, under no circumstances, consider "doing away with myself."

Money appeared to have triggered this particular crisis, for in reviewing his finances for the previous year, Charlie realized that without cash bailouts from his parents and the sale of some capital assets, he could not have remained afloat. Even so, the future looked grim, with $1,000 worth of bills piled up and only $75 in the bank. Charlie had always regarded money as something that just *was* . . . something that came to someone if they did a competent job. It was not something that "nice people either worried about or made their goal in life," and it bothered him greatly to worry about money. This attitude naturally followed a background of privilege; Charlie's parents had always provided for his needs, whether for school, travel, or expeditions. But now it was he who was responsible for his family's financial future, and he didn't feel up to the job.

His worries inevitably led to reflections about what he saw as his "nonproductive" career. He began to question his decisions to work in small communities such as Exeter and Aspen, concluding that he had virtually eliminated any possibility of financial success or professional prominence. Additionally, he wondered if those small communities had provided him an escape—that he was actually afraid of playing in the bigger and more competitive urban centers. His self-assessment was brutal: "I was more promise than accomplishment. I've never been a brilliant doctor—never at the very top of the pile." He believed that his scientific work followed much the same pattern. Admitting that some of his work was original and ahead of its time, he felt he had always failed to follow through, not only to a clear scientific conclusion, but also to the point of accomplishment—and recognition. He appeared to lack the stick-to-it nature required to conclude these big, important projects.

The recriminating assessments of his professional career spilled over into that part of his life he held most dear—climbing. And here he was most cruel with himself: "I never quite came through on the promises: Crillon I missed, Nanda Devi I missed, K2 I missed twice, Everest I didn't really try." Not letting up on his self-reproach, he continued: "Though I have consoled myself with 'explanations' for each of these misses—the fact is that in all my mountaineering trips, only Foraker has been the total success." Finally, to complete the self flagellation, he dismissed even his mountaineering books and films with the assessment that they were "good, sometimes quite good, but never really what they could and should have been."

Reflecting on the 1953 K2 expedition, Charlie was convinced that it hadn't just been their determination that got them down off the mountain, but some kind of divine intervention—a kind of miracle. But if this were true, he wondered what purpose they had been saved for—not once, but repeatedly. He had often wondered if God had some plan for him to accomplish great things. And he felt ashamed that he hadn't.

He began to think that perhaps it was no longer his own accomplishments that were at stake, but those of his children. Perhaps the only way Charlie could extract himself from this spiraling funnel of depression was to concentrate on the future, and his children. In his journal he wrote, "My life is probably over so far as success is concerned, theirs is ahead, and I—we—must save them from my errors." But that brought him back once more to the need for a superb education for each of them, and full circle: of course, the problem of money.

Later that winter he recorded in his journal: "I sit here at 5:00 AM on February 12, 1962, in the blackest mood a man can bear, and try to think over last year and to foresee the years to come . . . My life is filled with blackness so much of the time, my hopes are dashed so often, my dreams occupy a larger and larger segment of life—and are more and more devoid of realization—that I begin to believe—almost—that I am sick." He had spun himself into a nightmarish vacuum of loneliness and despair and misery from which he could not fathom an escape. He fantasized morbidly of becoming "one of the amiably dreaming failures so bitterly drawn in the *New Yorker*."

In the depths of his heart, he knew that he was running away from himself. His parents had told him in a blunt letter six years prior that this was his problem, and it now appeared to be true. No matter where he lived, Exeter or Aspen, the problems returned and he was left with feelings of isolation and loneliness. He struggled with a vacillating need for solitude and independence, yet all the while craving friendship and security. "I feel now that unless I break the chains of my past, unless with one titanic revolution I free myself from my bad qualities once and for all, I will go under," he concluded.

Just in time to save Charlie, that titanic revolution arrived from the most unexpected place—India.

URINE AND JASMINE

Eggs are health. Eggs are strength. Eggs are so tasty too. Such fun to make. So don't waste your money on things that can injure your health. Like tobacco. Spend it wisely on eggs.
> —Slogan from the Indian Government's pro-eggs campaign, quoted in the *New York Times*

The wildly popular Democratic presidential candidate, John F. Kennedy, was returning from one of the Nixon debates when his plane stopped in Madison, Wisconsin, for refueling. Word spread quickly that Kennedy was coming, and as a result about 1,200 students gathered around midnight on a cold, wet night to hear him speak. He was tired and irritated, and in the process of delivering a lackluster speech unexpectedly asked, "How many of you would be willing to work in a foreign country for two years for the United States?" The crowd went wild. A journalist picked up the story and mentioned it to one of Kennedy's aides, who thought the idea might be worth pursuing. Kennedy floated this trial balloon a couple more times, and, each time he suggested it, the crowd went crazy with enthusiasm. It was clearly an idea for the times. Shortly after he was inaugurated in January 1961, he wrote an executive order establishing the Peace Corps and chose his brother-in-law,

Sargent Shriver, to run the program. By early 1962, the Peace Corps had begun to take hold, capturing the imagination of the entire country.

Washington was full of volunteer applicants, and it quickly became clear that this was going to be a boon for the administration. Kennedy was an idealist; he instinctively knew this would be good for the United States's image abroad. Shriver repeatedly stated that the Peace Corps would do far more for the United States than it would for the host country. Although Charlie was a Republican at the time, he had voted for Kennedy, based on Kennedy's sophisticated education, his background, his personal charisma, and his leadership potential. Although he had heard about the emerging Peace Corps, he initially scoffed at it, thinking it nothing more than a public-relations ploy.

Yet Charlie's old climbing buddy, Bob Bates, had just signed on to the Corps and was heading off to Nepal. He called Charlie, urging him to join up, too. Initially, it seemed completely out of the question. Charlie was openly skeptical of the program, and by this time he and Dorcas were responsible for not only their own family but one of his sister's children as well. They were in no position to pull up stakes on a whim. But Shriver thought differently. He knew from Bates, who had recommended his friend, that Charlie had been to India, that he was a doctor, and that he had a good track record as an organizer, having already started two clinics. He was unconditionally convinced that Charlie was the man for India. He simply ordered Bates: "Gotta have him. Bob, go get him."

But ultimately it was Shriver himself who called Charlie, and over the following two months he called over and over again. Charlie repeatedly explained to Shriver that he had responsibilities: a family, an important artificial-heart research project, and a medical practice. Charlie's answers were consistent: "Absurd. Impossible. Out of the question." Shriver brushed the objections aside, and edged steadily closer to Charlie's current salary. Laughing, Charlie said, "Bates put Shriver onto me and Shriver gave me no mercy."

When Charlie continued to say no, Shriver tried a new approach. He would act as if he truly understood Charlie's dilemma in one phone call, and then a few days later call back with new arguments. Charlie felt flattered, and finally agreed to go to Washington—just to talk. It was July 1, 1962. There he found an atmosphere charged with electricity. A young John D. Rockefeller IV conducted the interview, and Charlie met a dozen youthful, dedicated, excited, and impressive Peace Corps staffers. And then there was Shriver, the most charismatic person Charlie had ever met.

Charlie returned to Aspen and refused once again. But Shriver's enthusiasm and optimism had infected him, and his family knew it. Early one morning the three Houston children and Johnny traipsed into Charlie and Dorcas's bedroom, sat down on the bed, and offered their advice: Charlie should say yes to India. Their endorsement was the last straw. Charlie had a long and heartfelt private talk with Dorcas, who sincerely didn't want to leave Aspen for India. She eventually bent under the overwhelming pressure, as she had so many times before. Charlie called Shriver and accepted. "Come next week," Shriver ordered.

Before leaving, Charlie went back to his little office in the Aspen clinic, put his head in his hands, and moaned: "What, oh what, have I done to my family?" But at the same time, he knew this was a turning point in his life. He had become disenchanted with the routine of his medical practice, and the heart research had more or less wrapped up. He was restless and unhappy, and succumbed once again to visions of greatness, writing in his journal: "I feel that it is the big chance that will never come again to do something of value, to be the leader I have never quite had the nerve to be, to do the big things I have never quite gotten done, to change myself, and through me, my family." The question was: could he do it?

It was left to Dorcas to rent out the house and sell the car. She packed up their belongings, shipped some of their furniture to Delhi, and worked with Washington to arrange travel for the rest of the family. They would join Charlie in India two months after he got there. Sadly, only immediate family was allowed to accompany Peace Corps volunteers, which meant that Johnny couldn't join them. Charlie and Dorcas made arrangements for him to attend a private school, but instead he returned to Tarrytown, New York, to help his mother re-establish their shattered family.

On September 5th, Charlie left for Washington, where he tried in vain to assimilate all that the bureaucrats explained about this new assignment. Meeting with dozens of Peace Corps staff, he was asked at one point if, as a Himalayan explorer, he thought the abominable snowman really existed. Without a moment's hesitation Charlie replied: "I know he does . . . he lives in Washington and his name is Shriver!" His commitment was for two years, his rank was equivalent to that of ambassador, and he would report directly to Shriver. Shriver's directions were clear: "You are not to frequent the embassy. You don't work for the American ambassador. You work for me." American Ambassador John Kenneth Galbraith had a formidable reputation, which may have prompted Shriver's words of warning to Charlie: "He is a very talented, brilliant, charming man, but he is a very strong person. He'll tend to dominate you. If you have any trouble on that score, just stand up to him. Get in touch with me at once, and I'll back your position and authority all the way."

Charlie casually mentioned his contact with Frank Thomas in India twelve years before. This caused a ripple in the hallowed Washington offices, since it turned out that, unbeknownst to Charlie, Thomas was a spy and the Peace Corps was strictly forbidden to have contact with any intelligence agency; senior officers in particular could have no history of that kind of contact. Shriver was clear: "You must not have any contact with the CIA under any circumstances. Hello and good-bye to those fellows. If they try to contact you, approach you, report it to me directly." After hours of cross-examination, Charlie convinced them that he had been an innocent bystander in the Thomas affair. What Charlie failed to mention was his special interview with the CIA following his 1950 expedition to the Everest region of Nepal. But Charlie had been sworn to secrecy, and he honored that oath. He was on a plane to India the next evening.

The long flight provided him ample time to think. He was totally drained. He had leapt into space again, away from a secure home, family, and future. He had left Dorcas, as he so often had, to pick up the pieces. He was heading into the unknown. Three previous directors had been fired or quit within eight months. "I wept. I despised my weeping. Which made me weep more. Which made me despise my weeping even more."

Twenty-seven hours later, at 5:00 AM on October 1, 1962, Charlie arrived in India. He was met by his predecessor, Joseph Wheeler, a hardworking, unimaginative government employee, who promptly announced that he would be leaving India the next day. In the six-hour debrief Wheeler gave Charlie before he left, he explained that the Peace Corps volunteers were demoralized; there was no cooperation from local authorities; there was no help from the government; and the programs were poor at best. The Peace Corps in India appeared a shambles. Within twenty-four hours Charlie spiraled out of control. He developed diarrhea and a fever, together with a panic attack. Overwhelmed and frightened, he ignored Shriver's orders and asked for an urgent appointment with Ambassador Galbraith.

Canadian-born John Kenneth Galbraith was a tall, thin man of towering intelligence and with a razor-sharp wit. He was a world scholar, an intimate of Kennedy, and completely enchanted with India. Charlie was too sick and worried to appreciate Galbraith at this first meeting, but began by begging to be sent home at once, before he did irreparable harm to the

United States. Charlie told him he had no idea of what he was supposed to do, or where, or when, or how. Galbraith listened quietly, did not argue or persuade, but instead spent forty minutes telling Charlie about his own situation, faced with a looming Soviet threat on the northwest frontier, and a shaky Indian parliament. Charlie only half heard him. Then Galbraith put his hand on Charlie's shoulder and asked him to go visit a few volunteers near Delhi, promising to send him home after that if he still wished. So Charlie went back to his office couch, grabbed some fevered sleep, and planned his next steps—a tour of some of his volunteers.

Together with his Peace Corps driver, Charlie headed out on a 1,200-mile trip north into the Punjab region. In the rural towns and villages he found mostly poverty and dirt. Everything was in need of repair. But he also saw people working hard, which he referred to as "the miracle of modern India." And between those villages on the rough, dusty roads, Charlie became mesmerized by the parade: monkeys, vultures, trained bears, camels, elephants, and people—endless throngs of people.

India had changed dramatically in the twelve years since Charlie's last visit. In the 1930s the British Raj held India much as it had been in the days of Kipling. It was a romantic land, half myth and half reality. But World War II, religious unrest, and the abrupt cruelty of partition had sliced the country in two. Surprisingly, even though millions had died and a hundred million had been displaced, much of the British infrastructure had survived. Since Charlie's first visit the population had doubled, mostly in the sprawling cities. Food production was inadequate, and famine, flood, and sporadic conflicts were endemic. It was to this India that the Peace Corps had sent a few dozen young American idealists, and now Charlie—previously an avowed colonialist—to shape and lead them. At the same time, the United States Agency for International Development (USAID) was sending hundreds of professionals and billions of dollars to India to build a self-sustaining economy. The contrast between the two organizations was stark.

For five days Charlie visited handfuls of volunteers in several villages. As Wheeler had intimated, all were discouraged and complained about the lack of support and understanding from the head office in Delhi. Their jobs were ill-defined, and they had received little direction from the previous Peace Corps directors, who had come and gone in quick succession. To Charlie they seemed suspicious, complaining, cynical, indifferent—and *rude*. But without exception, he noted, they always ended their tirades with the statement that, "with a little help great things might be done." Charlie recognized these statements as "small straws in a wind of bitterness," and he pressed for more. What would it take? What tools did they need to reshape their jobs in order to be productive? At each stop he understood the problems more completely. He saw a situation with great potential, and that potential excited him.

This first tour set the tone for Charlie; he realized that personal contact with the volunteers was absolutely vital. He resolved to go back to each volunteer once every four weeks—an exhausting program, considering the vast distances within the country, made more so as the program grew. In time, he would obtain more help, first a deputy and then an assistant, yet even after the program had grown substantially, he insisted on seeing each volunteer at least once every six weeks. Admittedly it was a somewhat paternalistic approach, but it seemed to work. As a doctor, as an expedition leader, as a medical researcher, and now as a Peace Corps leader, Charlie always focused on the individual.

⁂

Only six weeks after arriving, Charlie received an urgent call from Nepal: a volunteer had fractured his skull in a fall. Charlie had been chosen for this role in part because of his medical skills, and this would prove the first of many times he would be called upon to use them. He was directed to fly to a small grass airstrip and rescue the patient. He was to leave at dawn the next morning with the embassy plane.

He flew north in the clear, cold morning, first to the foothills and then eastward, parallel to the great, snowcapped Himalayan peaks. The mountains were a magnificent contrast to the heat and dust of the Indian plains, reminding Charlie of his earlier climbing adventures. He landed at a primitive airstrip alongside the road on which he had walked into Nepal in 1950, and was met by a Jeep to proceed to the British hospital. There, Charlie examined the unconscious volunteer, who had fallen off a steep trail. His condition appeared serious. They flew back immediately to Delhi, and Charlie admitted the patient to the Holy Family Hospital, one of the best in India, where he could do a more thorough examination. Convinced the patient urgently needed expert care, he exchanged a flurry of cables with Washington, and finally received permission to take him back to the United States on the earliest possible flight.

The patient remained unconscious throughout the flight, but as they arrived at Kennedy Airport he began to regain consciousness. He became so agitated and violent that Charlie was forced to hit him in order to knock him out again, just to regain some control. The public health officials then boarded the plane, asking for the patient's international vaccination certificate—which he didn't have. "Well," they said, "then he can't get off."

"Nonsense," said Charlie. "He's brain damaged, we've got to get off this plane."

"No, we can't let him off the plane—he's got to go to quarantine." Charlie exploded. He got on the phone to Washington and, within minutes, obtained permission to take the poor unconscious man to a hospital.

This unexpected trip to Washington provided Charlie the opportunity to attend a Peace Corps staff meeting that ultimately changed the direction of his work in India. During the meeting Shriver introduced Charlie to the group and then added, "Charlie, I hear your volunteers are doing great things in the poultry business." Charlie was stunned. He had no idea what Shriver was talking about. He mumbled a vague, "Yes, Sarge."

Shriver continued enthusing: "I hear they're making their own feed and manufacturing vitamin B-12 and penicillin. That's terrific!"

"Yes, Sarge," Charlie responded. Before he could catch him at the end of the meeting to find out what was going on, Shriver slipped away to another appointment. As Charlie was leaving the building, he bumped into a prominent Texan named Manning Grinnan. It turned out that Grinnan had just returned from India. While there, he had visited some of Charlie's volunteers, and it was he who had told Shriver the poultry story. Charlie soon learned that Grinnan had visited a group of volunteers in Nabha who had told him all about an ambitious poultry program. Not only had he talked to them, he had returned to the United States with the good news and read his report on the successful India poultry program into the *Congressional Record*. Congress was apparently quite impressed with the phantom program.

Charlie was aghast. Upon his return to India, his first task was to make the four-hour drive to visit the Nabha volunteers who had fabricated the entire story. He arrived unannounced on a hot, dry and dusty day to find the four volunteers sprawled out in the shade, drinking beer. Charlie was livid. "I'm Charlie Houston. I'm the director. What's going on here?"

"Well it's a hot day and we're having a beer," the insolent volunteers replied. Charlie told them what had happened in Washington and demanded an explanation. After some time, they finally admitted there was no poultry program. Charlie exploded: "Well you've lied to Shriver and there has been a note put in the *Congressional Record* about what you're doing and you've falsified everything." As he turned to leave, they pleaded, "Wait Charlie, wait a minute," and began explaining just what had happened. Tired of visitors from the United States coming by to see what they were doing, as if they were animals in a zoo, they had made up the story, and the Texan had swallowed it. It was brilliant. Their story was logical enough that it could be easily accepted by the unsuspecting visitor.

Charlie's anger intensified. But when he threatened to send them home they responded with, "Charlie, there's a really great chance to do poultry here." They explained that Indians raised lots of free-run chickens, but egg production was a very poor thirty percent. The volunteers were convinced that if they could get the villagers to make proper chicken houses, keep their chickens confined and keep the roosters away, they would see vastly improved egg production. Charlie asked them what they needed, and together they compiled a list. As he left, he said, "I'll give you a couple of months and I'll be back again. If you have something going, I'll give you what you want . . . if you haven't . . . I'm sending you home."

Back at headquarters, Charlie wasted no time. Although the Peace Corps was specifically forbidden to work with other agencies, such as USAID, Charlie had developed a good relationship with USAID Director Tyler Wood, and together they moved the poultry project along. Wood agreed to provide money to enable local people to build their own poultry houses. With the $150 cost of the house provided by USAID along with free day-old chicks, poultry farms could be created at no cost to the villagers. USAID also provided handbooks on raising poultry, which, after they were translated into the various dialects, proved quite useful.

Within a couple of months, the poultry program began to flourish. Once the program was underway, volunteers often found free sources of day-old chicks from Greece, Turkey, and elsewhere. One night Charlie received a call from the airport telling him that his chickens had arrived. To which Charlie answered, "What chickens?"

"The baby chicks you ordered."

"I didn't order any baby chicks."

"Well, there are five thousand here and you need to come pick them up." When Charlie and his assistant went out to the airport, they found boxes and boxes of day-old baby chicks. Slowly comprehending that they actually needed to take these chicks home, they began to gather them up, when the customs man abruptly stopped them:

"Oh Sahib, you have to sign some papers."

"Fine, give me the papers."

"Oh Sahib, first you have to get a customs clearance and you have to pay the duty."

It was Saturday night; Charlie clearly couldn't get customs clearance. When he pointed this out, the answer was, "Then, Sahib, you can't take the chicks." Charlie suggested calling the superintendent but was told he had gone home. Moreover, he wouldn't come out on a Sunday.

Charlie said, "But by Monday, they'll all be dead."

"Yes Sahib, they'll all be dead." After a whispered consultation, Charlie and his assistant began taking the lids off the boxes. Scores of adorable, pale yellow balls of fluff began tumbling out, running helter-skelter around the airport. The customs agent threw up his hands: "No Sahib, don't do that . . . no Sahib, don't . . . Sahib . . . please take the chicks." The chicks were theirs.

The next day a volunteer showed up at Charlie's office and the mystery was solved. For months, this volunteer had been receiving baby chicks donated from Greece, slipping them easily through customs because they were "gifts." But this shipment was too big, and it had caught the attention of the agent. The chicks were ultimately safely delivered to the project site, where they matured and duly began laying eggs, just as planned. Charlie never did pay duty on those chicks.

Within two years the poultry program would be the best in the world, gaining such notoriety that over twenty years later *The New York Times* would reference the pro-eggs campaign in India that amusingly proclaimed: "Eggs are health. Eggs are strength. Eggs are so tasty too. Such fun to make. So don't waste your money on things that can injure your health. Like tobacco. Spend it wisely on eggs."

After a couple of months Charlie began preparing for Dorcas and the family's arrival, which was scheduled for December of 1962. He was now confident that he could provide them with enough support to make their life in India comfortable. Charlie and his assistant, Pamar, began looking for a home for them to rent. Much to Pamar's horror, Charlie insisted on looking in the slums of Delhi. After seeing the appalling conditions up close, he quickly acquiesced to Pamar's urgings to modify their search to a more upscale area. They settled on 61 Sunder Nagar in New Delhi. It had a small front yard, a larger backyard, a laundry, kitchen, living room, and three bedrooms on the ground floor. The second floor would function as the Peace Corps headquarters office. From their low-walled roof they could gaze out over the trees of the neighboring zoological gardens to the ruins of a 500-year-old fort that captured the dawn and dusk light beautifully.

Upon signing the lease, Pamar generously offered not only to continue as his administrative assistant but to oversee his domestic staff as well. Charlie exploded: "Domestic staff? What domestic staff?" He bellowed at Pamar that he had never lived with domestic staff and certainly didn't intend to begin now. This was, of course, not true. Charlie had grown up with domestic staff in his own home on Long Island. Perhaps he felt uncomfortable as a white American in poverty-stricken India. But Pamar wouldn't budge. He patiently explained that the house came with servants—they weren't an option. He was convincing: How could Charlie expect to be on the road for long periods each year and leave his family with no help? How could he send these people who so desperately needed work out into the cold without a job? Charlie began to relax about it all, but then recoiled in horror once again when he was informed of the scale of the operation—there would be five of them: a laundress, a gardener, a part-time sweeper, a cook, and a driver. But it was settled, and Pamar got his way.

Before Dorcas and the children arrived, Charlie received a cable: "MOYERS IS ARRIVING DELHI." Then, more urgently: "MOYERS IS SICK. TAKE CARE OF HIM." At the time, Charlie knew nothing of Shriver's second in command. Bill Moyers had grown up at the feet of his political master, Lyndon Baines Johnson, having begun working for him as a nineteen-year-old college student in Texas. Vice President Johnson valued the brilliant young man greatly, as did Kennedy. When Moyers expressed an interest in leaving to work with the newly formed Peace Corps, Johnson was extremely reluctant to let him go. So was the president, who valued Moyers as a buffer between himself and Johnson. But Moyers pushed hard, and landed an appointment as deputy director under Shriver.

Charlie met Moyers's plane and found him mildly ill. Rather than admit him to a hospital, Charlie took him home, cared for him, and cheered him up. Their lifelong friendship was cemented in those three days. Though differing accounts have Moyers suffering from everything from hallucinations to an injured back to a bleeding ulcer, Moyers always claimed that Charlie saved his life. Charlie disagreed, but said, "Perception is reality and I'm quite happy that he thinks I did."

〰

Meanwhile, world politics took a turn for the worse. As a taut standoff ensued with the unfolding Cuban Missile Crisis, the Chinese attacked India along her northern Himalayan border and Delhi was plunged into a state of shock. Hysterical bulletins warned that Delhi would be bombed and that Chinese troops would overrun the city. Thousands of air-raid trenches were dug throughout Delhi and in the *maidan* (the large grassy area in front of Charlie's home). The trenches quickly became latrines. It was utter mayhem: futile blackouts were attempted; spies were denounced; the government claimed victory and then demanded sacrifice and warned of disaster. "Had it not been so tragic for a nation only recently recovered from a civil war, it would have been a comic opera," Charlie said.

With this political situation in mind, Charlie flew back to Washington to make the final arrangements for the family to join him. Once he arrived, Moyers shepherded them around and smoothed the way. In a desperate last stand, fifteen-year-old Robin announced that he would not go to India unless their dog could go, too. Thanks to Moyers, Thrice, the third in a long line of retrievers, was with the family when they arrived on December 23, 1962.

Charlie promptly went back to work, leaving Dorcas to settle in as best she could and hastily prepare for their first Christmas in a strange land. Unbeknownst to her, Charlie had invited a few team members and Indian friends over for Christmas dinner, wanting to introduce his family. And unbeknownst to Charlie, the Peace Corps volunteers had gotten wind of it, somehow interpreting the occasion as an "open house" at the Peace Corps director's house. Word spread throughout India, and they flocked to Delhi, over eighty of them arriving for Christmas dinner.

The normally unflappable Dorcas was horrified, running frantically between the dwindling food supplies in the kitchen and the door to properly greet people as they arrived. It was chaotic, more so when they ran out of food after about sixty people. The chaos continued when, the next morning, they were awakened by a cacophony of unusual sounds—not just the usual howling jackals. This time it was a five-piece brass band, playing some completely unidentifiable tune. After fifteen minutes Charlie realized that a tip was expected for this atonal performance. Hoping for some silence, he gave generously. Big mistake. For the duration of the morning approximately forty additional bands appeared, along with beggars, snake charmers, and monkey dancers. Word had spread: the Houston residence was the place to go.

Although Charlie thought Christmas "a great party," it strained the limits of what Dorcas could endure. Only two days after being uprooted from her home in Aspen and moving halfway around the world to India, she had entertained more than eighty people, none of whom she had ever met before.

After the initial shock and exhaustion had worn off, Dorcas realized that she would need to brace herself for household challenges she couldn't as yet even imagine. Yet she was determined to run her home as best she could.

As a very efficient housekeeper, Dorcas struggled with the Indian way of doing things. The laundry in particular bothered her—and there was never a shortage of laundry, what with a family of five, the stifling heat, and white being the predominant color for clothes and linens. Each day the laundress would carry their dirty clothes down to the Ganges River, where hundreds of people gathered, scrubbing their clothes in the muddy, filthy water into which everything—from garbage to corpses to ashes of dead bodies—was dumped, and then beating the clothes on rocks. The clothes were then duly spread out on the grass, urine-soaked from the endless cattle that cropped it short. Somehow the combination of filthy Ganges River water, urine satura-tion, and the blazing Indian sun produced clean and blindingly white clothes. Nevertheless, Dorcas was aghast.

Despite her misgivings, Dorcas seized control of the household, demon-strating her determination to manage this new domestic challenge, as she had done each time before: first in Pensacola, then Exeter, then Aspen. The next summer, Dorcas decided they must have air-conditioning in order to bear the unrelenting Indian heat. Charlie was adamantly against it, con-vinced it would be unacceptable for their down-to-earth Peace Corps im-age. The formidable Dorcas fired off a telegram directly to Shriver, point-ing out that the Peace Corps director couldn't do his job adequately in the stifling heat and that if he didn't get an air conditioner soon he would probably be dead or, at best, be left without a wife. Shriver promptly re-sponded: "TOO FEW HEART SPECIALISTS IN WORLD FOR US TO RISK YOU BUT WIRE UNCLEAR WHETHER PRESENCE OR ABSENCE OF AIR CONDITIONERS MOST CONDUCIVE TO MENTAL PHYSICAL HEALTH OF MY ESTEEMED DIREC-TOR OF PC IN INDIA. SARGE." The air conditioning was duly installed.

The India program was turning out to be very interesting to Washing-ton, and a steady stream of visitors came to Delhi, all of whom stayed at the Houston home. Evaluators from Washington came through every three or four months, as well as volunteers. Dorcas once remarked bitterly to Charlie that she could remember only three nights when they didn't have someone staying with them. And one night Robin implored his father over the dinner table, "Can us boys have two minutes to talk?"

While Dorcas took care of the house and endless visitors, Robin and David attended an international school for foreigners in Delhi, based on an

English model. Eventually Robin returned to the United States to attend Exeter Academy in preparation for entrance to a good university. Penny, who was already in university at the time, tried to attend classes at the University of Delhi, but found the language barrier too daunting. She eventually returned to the United States to attend Milton College. But each summer the entire family came together, often traveling throughout the country. Robin and Penny also traveled independently. When she was only seventeen, Penny ventured out alone for an extensive trip throughout India, walking from village to village, sleeping in people's houses, and eating local food. She also spent three weeks in an ashram. Although Charlie and Dorcas were nervous, they didn't hold her back, believing that "a life without risk is not worth living."

As Charlie endeavored to make positive change through this work, he revealed wildly fluctuating feelings in lengthy monthly letters back home to his American friends. At times he felt "hopeless, exhausted by the futility of doing anything here" and then, just at the worst moment, he would be catapulted into optimism by some individual event or scene. He expressed frustration at the deeply ingrained deviousness that he found in what he referred to as "the typical Indian personality," as well as the maddening habit he saw of starting things and letting them fall by the wayside.

"Those days were the busiest, most varied, complicated, exciting, and frustrating period I can imagine," Charlie reflected. "Every day was different; I never knew when some crisis or pseudo crisis would erupt." Probably his most difficult task was dealing with his Indian counterpart, U. S. Rana, who was responsible for winning internal approvals for Charlie's plans. A man Charlie described as evasive, elusive, secretive and self-serving, Rana was also a necessary evil—the portal entry for all Peace Corps programs—and Charlie simply had to learn to work with him. Because Peace Corps policy stated that it would respond to an idea only when a state or country made a specific request, in order to implement the poultry program it was up to Charlie to convince Rana that the project would make him look good. The requisite appeal then came from India—not Charlie.

It wasn't just Rana; corruption was a part of Indian life. Charlie routinely heard stories of high government officials telling American firms that the official would approve a certain installation, provided the American executive guaranteed a college education at a good American university for his two children. Honesty appeared to be a rare commodity. But despite all its shortcomings, he realized there was much to learn from this country: "To

India we must somehow give strength and leadership; from India we must learn patience, wisdom, and a change in our own values."

Much of Charlie's time was spent traveling, since the volunteers were spread throughout the country. He slept on their floors, met with the locals, and discussed new plans and projects. Gradually, the program grew. Washington sent more volunteers, and the program diversified beyond poultry; they now had teachers, nurses, and mechanics. But poultry was what they did best, and it remained the signature program. Over time it grew exponentially: chickens, eggs, broilers, feed production, and distribution channels.

As he crisscrossed the nation, the masses of people affected him profoundly: "They weigh physically because you are never away from them, anywhere, anytime. They weigh emotionally because they are all so thin, so ragged, so worn and on the edge of life. They weigh mentally because you always seem to be struggling about one thing or another." The struggles were mundane and tedious, often around money. Although bargaining was expected, Charlie hated it because he felt ashamed to haggle over pennies: "You with your fat American bottom and purse trying to beat down a thin bedraggled Indian." But he also hated being played for a sucker. He eventually began to discern a pattern among the people he visited: "the hospitality and kindliness in the villager, the oily deviousness of the middle official, and the lightning quickness of the top men."

Politically, Charlie sensed a growing tension in Kashmir, which he called "a smoldering bomb which could ignite all Asia." The sentiment was strong that Kashmir must be an independent state, and Charlie himself saw no other solution. And in Delhi, politics were becoming messy. Jawaharlal Nehru, leader of the Indian National Congress, was widely respected and loved at the time, but some government ministers were asked to resign and others were charged with corruption or political malfeasance.

Despite living through this tumultuous period, Charlie remained curiously apolitical, too caught up in his work. As a Peace Corps volunteer, he was discouraged from talking about or interfering in any way with Indian politics. He was there to help. Then, on November 21, 1963, the world was stunned with the assassination of President Kennedy. The Indians, who held Kennedy in great esteem, felt the loss as well. At that historical moment, however, Charlie and his family felt isolated and very far away from home, learning what little they could from Indian newspapers.

What they couldn't imagine was how the event would impact the Peace Corps itself. With Kennedy's death, Johnson assumed the presidency and immediately called upon Bill Moyers; when the new president disembarked from Air Force One at Andrews Air Force Base on the night of November 22, 1963, twenty-nine-year-old Moyers was at his side. No one at the Peace Corps offices begrudged Moyers returning to his mentor in this time of need, possibly thinking it would be a temporary situation. For more than a year Johnson chose not to appoint a vice president, instead relying on Moyers as his unofficial "deputy president." Moyers's role was such that when President Johnson was hospitalized for two days, it was Moyers who stood in. In a poignant note written to Charlie, Moyers asked: "Dear Charlie, I had to do it, but where does a 29-year-old go after he has been acting president of the United States for two days?" Moyers never returned to the Peace Corps.

For the rest of 1963 Charlie continued traveling the country visiting his more than 350 volunteers: a 1,600-mile journey through Mysore, a 1,200-mile tour of Punjab, up into the Kulu Valley rimmed with 13,000- to 20,000-foot peaks; five days in lush Maharashtra above Bombay; three days in Jaipur. A complete tour was 5,000 miles, and Charlie used planes, trains, and local vans to visit the volunteers, most of whom were fresh out of school and away from home for the first time. They lived simply in the villages, in a house supplied by the Peace Corps and on enough money to engage a cook and buy food. This freed them up to do the actual work required.

Besides the work, Charlie reveled in the joy of travel, indulging his love of adventure and his genuine passion for meeting and interacting with individuals. He was a nomad with a purpose. And with each passing day spent exploring yet another corner of India, he fell more deeply in love with that massive, complex, and beautiful country.

One of these trips was to the hill town of Mussoorie, on a road that was by far the most crowded he had ever seen in India. For eight miles it ran straight across the broiling plains, then into the dwarftree-covered foothills, through the army town of Dehra Dun and up to the cool, green oasis of Mussoorie, 3,000 feet above the plain. Mile after teeming mile, the road was choked with gray-swathed people: walking, cycling, sleeping, or sitting. Bullock carts moved at their traditional speed of two miles per hour. Camels shuffled along silently in the dust, and skeletal horses gamely trotted along with their overloaded carts. Even water buffalo could be seen from time to time. And through this maze came careening, roaring, stinking trucks, with their horns blasting.

On a trip to Rajasthan, Charlie marveled at the heavily bejeweled women in brilliant red and green saris carrying tarred gravel on their heads in order to mend the roads. Workmen carried their entire families on the backs of their bicycles and on the handlebars. One cyclist carried a complete load of wood and a string bed on his head, and a ribbon-bedecked miniature horse miraculously hauled a *tonga* with twelve passengers.

Another journey took Charlie to Darjeeling. He flew first to Bagdogra, from which a road ran along the plain and then up through miles of neatly cropped tea plantations. As he continued up, the foliage changed to rhodo-dendron, oak and holly, all dripping with moss and orchids. Here the people looked different: they were of Nepali, Tibetan, Sikkimese, and Bhutanese origin. Then suddenly, rounding a corner, Charlie was assaulted with the overwhelming bulk and beauty of the Kangchenjunga massif floating above the misty valley, third-highest mountain in the world. He was instantly overcome with poignant memories of his earlier days, high on the Himalayan peaks.

Wherever he went, his senses were overwhelmed, particularly his sense of smell: jasmine and orange; the sweet, pungent smell of dung smoke or cedar wood; tobacco smoke from hookahs; the hot smell of frying food in bazaars. Not everything was fragrant; there was also the stench of feces from open fields, and the acrid bite of urine. And everything was shrouded with the ubiquitous dust, finer than flour, that created such spectacular sunrises and sunsets.

When he wasn't traveling around the country, or negotiating with the Indian bureaucracy back in Delhi, or writing reports for Washington, Charlie was inundated with visitors or new volunteers. One of these was a new Peace Corps doctor named Bill Foege. During his tenure, Charlie had come up with the idea of installing portable latrines in the slums of Calcutta in order to get people to stop defecating on the streets. Charlie was convinced that this plan could eradicate cholera. He talked with Foege about his plan, saying he was sure that people could be taught to use them. Foege agreed. It was Foege's first assignment overseas, and he latched onto the latrine idea with a vengeance. A delightful and motivated person, he was devastated when the latrines were instead used for storage. But Charlie's infectious enthusiasm had worked its magic, and Foege stayed on in India for his entire two-year term and then returned to work on a smallpox eradication project in Ghopal. From there he went on to northern Africa, and for the next ten years he became one of the most influential people in eradicating smallpox throughout the world. After he left public service he became director for the Carter Center, then a professor of epidemiology, and finally a medical advisor to the Bill and Melinda Gates Foundation.[29] When Jimmy Carter went to Oslo to accept his Nobel Prize, he took Foege with him, stating that without Foege he couldn't have accomplished what he did. And when Foege was given the prestigious Mary Woodard Lasker Award for Public Service in Support of Medical Research and Health Sciences, he explained in his acceptance speech that he had first become interested in international health when he was a Peace Corps doctor for Dr. Charles Houston in India. "And that electrified me—if it hadn't been for Charlie Houston and PC in India, I probably wouldn't be here today," he said. Just as Shriver had inspired Charlie, it was now Charlie's turn to motivate and inspire others; Foege was one of the most spectacular examples, but there were many others. This was Charlie's legacy.

Then, in the summer of 1964, Nehru died. Though it had been clear that the great man was failing, his death still came as a shock. Everyone held their breath. Would China renew their aggression? But India remained calm and succession was swift and sure. A distinct easing of tensions with Pakistan appeared at once and Kashmir cooled off. The infamously corrupt government of the Punjab was swiftly replaced.

That summer, Shriver called a meeting in Pakistan for the Peace Corps directors from eight countries to exchange experiences and plans for the future. They shared stories and statistics. Charlie reported that at last count he had examined 17,659 chicken coops and 456 schools and had consumed 11,687,433 cups of tea. At the end of the meeting, Shriver took Charlie aside with a new proposal: would he like to start a doctors' Peace Corps, to send doctors all over the world? Though Charlie didn't want to leave India, the plan Shriver presented was so appealing, so breathtaking in its vision, that Charlie knew he would say yes.

Some months later, after returning to the United States, Charlie gave a presentation to the home office of the Life Underwriters Association in which he tried to sum up his life-changing experiences in India. He called his presentation "Urine and Jasmine," and it became one of his most famous speeches. To Charlie, urine and jasmine was what the Peace Corps was all about: the bitter and the sweet. He eloquently described bringing in a new group of volunteers to Delhi in the gray light of dawn. As they entered the city, they would encounter thousands and thousands of men, women and children squatting along the road, relieving themselves in this, the busiest, most prosperous city of India. The sight would be staggering, and the stench even worse. The impressionable volunteers never forgot it. But those same volunteers soon saw that flowers, too, flourished in this chaos, and that the scent of jasmine was also unforgettable. In time, they became oblivious to the urine, but never to the jasmine.

In truth, Charlie had been totally unqualified to do what he was asked: namely, administer a difficult program in the biggest and most complex democracy in the world. Prior to his departure, Charlie and his deputy, Brent Ashabranner, wrote a vision statement for the Peace Corps in India. "It was an exciting exercise," said Charlie, "me diluting his prudence and he cooling my ardor to shape a design to train 5,000 volunteers to serve all over India." As in the past, Charlie's grand vision was not realized, though many of his ideas and plans were carried out by someone else. Still, Charlie had inherited twenty-five volunteers in India, and left with 300 in place.

During his time in India, Charlie became painfully aware of the arrogant imperialism and intellectual condescension of the United States. He became convinced that Americans could not transpose their own ideas and accomplishments into any other culture and achieve real success. "They have to be adapted to, not adopted by, the countries that we are trying to serve," he said. He realized that many volunteers had never even heard of the countries to which they were assigned and he felt this had to be changed: "It's important that we know about these countries. It's important that we understand them." What he didn't say was that it was also important to allow oneself to be affected by them, something he surely believed.

The transition from India to the United States was difficult for all, and especially wrenching for Charlie. "Our lives had been so full of so many rich experiences. I knew nothing at home would even approach this. The heat, the dirt, the poverty, the bureaucratic frustrations had almost disappeared from our consciousness, replaced by bird-song, the colors, the endless variety of the street scenes." The night before they left, Charlie lay awake for hours, listening to the night noises of Delhi—the murmurs of people, then the whistles of the night watchmen. There were distant drums and pipes, then mongrel dogs, and finally the usual pack of jackals with their curiously human cries. Then, just before dawn, he heard lions roaring in the zoo two miles away. He arose, went to the window and inhaled: an occasional whiff of jasmine, a trace of smoke from dung and aromatic wood fires. The city was beginning to waken. It was a night he would remember as "being India."

The next morning, December 1, 1964, the Houston family was assembled at the Delhi airport, awaiting their flight to Athens. Unexpectedly, the gardener from their home appeared with garlands of flowers for each of them, solemnly giving them a traditional farewell. They swallowed hard and boarded the plane. As Charlie buckled up for the flight, he fought his emotions: "I wept my way over here. I'm just *not* going to weep my way back. What am I? A man or a mouse?"

TERROR ON THE HILL

A wheel cannot be turned by carried water.
—Turkish proverb

Charlie arrived in Washington with a lot of emotional and political baggage from his days in India, but also with considerable status. As an assistant to Sargent Shriver, he had entrée into some of the highest social circles in Washington. Diplomatic embassy dinners were common, and a social evening at the Houston residence typically included influential politicians. Charlie remembered Eunice Shriver getting down on the floor one evening in order to demonstrate her current exercise regime. There was even one carefully engraved invitation to the White House with precise instructions, time, and dress code. Charlie shook hands with Johnson and desperately tried to make small talk the entire evening.

However, there was a dark side to all that power, which Charlie occasionally glimpsed. Betty Harris, an old friend from India, was high up in the Johnson administration. Because of her close proximity to LBJ, she was treated royally throughout the city. One day that royal treatment ended. She called Charlie in hysterics: "I lost favor with LBJ yesterday and today all the invitations I had have been rescinded." Her expulsion was swift and cruel, and she was destroyed by it. Charlie could do nothing but try and comfort her. He learned then that once you have power in Washington, you must keep it. If you lose that power, you're dead.

But Charlie had a job to do—a difficult one at that—starting up Shriver's Peace Corps doctors' program. From the beginning, the project was plagued with difficulties. There were several roadblocks, the first of which was a Peace Corps policy that volunteers could not be sent abroad with children—or even a spouse—unless the skills of that spouse could also be used. Many doctors who responded positively to Charlie's call for volunteers had children, and eventually the Peace Corps did relax that rule. The second problematic regulation would not give draft clearance to join the Peace Corps. Most of the doctors recruited by Charlie were also being drafted for the Vietnam War under an emergency measures program administered by Dr. Shirley Fisk, a friend of Charlie's from Columbia and now a senior naval officer. When Charlie requested doctors for his program, he was turned down by Fisk.

So Charlie picked up the phone and called Robert McNamara, his friend from Aspen days, now Secretary of Defense McNamara. McNamara was completely immersed in the war and could justifiably have ignored the call, yet he gave Charlie a fifteen-minute appointment. They sat together, talking about Aspen, and then McNamara asked Charlie what he wanted. After Charlie's pitch, McNamara called in his secretary, dictated a memo to Fisk directing him to give Charlie what he wanted, thanked Charlie for coming, and said goodbye. Charlie was elated. The next morning Fisk called: "What have you done, Charlie? You know that it's impossible to do what the Secretary wants." Charlie laughed, "Just do it, Shirley." And so he did.

While recruiting medical personnel, Charlie also met resistance from doctors who were intent on their individual careers. But his Peace Corp's enthusiasm was infectious, and he would counter with: "Your experiences abroad will add to your life much more than is lost . . . human development cannot be hurried . . . two years spent with the Peace Corps form part of the foundation which makes the doctor truly a physician and healer." He believed these precepts, based on his own rich experiences in India. He was committed to the program because he felt that the Peace Corps experience was not only the United States's most effective means of providing foreign assistance, but also a profound instrument for personal development. He knew from experience—his own and that of other volunteers he had worked with in India—that two years of grassroots living created an important awareness of the privileges that existed in America. He worried that, as the American standard of living continued to outstrip that of most of the world, and the

On the way to K2 (1953)

K2 1953 ascent route and camps (illustration by Dee Molenaar)

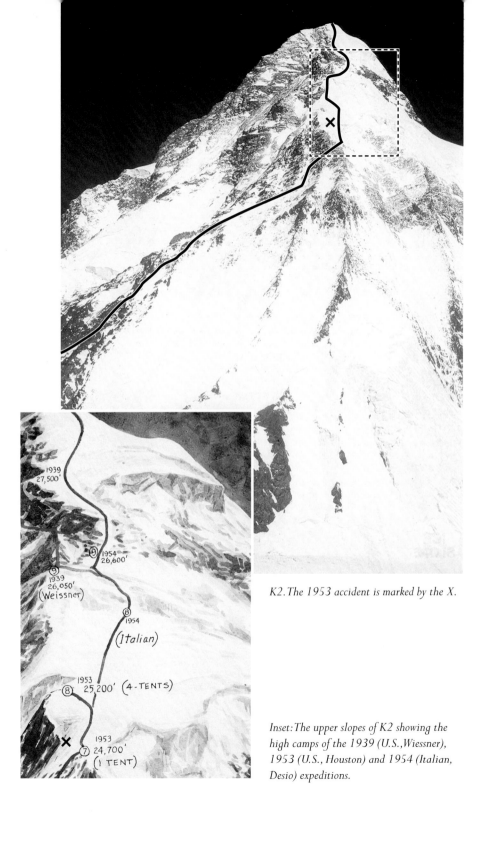

K2. The 1953 accident is marked by the X.

Inset: The upper slopes of K2 showing the high camps of the 1939 (U.S., Wiessner), 1953 (U.S., Houston) and 1954 (Italian, Desio) expeditions.

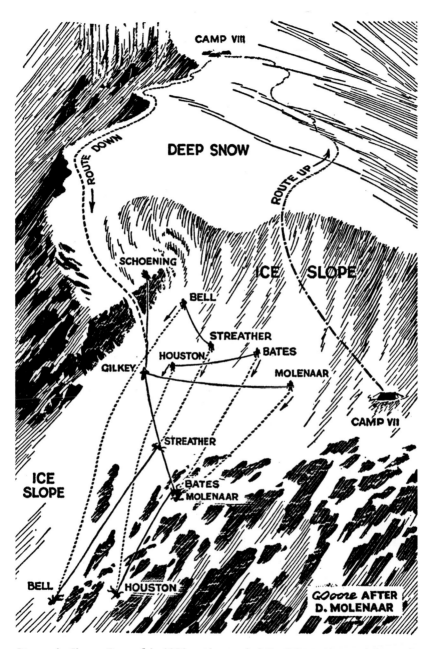

Diagram by Clarence Doore of the 1953 accident in which Pete Schoening's ice-ax belay saved the lives of his six companions. (Reprinted from K2: The Savage Mountain.) Schoening was holding the injured Gilkey; Molenaar was loosely tied in. At the critical moment Bell slipped, pulling off all the climbers, except Schoening and Gilkey, in rope tangles. Schoening, from his secure position, held the weight of the six others averting a terrible disaster.

Navigating steep ground on K2 (1953)

Charlie Houston bathing in a hot spring under the shade of the K2 umbrella (1953)

Brotherhood of the rope on K2 (1953)

Charlie Houston removing a decayed tooth on K2

The Art Gilkey cairn at the base of K2

Charlie and Dorcas Houston embracing at the end of the K2 1953 expedition

Charlie Houston inspecting the Peace Corps poultry unit in Kairon (1964)

Approaching Logan High Camp (1976)

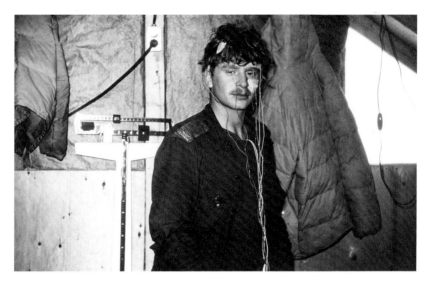

One of the Canadian Forces subjects wired for electroencephalographic tracings at Logan High Camp (1975)

One of the Canadian Forces subjects wired and on an exercise bike at Logan High Camp (1975)

gap between rich and poor countries widened, America appeared to be losing friends abroad, despite an incredibly generous assistance record.

These obstacles notwithstanding, Charlie did find willing doctors, and the
first recruits headed out in 1966 to Afghanistan, Iran, Turkey, India, Malawi,
Ethiopia, and Tunisia. Before departing, they were subjected to an intensive
twelve-week program that included classes in tropical medicine, preventive
medicine, sanitary engineering, and environmental health. Special emphasis
was given to the diseases common in the assigned country.

Three doctor couples started it off in Afghanistan, working in Jalalabad
with a young local doctor who had started his own rural medical school.
The first patient through the door was an elderly man with a spear wound
in his abdomen. When Charlie returned six months later, he marveled at
the transformation before him. With 100 students, they had supplemented
a regular curriculum with field trips to villages where they concentrated on
preventive medicine. The Peace Corps volunteers functioned as teachers,
doctors, and paramedical personnel. It was now a decent, clean, modern
hospital poised for the next step—an immunization program for smallpox.
Charlie was adamant that there would be no wholesale transplantation of the
United States's fully developed medical standards into this project, pointing
out that they were "inappropriate or unwanted in countries where the needs
are so basic." The comparisons were staggering: the United States averaged
one doctor to 750 people at that time, while in many of the Peace Corps
countries the ratio was one to 50,000 or 100,000, or even more.

Preventive medicine was the key. It meant helping build good latrines—
and convincing people to use them. It meant demonstrating how to purify a
water supply, how to control insect vectors of disease, and improving child
nutrition. The volunteers initiated massive campaigns to immunize against
prevalent diseases. When recruiting young doctors for the program, Charlie rightly emphasized the rewards of making a difference: of substantially
reducing the incidence of meningitis, polio, or encephalitis. And he insisted
that the program must be self-liquidating; a doctor's greatest goal was to
teach himself out of a job. Charlie knew that in the long run, the country's
medical needs must be met from their own resources.

A young volunteer family in an early placement in Addis Ababa, Ethiopia,
narrowly avoided tragedy, thus complicating support for the program. Both
husband and wife were volunteer doctors and, much to their horror, upon returning from the clinic one day, found their two young children under the bed
with an empty bottle of anti-malarial pills lying beside them. They induced

vomiting and saved the children, but the incident marked the end of doctor pairs with young children and hastened the demise of the doctors' program.

The work environment in Washington was stressful. Each week Shriver held a staff meeting with his senior staff gathered around a table where they talked about almost everything in their work world. Shriver tended to pit people against each other and would encourage heated debate. The predominantly male group was tough with each other; Shriver's management style promoted that kind of behavior and Charlie found it rough going.

Another Shriver ritual was something called the "murder board." The aptly named meeting included the national and regional directors of each Peace Corps country, gathered around a large table in order to defend their individual programs. The murder board was where programs were funded, where numbers were defended, and where staffing decisions were made. The process was, by necessity, very competitive. In Charlie's words, it was "bloody."

Shriver used Charlie to best advantage, calling on him to speak for the programs around the country and, once, in a congressional hearing. When Shriver called Charlie to "go up the hill," Charlie happily joined him, blissfully ignorant of what was in store. In the car along the way, Shriver explained that they were going before a congressional committee and that a senator who was very opposed to the Peace Corps would be cross-examining them on India. Although Shriver needed Charlie for credibility, he instructed him to say as little as possible. When Charlie learned it was Senator John Stennis, he wasn't worried, since Stennis had been to Delhi and Charlie was sure he had been impressed with all the good work being done in India. When Shriver and Charlie chatted with Stennis before the beginning of the session, the senator appeared informal and friendly. As soon as the gavel banged, his entire mood changed. He turned on Shriver and Charlie, attacked them and their fiscal management, and tried to catch them off guard with a maze of trick questions. Charlie was sweating profusely. After it was all over, Shriver congratulated him: "You did pretty well, he wasn't hard on you at all." Charlie was shocked. It was his first—and last—appearance before a congressional committee, an unpleasant event that represented the tenor of the political game.

It's possible the Peace Corps doctors' program was doomed from the beginning. It wasn't just the war and the shortage of doctors and the near-miss incidents in the field that caused Charlie's political downfall; so too would the suspicion by Peace Corps insiders of Charlie's motives and aspirations.

While Charlie was in India, Shriver had often mentioned his name in a positive light, and he continued to do so. Many suspected that Shriver had brought him to Washington to promote him into a top position, possibly as his deputy. Nobody in Washington believed Charlie when he said that he had absolutely no desire to remain in Washington, nor any ambitions of climbing the Peace Corps ladder. But Charlie was not politically astute and he didn't know how to handle the jealousy and gossip swirling around him. He ignored the rumors, enjoyed the privilege that Shriver's approval afforded him, and ran the best program he could—as always, pushing hard for what he believed was right. But the pressure wore him down, and Charlie sought help from a staff Peace Corps psychiatrist for the stresses that were finally beginning to overwhelm him. Charlie later learned that instead of counseling him, this man simply passed on his complaints to staffers further up the line. After this betrayal, Charlie's world fell apart: Shriver left the Peace Corps to become the first director of the Office of Economic Opportunity. With Shriver gone, Charlie's departure was inevitable.

Jack Vaughn was appointed Shriver's successor, and Charlie couldn't stand him. Vaughn didn't like Charlie, either, but largely left him alone. They came from opposite ends of the political spectrum and their styles didn't mesh. After a rancorous trip to Africa with Vaughn, Charlie announced that he wanted to leave, perhaps half hoping that Vaughn would insist on his staying. Vaughn didn't, saying only, "Suit yourself."

The eighteen months in Washington had been an incredible learning curve for Charlie—perhaps a bit too steep. Despite his passion for the program, he had probably been too unsophisticated to completely understand and influence what was happening in the power corridors of Washington. With Vaughn's ready acceptance of Charlie's resignation, the Houstons were in trouble. They still had a home in Aspen and another in Virginia, both with sizeable mortgages. Charlie had a family of dependents with growing financial needs—and he had no job. Although he had enormous experience and even considerable profile, they were in wildly differing fields: Peace Corps, family medicine, high-altitude research, Himalayan expeditioning, and artificial-heart construction. What could he possibly do next?

Soon after, Charlie was invited to attend a large meeting on international health where he participated in a small discussion group with the dean and the assistant dean from the College of Medicine at the University of Vermont. They got along well, and the two invited Charlie to come up to Burlington and take a look; it turned out that there was a vacancy at the university. As he began working his network around the country, other options presented themselves: a high-level position with the American Medical Association was offered him in Chicago; a position was offered at the Palo Alto Clinic in California; and of course there was always Aspen—he could still go back.

Or could he? The Houstons returned to Aspen to visit his partners, and Charlie informed them that he might wish to return. But while Charlie and his family were warmly welcomed back by the community, his medical partners displayed a distinct coolness. Shortly after, the three partners wrote him a letter explaining that he would not be welcome back. Not only that, they told him that if he tried to practice in Aspen on his own, they would fight him. "It was a bitter blow," said Charlie. He was sure this was just another example of a recurring pattern that haunted him: in Exeter, in India, and now in Aspen. "They had built a new clinic—just as I had pushed for, had added another doctor or two—again as I had hoped. They were clearly on a roll. But I would not be there." Charlie couldn't believe the letter, so he went back in person, going directly to Oden. But even his old partner said, "Charlie, I'm sorry but we don't want you back." As Oden saw it, Charlie had initially said he was leaving for two years, and was gone for four. Because the practice couldn't remain dormant, Oden had brought in another doctor and now insisted that there simply wasn't room for two internists. Charlie argued that it was he who had found his own replacement, who apparently had said that, if Charlie wanted to come back and there wasn't room for both of them, he would be the one to leave. The disagreement caused a deep rift in Oden's and Charlie's friendship and forced Charlie to look harder at his other options.

Throughout the uncertainty of where to work and live, Charlie was in a severely distressed state of mind, something that Dorcas, once again, endured. The family duly packed up, placed their belongings in storage, and rented out their house in Virginia. They were now owners of two lovely homes, neither of which they lived in. They headed north for the family womb—or taproot, as Charlie described it: Honnedaga.

The summer of 1966 went badly. The children were restless and bored: Charlie was frightened and irritable. Instead of enjoying their favorite place on earth, they simply endured it. Then, in early August, Charlie's sister Barbara sent word that she and her friends would be coming to camp for a week, despite having promised him exclusive use of the camp for the entire summer. Charlie protested vehemently, but she wouldn't budge. Furious, he packed up his family and moved in with some friends in Burlington, Vermont. The University of Vermont invitation was maturing by this time, and after two more meetings it was formalized. Charlie accepted, with a start date after Labor Day.

By the time Charlie reached Vermont, he was fifty-three years old. He was now well aware of his sometimes difficult personality and, once again, he resolved not to repeat the same mistakes. He was determined to make a fresh start in a new and different environment. And for a time, it worked.

It was late August 1966 and his family had no place to live, but Charlie was excited: he had left the turmoil of politics behind him; it was his first experience in academe; it was a chance to affect the future of medicine through teaching. A university colleague rented the Houstons a summer cottage on expansive Lake Champlain, and they settled in while Dorcas set about finding something more permanent.

Charlie's office was just off the edge of campus, occupying two of the three floors in an old Victorian building said to have been a haven for escaped slaves during the Civil War. His department included a secretary, a Ph.D. student, two MDs, and a statistician. He was given a prestigious title, Professor and Chairman of Community Medicine, and a salary of $22,000. But he lacked a job description, or even expectations; he had no existent models to follow.

Charlie's predecessor had been an imaginative and aggressive physician who had procured a large grant to develop a family-practice teaching program. With that money he had set up a small clinic that was well equipped with examining rooms, X-rays, and a small laboratory. Initially the response was positive and several hundred patients had enrolled, but even before Charlie arrived they had gradually drifted away to other doctors. Although it was unspoken, Charlie instinctively felt that he was not to reopen this family practice. It also became clear that he was to get rid of one of the doctors who was now regarded as dead wood. Since this doctor was tenured, it was obviously going to be a challenge. He also sensed that his role was to work more widely within the community while tightening up the department and making it more productive. But at what?

Unbeknownst to Charlie, there had been a messy political battle within the College of Medicine just prior to his coming. Professors had been replaced and wrists had been slapped. Charlie, however, had assumed that this school was mercifully free of guerilla warfare and politics. He now faced two dilemmas: determining the department's vision and negotiating a political minefield—something he thought he'd left behind in Washington. He idealistically went about his business, initiating strategy talks with his department members and enlisting the help of Dr. Kurt Deuschle of the Mount Sinai Hospital in New York. Among the good advice he received from Deuschle, one bit was ignored: to avoid intruding on other faculty members' turf. In fact, Charlie's personality was incredibly ill-suited to the structure and constraints of academia and a large institution, even though he was highly motivated to teach.

At about this time, Charlie became aware of two federal programs that could—or, as he felt, should—involve his department. The Regional Medical Program (RMP) was President Johnson's mandate to make widely available the latest advances in heart disease, cancer, and stroke. The program was very well funded, and Charlie felt sure he could develop some valuable teaching modules around the RMP. But it was chaired by an epidemiologist who happened to occupy the third floor of Charlie's building and who felt a certain amount of ownership in the program as well. They talked together rather warily, but never succeeded in working together. The second program emerged a year later and was called Comprehensive Health Planning. It contained strategies for delivering health care in rural Vermont, another area around which Charlie felt he could build a program. The director and Charlie got along well, but again, it was someone else's program. So within eight months of his arrival, Charlie had discovered two attractive areas where he should *not* go. What remained was for him to develop his own direction. He began to do so, in somewhat unusual ways.

One plan consisted of inviting a handful of first-year medical students to advise some of Burlington's needy families. Charlie would introduce a student to a family and instruct the family to call the student any time they had a medical issue. The student would then assess the situation and call Charlie only if he was needed. Four or five took up this task, relishing the responsibility. The program worked well, and the student interventions made a positive difference in the lives of the families who used them. Charlie recalled one instance of a poor, blue-collar family of four children, including one girl who displayed great promise. The medical student took the girl under his wing, worked with her on her classes, somehow got her admitted to a small college, coached her through drugs and pregnancy, found her a scholarship to the University of Arizona, and celebrated with her upon her return to

Burlington. Charlie celebrated, too: the first member of their family had made it past high school, and earned a university degree at that. Though Charlie was convinced that the program was effecting positive change, the university soon terminated it, stating that medical students were too young for that level of responsibility.

Charlie then borrowed from previous successful experiences in Exeter, recruiting practicing doctors in rural Vermont to mentor a medical student for a month. The student lived with the doctor and shadowed him as an apprentice. Soon this program too was terminated. Charlie began to question his style. Were his ideas too radical? Was there a step in the academic approval process that he was missing? Was he not consulting enough? Whatever the reason, his groundbreaking programs were always somewhat short-lived.

Yet some of Charlie's other ideas took root and found success. In a program called Combined Clinics, Charlie assembled the entire freshman class in one of the old amphitheatres. A patient would take center stage and tell the story of his or her medical problem. The case was always described from the patient's point of view. Charlie would then introduce various doctors who had worked with the patient, and they would describe what treatment they had provided. The faculty was cooperative and supportive, and the patients were delighted to appear. The program turned out to be quite successful.

One particular Combined Clinic event moved beyond the amphitheatre in the form of a simulated auto accident. The scenario was prompted by a severe crash on Highway 7 near Burlington. When Charlie asked the students what experience they had in first aid, they answered "None." There was no Emergency Medical Training available in 1965 in Burlington, and there were no rescue agencies other than the hospital and the fire department. So Charlie decided to rectify the situation. He found an old wrecked car, had it towed outside the faculty auditorium building, and piled it up against the tree just as class began. He then enlisted two local actors to be made up as victims, and coached them on what kind of injury they should simulate. About ten minutes into the class, the car was crashed into the tree and the ambulance siren sounded. Charlie looked out and announced that there must have been an accident. The students rushed out and the ambulance crews were very cooperative. After some confusion, the students realized that this was all a sham, so they went back inside and had some serious discussions about how to handle first aid: shortly thereafter, formal first-aid training began.

All of this was interesting, but Charlie still hadn't found a focus for his department. He felt trapped by the institutional constraints of the university, and his free-wheeling style and natural creativity were too reined in. It wasn't as bad as the disastrous experience of the Peace Corps doctors' program, but it was frustrating nonetheless. His institutional frustration created fertile ground for an exciting new idea that would soon provide him with professional and emotional satisfaction.

It began in October of 1966 with a phone call from Walter Wood, a prominent explorer, geologist, and climber. Wood wanted to assemble a small group in New York to discuss an exciting new idea—an altitude-research laboratory on the high plateau just below the summit of Mount Logan, Canada's highest peak, located in the Yukon Territory. Most scientific studies on the effects of altitude hypoxia had been done in decompression chambers up to this point, although limited research had been done as high as 19,000 feet in the Sierra Nevada, the Andes, and the Himalayas.

The frequency and severity of altitude-illness cases were increasing as mountaineering grew in popularity. The Indo-Chinese border war also vividly revealed the need for practical information about the impact of high altitude on soldiers trying to live and fight on the Himalayan glaciers. In addition, there were millions of patients with heart or lung disease who experienced shortness of breath at sea level. Wood thought that lessons learned at altitude might address these problems, and he was convinced that this new study would bring valuable research and solutions to these unanswered questions.

The Army Research Office, through the Arctic Institute of North America, had agreed to sponsor the project, and both the U.S. and Canadian armed forces were interested in participating. Wood invited Charlie to come up and visit Logan the following summer. How could he refuse? As Wood described it, "The trap had been baited with an irresistible cheese that Charlie promptly swallowed," an opportunity to combine two great passions in Charlie's life: mountains and medicine.

LOGAN LANDINGS

Women do just as well as men—they're much more difficult—but not in terms of altitude.

—Charles Houston

Little did Charlie, or even perhaps Wood, know that this proposed High-Altitude Physiology Study—or HAPS as it came to be known—would occupy Charlie's summers for the next twelve years. In the end, HAPS would turn out to be one of the most gratifying things Charlie ever did, almost as productive as Operation Everest in terms of research findings, and would put him forever on the map in terms of high-altitude medicine.

In July of 1967, Charlie flew first to Whitehorse, Yukon Territory, and then on to a camp on the shores of Kluane Lake, only ninety air miles from the Mount Logan massif. For many reasons, Logan seemed perfect for the project. Its multiple summits surrounded an enormous plateau that extended fifteen miles by six miles, sloping gently from 19,000 feet down to 11,000 feet. Partially sheltered from the high-altitude winds, the plateau appeared almost free of crevasses, providing an ideal space both for landing a short take-off and landing (STOL) aircraft and for a well-equipped camp that became known as Logan High Camp.

But there remained many unanswered questions about this great experiment. Would the weather cooperate sufficiently to allow regular flights back and forth to Logan High Camp? What would the snow be like for landing—would it be too soft, too wind-drifted? What kind of scientific studies could actually be accomplished in a camp situated that high? Would the results be of any use to anyone? Could it be made safe?

Charlie was about to find out, with help from some extremely talented people. One of the most vital members of the team was Phil Upton, a man who had more high-mountain flying experience than anyone in the country. A tall, lean, handsome fellow, Upton had a quiet sense of humor and a deceptively calm way about him—typical of pilots. He had served in the Royal Canadian Air Force during World War II and was an experienced bush pilot; he knew exactly when to fly—and when not to. At times his style and Charlie's were in conflict, since he refused to be hurried and, as one of Charlie's protégés said, "Charlie's always in a hurry."

Years earlier, Upton had stood on the "divide" between the Kaskawulsh and Hubbard glaciers and gazed over at the massive bulk of Mount Logan thirty miles away: "If we had an airplane with enough power we could probably land and take off on that flat-looking area below the summit. It must be over 16,000 feet high." With his new Helio Courier aircraft, Upton did just that. He could take off from the rough gravel strip at Kluane and land on skis high up on the glacier. He promptly had the plane modified with turbo chargers, and installed oxygen equipment and a high-frequency radio.

On only his second reconnaissance flight in the area, Upton was challenged by one of his passengers, Everest climber Barry Bishop, to "go down and see what it's like." This was the moment of truth—would the plateau work as a landing strip? Upton brought the plane around for one more look. The snow surface appeared smooth, the wind was calm, the day was clear, and the altimeter read 18,000 feet. He sailed out over the end of the plateau, the void increasing below him from 100 feet to 9,000 feet in a split second. He turned once again and prepared to land the plane upslope. Upton knew he was taking a chance, because scale, distance, and perspective were almost impossible to determine in that environment. But he was committed now; the flaps were down, he lost altitude, and smoothly touched down. Before losing too much speed on the snow, he instinctively turned the plane around, readying himself for a downsloping takeoff. As he slid to a stop, the propeller stopped. Bishop casually commented: "You didn't have to stop the engine." With his heart in his mouth, Upton responded: "I know. I didn't. It quit."

They got out. Bishop and the other passenger, Dan Taylor, wandered around a bit, taking pictures and confirming that this was a good spot for the camp. Upton wandered around too, but not without his oxygen bottle. After a few minutes they piled back in. They all waited nervously: Would the plane start? Upton fired it up and, miraculously, it ran, but only for two seconds. Same result the second time. Then it occurred to him—the fuel mixture was too rich for this altitude. After an adjustment, he found the correct balance and they were off. They had been lucky. Landing on an unknown glacier with no ground crew to help them if things turned nasty, was a dangerous activity, but this project was not without risks.

It was two days later when Bishop and Upton headed up once again. This time about four inches of new snow had fallen on their high-altitude landing strip, preventing them from taxiing around to have the plane facing down the slope for takeoff. By the time Bishop had finished unloading the plane, clouds were obscuring the sun. They piled back in and Upton opened the throttle—nothing happened. Upton unhooked himself from his oxygen supply, stepped outside and man-handled the wings in order to free the skis from the new snow. He tried to take off again, but without success. They both disembarked this time, wiggling the wings and jiggling the tail enough to free the skis. Meanwhile, the clouds continued to descend. Upton opened the throttle a third time; they held their breath, and the plane taxied down the glacier. By the time they were airborne, the entire mountain was cloud-covered.

The next two landings at Logan High convinced Upton never to land without a support team on the ground. He learned through trial and error that it was equally important to ensure the team was well acclimatized. A couple of weeks after the initial run, he flew a team of three to set up the campsite and stockpile materials via shuttles throughout the day. The support team was to unload the aircraft, turn it around, help get it unstuck if necessary, and then wait for the next flight. After a few hours Upton could see that the three on the ground were deteriorating quickly—stumbling around the aircraft in a hypoxic state, communicating incoherently, and taking longer to crawl out of the tents each time the aircraft landed. Luckily, that day there were no major problems with the snow conditions.

That was not the case a few days later, when a two-day storm dumped more than three feet of snow on the mountain. After landing with a full load of supplies, Upton knew he would need the help of the ground crew to turn the plane around. It was also obvious that a landing strip would need to be tramped out, as the deep snow simply bogged the plane down to a crawl.

For hours, the crew tramped up and down on snowshoes, creating an airstrip about 400 feet long. Slowly the plane began to move, but by the end of the runway, it was still wallowing dangerously in soft snow. It floundered to a stop just short of the drop-off. The exhausted team now had to come down to the end of the runway, drag the plane up the slope, re-tramp the original airstrip, and increase its length. Several hours later, Upton finally became airborne. It was that takeoff that convinced him he needed a minimum of six to eight well-acclimatized people on the ground to get out of a similar situation.

Charlie was one of a dozen doctors, scientists, and army officers on the project, and the one with the most high-altitude experience. But like Upton, even with his extensive knowledge, the limits of this experiment would soon be tested. Barry Bishop was leader of a small group of climbers who had been flown to 10,000 feet. From there they were to climb a long, steep snow and ice slope, cross the great plateau, and set up a prefabricated plywood building that was being flown up in sections. Charlie admitted, "It was a crazy, ambitious plan, and trouble soon began."

About halfway up to the plateau, three of Bishop's team were in a well-stocked camp on a level spot. They had a tent, food, and radio. But instead of recovering, one of the three (a biochemist) radioed down to Kluane Lake that the other (an orthopedist) was getting sick. By the next day the biochemist demanded an emergency evacuation because he claimed the orthopedist was "sinking into a coma." Charlie didn't know any of them; his only reference was the radio contact with the biochemist, whose cries for help became more shrill and urgent with each passing minute.

The problem was access. Their Kluane Lake plane couldn't land anywhere near the climbers, and it would take hours to find a helicopter. Charlie radioed throughout the Yukon Territory trying to secure one; meanwhile, the calls from the biochemist became increasingly frantic. All the choppers in the area but one were flying members of the Alpine Club of Canada into a number of climbing camps, luckily in the Kluane region. It took some convincing, but Charlie finally persuaded the leader to lend him their chopper.

The three were rescued from their airy platform and soon arrived back at Kluane. Immediately Charlie sensed that something was amiss. The biochemist staggered out of the chopper and began talking erratically, the orthopedist seemed perfectly normal, and the third man—the climber—said nothing. Charlie instinctively examined the biochemist first and discovered it was *he* who had pulmonary edema, not the orthopedist. "I realized that the cries for help had come from the man who was mentally affected, while the alleged victim lay next to him, making no protest. We had done the right thing to rescue the wrong man," Charlie said. That experience taught him the critical lesson that, because judgment can be severely affected at altitude, reports from people up above were unreliable.

The Bishop team did assemble the hut that summer, although the weather was abysmal. Charlie went home, excited by the possibilities. "I was hooked," he said. "I thought this could be a great chance to study altitude under field conditions. But I didn't realize till a few years later that it would be painful and dangerous to fly people straight from Kluane (2,000 feet) up to Logan High Camp at 17,500 feet." This lesson was personal: Charlie believed that, since he had been higher than 17,000 feet many times in his life, altitude wouldn't bother him. On one particular visit to high camp early in the life of the project, Charlie became sick with a blinding headache and horrible nausea after ten hours. The weather then worsened, and he wasn't sure he would get out. He did, but learned first-hand how dangerous it was to go high too quickly.

The next year Charlie was asked to direct and finance the project. So he wrote grant requests to the National Institutes of Health and managed to fund the program for the next ten years. Since he was already working at the University of Vermont College of Medicine, it seemed a likely home for the project. But the dean would have none of it; he had no interest in altitude illness and felt it had no place at the university. Rather than bringing the project home to the University of Vermont—his first choice—it was embraced instead by the Arctic Institute of North America, located at the University of Calgary.

Over the next ten summers the project evolved; they gained experience, the medical studies changed, and so did the scientists. The U.S. Army eventually withdrew but the Canadian Forces stayed on, providing air support and supplies. In fact, the team loved watching the Canadian Forces supply planes come in. The enormous Hercules aircraft were designated STOL and would come in very low over the brush and debris at one end of the thousand-foot gravel strip, roar through an immense cloud of dust as they reversed their engines, and come to a halt directly in front of camp. Out would tumble dozens of people, tons of cargo, and the occasional Jeep. More importantly, members of the elite Canadian Airborne Regiment also volunteered as subjects.

Charlie had no problems finding climbers willing to climb the mountain and support the efforts of scientists who would fly up with their subjects and equipment. Each winter and spring the scientists would meet to plan their research objectives for the following summer. As the project gathered momentum, scientists vied to be part of it, bringing their own projects, and HAPS developed a momentum and life of its own. However, this also meant that Charlie had to be away from home and his family every summer for the month of July. He felt guilty about that, but not a bit of guilt about taking time away from his job at the university. In fact, he didn't even ask permission—he just went, confident that the work was valuable and needed to be done.

While there were many outrageous episodes high on that mountain, they did result in important medical discoveries. In 1968, one of the support team developed high-altitude pulmonary edema (HAPE) and was flown out to the hospital in Whitehorse. He recovered quickly, but an alert doctor noticed that he had numerous tiny hemorrhages in his retina with no obvious explanation. Charlie said this would require further testing and told the man, who was complaining of vision problems, that he should stay off the mountain. As it turned out, his vision problems had nothing to do with the hemorrhages.

Charlie sensed he was onto something, so the next year he invited Doctor Regina Frayser to join the team. A brilliant physiologist, Frayser had a caustic tongue, but was bright, brave, and independent. When Frayser took retinal photographs of everyone at Logan High, she found hemorrhages in half the people, regardless of whether they had mountain sickness or not. These observations were quickly published as the High Altitude Retinal Hemorrhages report—the first major new medical finding from HAPS. Since then, retinal hemorrhages have been seen by many others on high mountains.

Other bizarre incidents occurred, resulting in new data on the high-altitude environment. During one storm in which a tent containing three inhabitants was almost completely buried, the occupants developed severe shortness of breath and headache. Surprisingly, the symptoms stemmed not from altitude sickness, but from carbon monoxide poisoning. The carbon dioxide from their breathing and the carbon monoxide from the stove they were using in the confined quarters combined to produce dangerous levels. The team also discovered a new symptom of altitude sickness: a "staggering," or drunken walk, that persisted for some time after a person returned from the high-altitude camp to lower altitudes.

The HAPS team was a diverse group, and the scientists were crucial. One of the scientists who joined early on, Drummond Rennie, was a kidney specialist from Chicago and also a climber. Charlie Bryan was a brilliant researcher from Toronto who, unfortunately, suffered badly from altitude. But one of the more surprising, and ultimately indispensable, members of the team was John Sutton. Charlie recalled their first meeting: "I was working in the log cabin at Kluane . . . the door flew open and in came a large, disheveled stranger, covered with dust, dragging a dirty duffel-bag. 'I'm John Sutton,' he announced in an extreme Australian accent, shaking my hand vigorously. 'I called you a few weeks ago and I want to join your party.'" This was an unpleasant surprise for Charlie. It was true that Sutton had called a few weeks earlier, but Charlie had told him firmly that there was no room for him; all the plans were in place for that summer, and they would certainly not allow him high on the mountain. But here he was. The brash young Australian doctor had flown from Toronto to Whitehorse on his own, hitched rides the 175 miles to Kluane—the last fifty in a rusty hearse driven by two hippies—and been dropped off at Charlie's door. "I was furious, but fortunately there wasn't anything to do but accept him—ungraciously," Charlie admitted.

Sutton was certainly qualified, having graduated in medicine from Sydney University in Australia in 1965 as a distinguished scholar. But Sutton was not just an academic; he was also an extraordinarily enthusiastic athlete. And Sutton was persistent. Within a week he was up at Logan High. And in another week he had proven his value. In the years ahead Charlie would describe him as "the strongest, most imaginative and innovative member of the team—and my very close friend for the rest of my life. . . . I often bless the persistence that led him to overcome my objections."

Charlie had his own unique volunteer recruiting methods for gaining new team members. "All I asked of the applicants was that they have some experience in mountaineering, preferably on snow and under cold conditions. Second, that they be fit and strong. Finally, I demanded seven letters of reference and a personal interview after I had read them." Many of them were medical students. And many of them were women. After some misgivings and great trepidation, almost certainly due to his age and generational biases, Charlie was finally persuaded to accept women. Unsurprisingly, it turned out to be a smart decision. They did excellent work and added greatly to everyone's enthusiasm. There was even the occasional romance—and marriage—as a result. About 120 young people volunteered over the years; Charlie referred to them fondly as the "Logan kids."

Regular radio calls were scheduled every morning and evening between Kluane and Logan High. Charlie would provide weather reports and conditions, and he and the scientists on Logan would swap stories and discuss plans for the following day. Charlie always tried to listen to what was *not* being said—to what lay behind the words—just in case things up high on the mountain were deteriorating without his knowledge. What none of them realized was that their conversations could be heard in Whitehorse and all over the Yukon, and that their regular chats had become famous as "the John [Sutton] and Charlie Show." As he recalled, "sometimes the exchanges got quite bawdy, and once we were told to clean up the act or the department of Posts and Telegraph would take away our license and close us down." Charlie defended himself, saying that although there were a few dirty stories from time to time, surely it wasn't that bad. The Department of Transport officer responded: "We don't allow that in Canada," and so they modified their language from that point forward.

As had been the case in the Peace Corps, the camp also drew visiting dignitaries. One day they were visited by a distinguished doctor, Claude Lenfant, and his assistant, Sue Hurd, from the National Heart, Lung, and Blood Institute. The first problem presented itself as soon as they arrived. Charlie wasn't sure of their "arrangement," so when he deposited their suitcases in the log cabin they would be sharing he simply placed them between the two rooms, leaving the logistics up to them. A few days later the visitors were ready to see more. Charlie was determined to show Lenfant a good time, so he offered to fly him and Hurd to the 9,000-foot halfway camp, called Eclipse, for an inspection and lunch. It was a perfect day and the view was spectacular. Logan loomed clear and beautiful forty miles away, and hundreds of icy peaks rimmed the horizon. Then suddenly the weather changed. The clouds rolled in quickly and it became clear that the pilot would not be able to return from Kluane to bring them down. They were stuck up in that cloud for five long days. Charlie was aghast, but his guests had a wonderful time, wandering about the camp, reading, talking with the volunteers, and pulling each other around in toboggans. They actually seemed in no hurry to leave. The weather finally cleared and they reluctantly returned to Washington.

Although there were frequent pleasant outcomes, even in the face of apparent danger, there were also several cases of serious altitude illness, especially in the first years. The worst was a twenty-eight-year-old captain in the Airborne who became ill just a few hours after flying up. He worsened rapidly, and thirty-six hours after arriving at Logan High was deeply unconscious. Upton flew Charlie directly to Logan High at eleven o'clock that night, skillfully landing immediately next to the small village of tents and lab. They loaded the unconscious man in the back of the plane and took off. "I was worried sick," Charlie recalled. "His periodic breathing was so pronounced that he would stop completely for what seemed like minutes, and then slowly begin again, deeper and deeper before he stopped once more. I honestly thought he was going to die."

Down at Kluane base, Charlie had to decide whether to transport him directly to the Whitehorse hospital or treat him there. After a brief and intense discussion with his colleagues, they realized they had more knowledge of cerebral edema than anyone at the Whitehorse hospital and decided to keep him there for immediate treatment. Charlie gave him intravenous steroids all night. At about 8:00 AM he came to, a little dazed. He staggered around a bit and walked out of the room, completely recovered. It was a very serious case of HACE—high-altitude cerebral edema—the worst that Charlie had seen. There were other cases too, although none so dramatic as Bob Lowry's.

Lowry became sick while climbing on the route above the King Trench and was brought to the camp located there. He was coughing blood, and both his lungs were filled with fluid. Drummond Rennie happened to be at the camp, administered the diuretic Lasix, which was commonly used for HAPE, and gave the twenty-one-year-old some oxygen. But he worsened, so Drummond called down for a rescue. Unfortunately, Upton was off getting the plane serviced and the weather looked bad. So Charlie called in a helicopter to do the job. "Well, this little chopper landed and out stepped a kid in a T-shirt and sneakers and a baseball cap. He hadn't ever flown in these high mountains but was cocky enough to try," Charlie said. There was no way he could find the Trench himself, so Charlie realized that he would have to go with him. The climber needed a doctor, and the pilot needed a guide; in each case, that person was Charlie.

It was late in the evening when they took off, flying straight up the long glacier toward Logan. The pilot seemed nervous; he kept wiping his hands on his pants and holding them out the window to dry. They could see nothing but the cliffs at the edge of the plateau; the top half of Logan was enshrouded in cloud. "I told him to fly straight at the cliffs, turn right and follow as close beside them as he could," Charlie said. He was sure this would eventually get them to the lower end of the Trench. But the map showed a long valley and a steep ridge in their way, so they turned up the valley. As they climbed up toward the mountain, the pilot became increasingly nervous, as did Charlie. "Can we get out at the end of this?" the pilot asked. Charlie wasn't sure. "The valley ended, sure enough, in a narrow pass, like a gun sight, off to the right."

The pilot became very quiet. He spiraled slowly upwards, laboriously gaining altitude until he felt he might be able to skim through the frighteningly steep and narrow pass. Charlie held his breath—and they slipped through. The altimeter read just below 11,000 feet. Soon they came to the Trench and landed at their 10,500-foot camp. The pilot hadn't said a word.

By this time it was getting dark. They loaded the unconscious boy in the chopper, and when Charlie tried to place him in the middle seat between himself and the pilot, the pilot broke his silence with "Don't put that man there, he's dead." So Charlie rearranged the seating, taking the middle seat himself. Though the situation was desperate, Charlie added, "I give that young pilot a lot of credit. With the extra load, he had great trouble taking off, and had to bounce a couple of times before almost falling off the steep end of the valley. We made it back through the gun sight and onto familiar terrain." At this point, the pilot regained his composure and began to talk—and continued nonstop until about twenty miles from Kluane when he said they were running out of gas and would have to land and fuel up from an extra tank they had brought. They landed on the rough glacier, and the pilot refueled. At that moment, the patient, Lowry, stirred and said he had to pee. He stepped out of the chopper and, as Charlie remembered, relieved himself of about two gallons of liquid.[30] They climbed back in and the pilot casually lit a cigarette, throwing his match out onto the spilled gas! Charlie fully expected to go out in a blaze of glory, but the fuel didn't catch. By the time they reached Kluane, Lowry had recovered enough to get out and walk by himself. He had descended 7,000 feet and that was enough to do it. A day later he was fine. Strangely, he immediately launched into a very critical tirade against doctors—in a general sense. Dorcas, who was at Kluane for the first time that summer, finally heard enough and launched into her own tirade: "My husband risked his life for you. You could at least be a little more respectful!" A few years later, he gave his first-born son the middle name "Houston."

※

By the end of the summer of 1969, the HAPS program was well established, with well-researched and relatively safe protocols and experiments that were producing results. As the 1971 season drew to a close, the scientists all agreed they needed to take time to review their data, write their papers, and plan for the future. They were also beginning to be concerned about the dangers of flying subjects directly to Logan High. As a result, there was no program in 1972, and for the following years they found an ideal staging area at 9,500 feet on the Badham-Donjek Plateau. Their goals changed as well: from studying the symptoms of acute mountain sickness (AMS) to exploring the changes that make up acclimatization. As the years passed, a wealth of new data emerged from their studies.

The study had broken scientific ground in a number of areas, including in the field of retinopathy. They firmly established that everyone experiences a considerable increase in retinal blood flow above 17,500 feet, and that about half develop retinal hemorrhages. They determined that hypoxemia becomes more pronounced during sleep. They were not successful in discovering a procedure to predict the susceptibility to altitude illness, but they did learn that it was exercise at altitude, rather than hypoxia alone, that was a major stimulus to the endocrine system, causing the greatest changes. They found that fit subjects, even after six weeks of acclimatization at 17,500 feet, could only reach seventy to seventy-five percent of their sea-level performance.

In an article written for *The Lancet,* October 18, 1975, Charlie summarized what they had learned thus far. He described acute altitude illness as one of a number of things: acute mountain sickness (headache, nausea, vomiting), pulmonary edema (cough, fluid in the lungs, death), retinal involvement (dilated vessels, bleeding, papiloedema), and cerebral edema (intense throbbing headache, staggering gait, double vision, coma). Of these, cerebral edema was the most serious, but pulmonary edema was not to be taken lightly either, as the tissue separating the air sacs from the capillary blood vessels in the lungs filled with fluid, eventually seeping into the air sacs, causing the person to have shortness of breath, serious coughing, and essentially to drown. AMS was probably the least serious; if the individual took aspirin for the headache, stayed somewhat active, and drank plenty of fluids, it would usually disappear after a day or two. In the case of cerebral and pulmonary edema, they found that it was crucial to watch the speed with which symptoms appeared—and worsened. Speed was the enemy; when things were changing quickly, the victim had to descend quickly—or risk death.

The study also produced information on Cheyne-Stokes breathing, common above 9,000 feet. Not terribly serious, it nevertheless elicited alarmed responses from tent-mates as the person suffering often went through a period of rapid, increasingly deep breathing followed by a period of shallow breathing—or no breathing at all—for up to ten seconds. Clearly, a climber, hearing absolutely nothing coming from his climbing partner next to him, would experience a moment of panic, until the pattern began all over again. This physical response to hypoxia, although not terribly serious, did result in some spectacular headaches in the morning. They found that periodic breathing could be reduced by taking Diamox just before bedtime, which smoothed out the swings in oxygen saturation and somewhat alleviated the accompanying morning headache. Previously, the drug had been reported as a good preventive against altitude illness in decompression chambers, but on the mountain it also made a difference, keeping the oxygen saturation of the blood higher at night and helping to alleviate the severe AMS symptoms that are worse upon waking.

They also observed less common manifestations such as hallucinations, double vision, and emotional lability, which occasionally become psychosis. In addition to recognizing and describing the disabilities, the scientists developed treatments. The most important was undoubtedly returning the affected person to lower altitude, where they would usually recover promptly and completely. Strangely, the benefits of oxygen administered at high altitude were less than stellar, although breathing bottled oxygen during the night seemed to alleviate morning headaches. Perhaps their most important conclusion was that the best solution of all was prevention, and prevention was best achieved by slow ascent, facilitating acclimatization.

The 1979 team agreed that it would be their last year and they vowed to make it special. They recruited specialists in cardiology, pulmonology, and ophthalmology to do sophisticated studies on the acclimatized subjects at Logan High. But of course everything depended on the weather. "It was a disastrous year," Charlie recounted sadly. "Everything went wrong, but mostly it was the weather—storm or deep snow every day we needed to fly." Days passed and they bided their time. Finally, sensing that the weather wasn't going to clear, Charlie hit on a new idea—crazy, but original. He bought a dozen cylinders of pure nitrogen and arranged for some huge meteorology balloons to be brought in. The plan was to fill these huge balloons with a combination of air and nitrogen equivalent to that of Logan High and run the tests down at Kluane. "The trick was to get the subjects to Kluane instantly," he explained. Unfortunately, the weather was too bad to fly, so the subjects had to descend on their own to the Trench, where they were picked up. By then, they had lost some of their acclimatization, and as a result the tests were contaminated. The researchers did the tests anyway, but didn't bother publishing the flawed results.

His many years of research had given Charlie the statistical data necessary to advance his own theories on how to survive with a decreased amount of oxygen—namely acclimatization. Although he expressed some

very general-sounding and even amusing theories: "Listen to your body—
mind you—if you listen too closely, you'll never climb a big mountain.
Women do just as well as men—they're much more difficult—but not in
terms of altitude. One of the few blessings of age is that fifty-year-olds do
better at altitude." He always backed them up with research. He offered
up countless examples of preventative and coping measures for the debilitating affects of HAPE. His findings were used by climbers around the
world, particularly those going to the highest range—the Himalayas. They
changed the way climbers planned their acclimatization programs and how
they treated and reacted to the early symptoms of high-altitude sickness. His
research firmly established Charlie as one of the world's leading authorities
on the subject—and undoubtedly saved lives in the mountains.

DRUMMER

To live without fear of death makes you capable of great things.
—Stephen Canning

W hen he wasn't in the Canadian North doing research on Mount Logan, Charlie continued with his innovative teaching programs at the University of Vermont, including a full-scale drug treatment program. Then, in 1970, Charlie was awarded a contract to describe the major health problems in the Northern Counties of Vermont and northern New Hampshire, and to recommend various solutions. Together with four other doctors, he produced a report called "Health Care in the Northern Counties." Charlie's memories of that work were bittersweet: "It was in the spirit of the times: a burning desire to help the underprivileged . . . in the belief that throwing dollars at problems would solve them! It didn't work." Nevertheless, it was exciting work and they were totally absorbed by it, blissfully unaware of the turmoil outside of Vermont—the civil-rights struggles in the South, and Vietnam. Meanwhile, there was a looming problem at the university for Charlie. After six or seven years of taking on several challenging and high-profile external projects, as well as developing his own unique teaching style, Charlie had sufficiently blundered onto other departmental turf to raise hackles among some of his colleagues. At times he appeared undiplomatic and inconsiderate. He often barged ahead on his own initiative without consulting anyone else. Quite understandably, some of the more established physicians resented him.

This was not the only problem; Charlie's passion was still family medicine, but the growing rage was specialization, making it increasingly difficult for him to attract students—and funding. By the mid-1970s the medical college was in serious danger of collapsing because there wasn't enough funding for salaries. The original purpose of Charlie's program—to train family doctors—shifted, and it became a tertiary-care center. Family practice quietly became unfashionable; it was replaced by specialty and subspecialty training. Teaching took a back seat to research for the simple reason that research brought in dollars. Any funding that did come in was jealously guarded. Friendly cooperation turned to competition, and departments began to fragment. Lectures became more formal, and the atmosphere more self-serving. Even the modest faculty salaries became impossible to pay, and faculty were required to write grant requests to help fund their own salaries. Like his colleagues, Charlie didn't have the fundraising skills required to pay his own salary; he could raise project funding, particularly for students, but salaries were a different matter.

By the late 1970s the focus changed once again. Family practice—Charlie's area of special interest—was resuscitated and became part of the department of medicine. His passion had now become a desirable prize for other departments. Although he had no direct control of the program because it had been moved out of his area, he was still pleased that it had been revived. But there was a difference. The university practice took it over, for a fee. Charlie now felt personally responsible for some of the changes he abhorred, because he felt that he simply didn't have the personal qualities to prevent them.

But major changes were looming, as the frightening cost of care made free care harder to provide. Those who needed medical attention were required to pay, in one way or another. Medicare and Medicaid became major players. The huge cost of some intensive diagnoses and treatments led to cost-shifting, which in turn led to higher premiums from insurance companies. Charlie felt strongly about these issues and spoke out. Many of his colleagues silently supported him and urged him on: "You're right. Keep up the good fight. We can't support you because . . . well, you understand."

Charlie began to receive unmistakable signals to cease and desist some of his activities; rather reluctantly he did so. But it was too late. In 1978,

Charlie had a meeting with Dean Bill Luginbuhl in which he spoke out, saying that the college was placing too much emphasis on research and not enough on clinical medicine. This did not sit well with the dean, who pointed out that the college was in dire financial straits and that research brought in a large amount of money. The dean had quite wisely gone about repairing the financial condition of the college and thus had saved it from extinction. Charlie should not have been surprised when, finally, he received a long letter from Dean Luginbuhl, terminating his position as Professor of Community Medicine. "Instantly I became a non-person. Few of my former friends spoke to me," Charlie bitterly recalled. Charlie still held his appointment of Professor of Medicine but ceased to find any pleasure in academic activities. He retreated in sullen anger, taught what he was told to teach, and avoided any other college activities.

Like so many times before, Charlie felt that he had wasted his opportunities in Vermont. For the first year or two everything had gone well. Then had come a repeat of the same old problems. As always, Charlie had great ideas, a grand vision, a vivid imagination. When others hesitated or were reluctant to go along, he pushed and cajoled and persisted. That same insistence—or arrogance—led him to tangle with others. Some thought he was empire building, and the inevitable result was conflict. Charlie had birthed, nurtured, and then was forced to abandon half a dozen projects over the years for one reason or another. Some of them were taken over by others. Others died. The ashes of some went on to fertilize projects that flourished later. But there was a recurring pattern, and Charlie knew it: "I continued to march to different drummers. But those different parades weren't going anywhere."

It was a time for reflection. For almost ten years Charlie had free-wheeled, wandering the state, planning and executing imaginative programs with enthusiastic faculty. But he had failed to recognize that some of what he was doing threatened other departments. He had failed to form alliances and share in what he felt was the prime mission. He had openly challenged the dean on priorities. He had not been diplomatic. And he had not guarded his back. By 1979 he had reached the age of sixty-five, mandatory retirement. Although Charlie understood his new reality, he was bitter for some time. It would be decades before he and Dean Luginbuhl spoke again. Though their next meeting was cordial, Luginbuhl admitted that the termination was painful and unpleasant for both of them—but necessary. "Charlie wanted to do things beyond the resources that were available," he explained. He admitted that Charlie was a visionary, a charismatic man, almost Messianic at times, but he felt that "the innovation that Charlie brought was, in the end, the seeds of his own destruction."

Despite his Messianic tendencies, or perhaps because of them, Charlie did make remarkable progress in a number of areas: high-altitude research, drug rehabilitation programs, community medicine. In some cases, his efforts produced immediate results that could be easily attributed to him. But many times he failed. It was this pattern that haunted Charlie and that caught the eye of a friend in Colorado. His friend called, asking Charlie to give the graduation address at the Colorado Rocky Mountain School in Carbondale, where he had briefly taught. Flattered, Charlie instantly began fantasizing his role, but asked, "Why me, Ed? You could easily get many people better known and more effective."

"You're ideal, Charlie," Ed replied. "You've had an unusually varied life, you've tried all sorts of activities, and you've done so many interesting things. But most important, you've failed in all of them, over and over again. I think the graduating class would be inspired by your philosophy."

Stunned, deflated, and bruised, Charlie turned him down, suggesting someone more successful in the conventional manner. But he couldn't stop thinking about it: "The more I thought over this rather unusual invitation, the more I had to agree. I have certainly led a varied life; at least three completely different careers have blended as do the braided streams in a glacial river. And I certainly have made a mess of things." Ed's words kept echoing in his head: "You keep coming back, you keep trying again, you never give up." Charlie called him back a week later and accepted.

The concept of retirement didn't resonate for Charlie, so although he remained in Burlington, he threw himself into other projects. It was outside the structure of universities and institutions that Charlie did his best work, much of it in the field of high-altitude medicine. In 1980 he wrote his first edition of *Going Higher,* the book that combined his love of medicine and mountains, and the first publication to connect those two topics. He wanted to create something that would be useful to climbers going into the highest ranges, as well as to a broad public, so his writing trod a delicate balance between medical terminology and engaging anecdotes, moving from a complete description of oxygen, to respiration and circulation, and finally to the meat of the book itself: mountain sickness. The first edition was self-published, cost him $13,000 in total and earned him

$25,000. He personally mailed out 5,000 copies of the book in the course
of filling orders. Its success took Charlie by surprise; there would be four
more editions. Then, in 1985, Charlie became involved in what initially
appeared to be a sequel to his work on Operation Everest I, but which
eventually assumed a dimension and scope far greater.

Much had been learned in the field of altitude research in the forty inter-
vening years since Operation Everest I. The National Heart Institute began
supporting altitude hypoxia research, namely through Claude Lenfant. The
Kingdom of Nepal had opened its doors to the outside world, and mountaineers had flocked to the Himalayan peaks, some of them well over 26,000
feet. The twelve-year HAPS study had provided critical information on altitude illness and acclimatization on 19,850-foot Mount Logan. The stage was
set for Operation Everest II.

Charlie first needed to find the money. Initially he asked the army, then
the Yosemite Institute, and finally the Arctic Institute, but each was either
uninterested or couldn't afford it. Then Charlie had dinner with a friend of
a friend, a two-star general in charge of the Army Research and Development Command. Charlie described the program, and the general listened
attentively. Charlie followed up with a letter stating the case. This was highly
unorthodox behavior; one did not go directly to the top guy in the army. But
it worked. A few days later Charlie received a handwritten note on official
letterhead saying: "Dear Dr. Houston, I have instructed my staff to fund your
project." Signed, Major General Rapmund.

Operation Everest II took five years to prepare and six weeks to complete.
It took another three years to publish the findings, using an early-model IBM
PC and a daisywheel printer in Charlie's home. Charlie, John Sutton, and Allen
Cymerman, head of the Altitude Physiology and Medicine Division at Natick,
Massachusetts, began the project on October 1, 1985, in the huge army
decompression chamber at Natick. There were eight subjects, twenty-five sci-
entists, and forty support people. For forty days, eight young men "climbed"
to the summit of Mount Everest.

Initially the tension was almost unmanageable: the subjects weren't
happy with the conditions of the chamber; the scientists jockeyed for position; equipment malfunctioned; and the costs soared. Because the army was
consistently late in paying their invoices, Charlie was forced to take out a
personal line of credit just to keep things moving. As Charlie desperately
tried to keep things under control, his colleague Jack Reeves observed:
"He is a difficult taskmaster and brooks no breach of discipline . . . lets it

be known that power issues from the top." Charlie became known as "The Commander," a title he secretly enjoyed.

Building on his earlier research, Charlie once again delved into the world of oxygen. Though his and others' experiments indicated there was probably an altitude beyond which human life could not be sustained, along the way they had proven that acclimatization could help human beings adjust themselves to an environment that was foreign to them—an environment with far less oxygen.

Although every individual was different, most Operation Everest II subjects experienced a headache between 10,000 and 15,000 feet, as well as a faster pulse and deeper breathing. Some of them became euphoric, laughing at silly jokes and functioning in a somewhat childlike manner. Some lost consciousness after 18,000 feet of rapid accession, many fainted at 20,000 feet, and most collapsed completely by 25,000 feet.

One important observation was that, as the subject went "up," he experienced a significant increase in his ventilatory exchange—basically, he breathed faster. This, among other factors, resulted in fluid loss, which subsequently produced thicker blood and increased the concentration of hemoglobin. This, combined with a greater heart rate, delivered more oxygen to the tissues. Essentially, the body was struggling to protect itself from the decrease in oxygen.

Years before, after the Operation Everest I experiments had concluded, Charlie had offered himself up for an experiment, climbing to 25,000 feet in one day, all the while controlling his breathing. He had acclimatized well by reducing his ventilation whenever he experienced tingling in his fingertips, and by increasing his respiration whenever his vision started to give out. But it wasn't just the clinical experiments that informed Charlie's growing knowledge of high-altitude acclimatization. As a climber with experience in the rarified air of the Karakoram, he knew that exercising climbers acclimatized more rapidly than did subjects in a low-pressure chamber. Living conditions were obviously easier in the chamber, so he was curious as to why climbers seemed to fare better. After years of observation, he attributed it to two things: motivation and increased fitness.

Two schools of thought had emerged on how climbers could best acclimatize. One was that they should arrive at the mountain in superb condition and move slowly up the mountain, carrying very little and resting frequently. Another approach was to arrive in superb condition, and then work hard from base camp, carrying heavy loads and breaking trail until higher elevations were reached, at which point the strenuous work would gradually taper off, leaving the climber to concentrate simply on the climbing. After considerable experience and observation, Charlie believed the second approach worked better.

On the other hand, he also knew that prolonged stays above 22,000 feet resulted in a slow but steady deterioration. This he attributed not just to lack of oxygen, but more so to prolonged exposure to cold, inadequate fluid intake, poorly digested food, and lack of sleep. On K2 he noticed other odd symptoms as well: hair and nails grew more slowly; hair lost its shine and its curl; and numbness and tingling were present in the extremities months after returning to sea level.

All of these physiological changes were tempered by the presence of risk. Whether perceived or real, danger or fear stimulated emergency releases of adrenaline into the bloodstream, revving the heart, brain, lungs, and muscles into high gear. The effect was swift, strong and brief, but was followed by exhaustion. Risk-induced stress also released longer-lasting hormones, namely endorphins, which dulled the feelings of discomfort or pain, quieted anxiety, heightened enjoyment or pleasure, and, as Charlie knew first-hand, were slightly addictive.

From his experiments in the pressure chamber, he knew that voluntary hyperventilation helped the acclimatization process, something he and his teammates had put to good use on K2 in 1953. He was convinced that hyperventilation had improved their sense of well-being and given them added strength. But even so, prolonged exposure to thin air was debilitating. Each man's concentration levels on K2 had become somewhat reduced, and each of them had eaten and slept poorly and steadily lost weight. Coordination had been impaired, making the simple act of dressing, fastening a crampon, or loading a camera, extremely slow and difficult. Loss of memory had also been common. A sense of proportion had often been lost; a climber would become emotionally unbalanced, laughing inappropriately, weeping for no cause, or lashing out at a fellow climber for an insignificant slight. What Charlie always marveled at was that the so-called "higher faculties"—the appreciation of beauty; perseverance in the face of disaster; consideration for others; courage and faith—had remained strong, or had even increased, at altitude.

Although the scientists were extremely important, in Charlie's opinion the subjects were the key. They in turn sensed Charlie's concern for them and trusted him; this spurred them on to greater efforts, despite their discomfort. The days wore on; the subjects grew wearier; and the scientists became ever more careful with their data collection. There were frequent crises; arguments ensued; and tempers inevitably flared.

In the lab they had experimented not only with breathing techniques but also with chemicals and drugs to counteract the debilitating effects of altitude. Diamox, for example, helped to eliminate periodic breathing at altitude and ameliorate acute mountain sickness (AMS). They found that drugs were effective some of the time, but concluded that no single chemical was as effective as the natural changes that occurred in the body of someone working, living, and functioning above 20,000 feet.

It was found that with gradual acclimatization, the number of red cells in a person increased, the amount of hemoglobin changed, and the equilibrium of the bodily fluids and gases with those outside the body reached a new balance. This adaptability worked best through a slow, steady ascent to higher altitudes, or, as Charlie explained, "The impatient are likely to become patients." This was as true for people going up to ski areas at 9,000 feet as it was for climbers in the Himalayas. In fact, fully twenty-five percent of visitors to "moderate" altitudes, those found at ski areas, experienced some level of AMS. It was equally true for miners and road workers and laborers in the Andes, the Alps, or any mountain region in the world, as well as for the Pakistani and Indian soldiers fighting each other high on the Siachen Glacier in northern India, where more soldiers died of altitude sickness than from battle wounds. Even train passengers in the Peruvian Andes experienced altitude sickness when they traveled from sea level to 15,000 feet in a day.

Charlie and his researchers had become a team, and after forty days the door was opened and the subjects emerged. Everyone was relieved that the study had been completed safely and that so many important scientific observations had been made. At the age of seventy-four, Charlie had artfully managed a challenging project with equally challenging people. Finally, it was time to go: "It was an emotional moment," he recalled. "We were completely exhausted, but standing by my loaded pickup truck we embraced, in the certain knowledge we had completed a major advance in the history of altitude research."

HAPS on Mount Logan had proved another inspiring—and independent—undertaking, which, in turn, sparked other critical studies of high-altitude sickness, including a study on Denali, organized by Peter Hackett. Hackett had come up to Logan to visit Charlie and his team and had taken a good, long look at the project. He subsequently went to Alaska and persuaded an Anchorage doctor, Bill Mills, to help him set up a laboratory on Denali with the help of the Parks Service and the U.S. Army. Hackett brought in his own scientific team, including Rob Roach, a young college student with an interest in nutrition and a passion for climbing. They soon began doing pioneering work in altitude sickness.

Another outcome of Logan was at McMaster University in Hamilton, Ontario, under the leadership of Sutton, now in their Department of Medicine. Here they developed a very systematic investigation of hypoxia, stimulated in a large part by the Logan work. An enduring legacy of HAPS was the annual International Hypoxia Symposium in Banff, a meeting between scientists and clinicians working in the prevention and treatment of hypoxia. The idea started modestly in 1979 with Charlie and Sutton, with leadership provided by Peter Hackett and Rob Roach. By 2005, under Roach's direction, the symposium attracted 250 people from thirty countries. HAPS was far from dead, although it had moved a long way from Mount Logan.

One of the most lasting outcomes was the friendship that developed between Rob Roach and Charlie. Roach first met Charlie in 1977, and their initial relationship was clearly one of mentor and student. But that all changed when Roach's father died. He went immediately to Burlington, where he unloaded his grief. Charlie listened and, finally, gave advice. Roach was astonished at Charlie's bluntness, but was eternally grateful for the wisdom. At other times, the wisdom came from Roach. He recalled the time Charlie purchased his first personal computer. It was 1983 and Charlie was already in his seventies. Roach helped teach him how to use it, and functioned for a time as his computer consultant.

Charlie and Roach developed a pattern of communication that, strangely, worked for both of them. Roach would present Charlie with an idea, and Charlie's typical response would be, "That's the stupidest idea I've ever heard." For Roach, that meant it was probably a good idea that needed work; this was Charlie's way of forcing Roach to strengthen his logic and challenge himself. As Charlie aged and mellowed, Roach reported that his response softened too: "Even though you came up with the idea, it may not be so bad."

Roach characterized Charlie as a typical New England Yankee, whose core values are to be frugal, to be self-effacing, to care deeply about other people, and to never *ever* show off your wealth. One of Charlie's mantras to Roach was to "not lose time." Many of Charlie's friends pointed out that Charlie has been in a hurry all his life. Roach remembered complaining to Charlie at one point that he didn't have time to peruse some scientific papers that he really needed to read. Charlie chastised him: "You go to the bathroom, don't you? Well, take them into the bathroom and read them!" Roach did.

Today Roach talks with Charlie on the phone at least once a week and be-lieves that Charlie's commitment to staying in touch is generational. "Char-lie understands the investment you have to make in a friendship . . . in his day it wasn't easy to stay in touch, but they made a real effort to do so. It's indicative of the values of that generation around the subject of friendship—and brotherhood," he says. Roach sees his own relationship with Charlie as a "metaphysical bond," something that is there through thick and thin. Perhaps the most poignant manifestation of that friendship came when Roach named his youngest son after Charlie.

Arguably the most important legacy of Charlie's high-altitude endeavors is embodied in the University of Colorado Altitude Research Center where the Charles S. Houston Chair was later inaugurated. At the inauguration cer-emony, attended by numerous government and university representatives and a congressman, the president of the university gave a speech stating how important high-altitude studies were becoming and that it was essential that Colorado recognize the importance of altitude sickness to its economy. Stand-ing next to Tom Hornbein, Charlie whispered rather loudly, "It's about time." The president stopped dead in her speech, looked over at Charlie and, with a smile, asked: "Dr. Houston, do you want to make my speech for me?" Charlie apologized profusely, and in the end they jointly cut the ribbon. Apart from the honor, which Charlie was pleased to receive, he pragmatically pointed out that the university was motivated by "clever, enlightened self-interest." He was correct; the university needed to raise money for the chair and knew that Charlie's name had the stature to attract donors.

But it wasn't self-interest that prompted the university to bestow Charlie with an honorary doctorate in 2006. The accompanying event was a parade of pure, unadulterated admiration by a host of respected friends and colleagues from the many facets of his prolific professional life: climbers, physicians, and researchers. When Charlie saw the lineup, he declared that he wouldn't miss it, even if they had to wheel him in, in a body bag. Hornbein turned the tables on Charlie when he ceremoniously presented him with just that—a body bag. Apart from the good fun, the assembled speakers had many affirming things to say about Charlie and his contributions, and Charlie was profoundly moved by the event.

((((

In these later years, Charlie has found himself routinely recognized for his pioneering work, mostly for his achievements in mountaineering medicine.

However, it is noteworthy that, despite not having been on a mountain since 1953, many of the most respected mountaineering organizations in the world lined up to honor him. Charlie received the American Alpine Club's highest honor, the Angelo Heilprin Citation, for his work in high-altitude medicine, bestowed on him after his nomination by Bob Craig. The Alpine Club in Britain awarded him an honorary membership, as did the American Alpine Club and most other major mountaineering clubs in the world. In 1996 he was presented with the prestigious King Albert Gold Medal in Switzerland. Charlie was characteristically self-deprecating about his achievements, dismissing the honors with, "You get old enough, you can get anything." Privately he was pleased, as he had worked hard to stay close to the mountaineering community, and his climbing memories remained among his most cherished.

Although Charlie graciously accepted his awards from the mountaineering community, he was sharply critical of some aspects of modern climbing. He acknowledged that many of the Himalayan routes now being climbed were significantly more difficult than those climbed in his days, and he could see that most important expeditions were studded with at least a couple of climbing superstars. But he also observed that many of those high-profile expeditions did not turn out well. He expressed shock and regret that some superstars felt comfortable abandoning their team and switching to another expedition if it was advantageous, even though they didn't necessarily know the members of their newly adopted team. He heard about these antics firsthand, along with drugs and alcohol at base camp, none of which he approved of. There were few superstars he truly respected, but John Roskelley was one. Charlie was fond of Roskelley, believing he handled himself very well in the face of much criticism, primarily for the Nanda Devi expedition on which Willi Unsoeld's daughter, named Nanda Devi, died. Charlie felt that Roskelley had been unfairly blamed for his role, and that responsibility for the tragedy should have been more evenly distributed to others on the team. He was particularly critical of Willi Unsoeld, a climber he and Bates had rejected for K2 in 1953. Although Charlie recognized that Roskelley was of the superstar status, he was direct in his praise: "John, you're one of the few superstars who emerged without being self serving."

Another superstar for whom Charlie had the greatest respect was Reinhold Messner. It must have been a sweet moment of vindication for Charlie when Messner and Habeler first climbed Everest without supplemental oxygen in 1978. Although Messner referred to himself as a "single, narrow, gasping lung,"

Charlie would have been pleased that his earlier conviction that it was possible to climb Everest without oxygen had finally been proven.

Despite his disdain for superstar climbers, Charlie had a soft spot in his heart for the equivalent of a superstar climbing club—the Welsh Climbers Club. It was on the occasion of the Climbers Club's 100th birthday that they invited Charlie to come over to Wales to speak about Nanda Devi. They met in an old hotel on a day that was typically cold, rainy, and gray. The place was crawling with famous climbers, and dinner was served in a huge tent. A wooden floor kept them dry, electric heaters kept them warm, and temporary chandeliers illuminated the celebration. Waiters in white gloves catered to the formally-attired group's every need. The weather was atrocious and the tent groaned under the force of the wind and driving rain. The audience loved Charlie's Nanda Devi presentation and he in turn was thrilled with their response: "I got a huge standing ovation . . . they wouldn't stop. From the Brits, that's really something." Immediately after that unusual British approval, the executive huddled and came back to name Charlie an honorary member.

As pleased as Charlie was to be welcomed into the Welsh Club, he was equally pleased to display a bit of one-upmanship with the French climbers. He was in Chamonix, invited by the legendary French climber Maurice Herzog to star in a television program about distinguished mountaineers. Set up in full view of magnificent Mont Blanc, the interviewer turned to Charlie and, with no introduction, asked: "Est-ce que votre amour des montagnes (de la montagne) est d'une nature homosexuelle?" (Is your love of the mountains of a homosexual nature?) Taken somewhat aback, but having learned the language well as a child, Charlie knew that "mountain" is a feminine rather than masculine noun. He responded without a second's hesitation: "Non monsieur. Vous savez que c'est *la* montagne; pas *le* montagne," pointing out the unlikelihood of a homosexual relationship with a feminine mountain. Everyone responded with howls of laughter, and Charlie felt it was his finest line in French—ever.

In 1991 Charlie was invited to star in a television program that involved trekking into Nanga Parbat base camp. On the trek he developed great respect for British climber Chris Bonington and a warm fondness for British climber, author, and filmmaker Jim Curran. Curran met him at London's Heathrow Airport and the two hit it off immediately. Charlie was convinced that on the Nanga Parbat trek he was suffering from pulmonary edema, and was grateful that Curran stayed behind to descend slowly with him to lower altitudes. Curran thought Charlie had edema, too, but his motivation for staying behind had more to do with getting to know the man: "I just wanted to be with him and talk with him." Curran felt there may have been another invisible bond between the two of them, for in both cases—and possibly on the same day in August—they had been on K2 when their close friends were killed: Art Gilkey in 1953 and Al Rouse in 1986. Several years later, Curran visited Charlie while working on his latest book. He recalled spending wonderful days lying on the living room floor, snuggled up to Charlie's retriever, Pooh Bear, writing diligently to meet a deadline.

But it was more than K2 and a snuggly dog that cemented their friendship. Charlie offered Curran wise counseling at a time he felt he needed it. Although Charlie was disarmingly frank, sometimes prickly, even critically sharp and judgmental, Curran felt his advice was sound: "He is moral and honest beyond belief . . . a kind of upright personality." Curran added that Charlie exemplified an attitude of "service to humanity" that reminded him of Bob Bates. Perhaps it was that the two of them came from a generation of chivalry. Something Curran particularly admired was Charlie's ability to "sniff out integrity and bullshit." Curran reflected on the K2 expeditions and concluded: "His two expeditions were the best possible human behavior in the mountains." Many others agreed. Some described these expeditions as the "touchstone of all that is best in mountaineering," while Messner described them as an "inspiration for a lifetime."

Some of Charlie's most judgmental and strongly expressed views regarding climbing were reserved for the effect that commercialized climbing had on the people of Nepal. While his opinions were not popular, he was troubled with the whole concept of development: clinics, schools, and electric generators. In Charlie's opinion these were all examples of Western climbers transposing their own set of values, wanting to "make it more like us." He was certain that, as the young people of Nepal become more and more Westernized, they would almost certainly have to go abroad to realize their ambitions. And this, he felt, was wrong. Charlie also declared money one of the greatest corrupting influences in modern climbing: "It's a great big ball of wax that sticks on everything." Despite all these misgivings, Charlie was sure that there were people doing trips in places and on peaks that nobody knew about: it was these he approved of the most. As for sport climbing, Charlie simply dismissed it as acrobatics. "I think it's great, but don't call it climbing." Although he was impressed by the athletic and sometimes artistic skill of the protagonists, it was what was missing that bothered him: "Weather, storm, exposure, the whole bit . . . scenery, the beauty, the tragedy . . . mountaineering is different from climbing and climbing is different from acrobatics."

Charlie didn't just rant about his thoughts on modern climbing and insensitive use of landscape to his friends. He wasn't afraid to state his case—publicly and passionately—as evidenced in a letter written to Jim McCarthy for the April, 1972 edition of *Summit* magazine:

> *Yes the mountain men have gone. . . . The mountain men roamed free and wild for only fifty years or so; they crossed the mountains and followed the streams and saw and used the land for the first time. They also trapped the beaver and slaughtered the buffalo, taught the Indian to love firewater and spread gonorrhea and syphilis like wildfire. They loved the wild country but most of them were rapists and the West will carry the scars forever. . . . The mountain men of our century are also going and will soon be gone. About time I say. Those who followed the cowboy economy of the old mountain men have turned that beautiful Yosemite Valley into a smog-filled garbage pile. They have littered almost every summit, polluted the woods and water and raped the mountains.*
>
> *How can those who profess to love the mountains be so wanton? Surely the litter and destruction is only careless rather than deliberate—but in either case, if not soon stopped, much of what calls us to the mountains will disappear.*
>
> *When competition or self gain is the primary motivation for climbing, the sport is no longer beautiful, but ugly and dangerous and damaging . . . though I hate the litter, the shattered trees and summits, the smog and the crowds, I dislike even more the almost desperate urge to do something harder, more extreme. Why does the young climber feel compelled to attack mountains?*
>
> *Though I support the generality that man should reach beyond his grasp, and that our restless surges have brought progress—I submit to whoever cares to listen that progress in today's world is a deceptive goal, a siren luring us to destruction. There seems little more to be gained or proven by climbing even longer and more difficult or dangerous routes; even the publicity gets tired.*
>
> *It seems to me that the motivation behind much of the climbing (rock acrobatics and expeditions) in recent decades has been to gain publicity, status, or money—not simply to test oneself. I believe this*

because so few extraordinary climbs are kept secret. If people wish to climb the impossible for self-realization—I say wonderful. But if it is to beat their neighbors or to be named Minister of Sports—to me this is another symptom of the sickness of our times."[31]

But Charlie went on to add with a wry smile: "It's easy when you're old and senile to say it was better in the old days."

In addition to writing, Charlie took up filmmaking. Earlier in his career he had produced his K2-1938 film, several Nanda Devi films, and a K2-1953 film. He then produced *Exploring the Heights*, which chronicles the major achievements of his high-altitude research. Though it played well at the mountain film festival in Trento, Italy in 2004, on the way home he decided that it was too autobiographical and didn't have quite the message he wanted. On the eight-hour flight back he began thinking about another film. By the time the plane set down in Burlington, he had the structure in place and it was just a matter of doing it. But Charlie had a problem: his eyesight was failing him. At first he struggled through the entire process himself, straining to see the precious archival footage he had amassed on each of his expeditions, editing a cohesive piece and, finally, doing the entire narration himself. As the project carried on and as time passed and his eyesight deteriorated, he relied more on a friend, Paul McGowan, whom he trusted implicitly. Charlie and McGowan would watch the raw footage together, Charlie would create the script, and under Charlie's guidance, Paul would cut and splice, mold and shape. Charlie described the film as "not about climbing, or even mountaineering, but a film about people." Ultimately, that's what K2-1953—and climbing in general—meant to Charlie, and this film, *Brotherhood of the Rope,* became his favorite. Charlie chose the Banff Mountain Film Festival for its gala world premiere in 2004. Canadian alpinist Barry Blanchard introduced Charlie that memorable evening, reading from a letter that Charlie had written to the editor of the *New York Times* on August 4, 1954, in response to Desio's K2 victory climb:

I applaud their courage and their perseverance, but I am too human not to be saddened . . . Both Everest and K2 were climbed by large, superbly organized expeditions with unlimited funds and resources . . . Both Everest and K2 were climbed with the help of oxygen. To me it seems that something is gone from the great sport of mountaineering when the undertaking becomes so complex, so

*professional. Now that the giants have toppled, I hope more climb-
ers will make expeditions for the love of climbing, rather than for
prize of conquest. I would not deny that the summit matters and
matters greatly, but I know that the rewards of climbing lie in the
venture and not alone in the triumph. It is the means which calls
us to the end, not the end which justifies the means. Climbers, all
men indeed, will be more rewarded by their exertions if freed from
the compulsion to win.*[32]

As Blanchard finished reading the letter, he invited Charlie to the stage.
A thousand people rose to their feet as one, and, although Charlie's eyesight
was failing badly and he could not see those who honored him, the applause
lingered in his ears long after the evening was over.

The friendships Charlie has enjoyed in his life are threads that never break;
they are strong, yet flexible. And the most successful and enduring of
those friendships were formed in the mountains. Bob Craig, K2-1953 teammate and Aspen colleague, ruminates: "What is the quality of friendship?
There has never been an expedition that exhibited such friendship." Teammate Dee Molenaar agrees, and more than fifty years later, still stays in
touch. "I just called Charlie earlier today [February 13, 2005] because every
now and again I miss those old goats," Molenaar laughs. Although Craig initially found Charlie somewhat intimidating, he eventually found him to be a
warm human being. Perhaps more importantly, looking back at the history
of mountaineering during those decades, he rightly points out that "Charlie
has come through with great respect and is pretty much unscathed . . . even
though he had to make some unpopular decisions." Charlie was undoubtedly a complex person: a dear person who could also be difficult and iras-
cible. But Craig was won over by his compassion, and cited a very personal
example. Craig's own daughter suffered from a number of serious health
conditions and at one point was in a very bad state while attending Middle-
bury College in southern Vermont. When Charlie learned of her condition,
he took her out of school, admitted her into the Burlington hospital, and
then brought her into his own home, where he and Dorcas nursed her back
to health. Craig never forgot that she was treated like one of the family.
The overriding frustration surrounding their friendship is that Craig feels he
can never live up to Charlie's expectations. Charlie is a communicator—a

frequent one—and his style assumes that he and Craig be in frequent touch. That's not Craig's style and he senses disapproval and disappointment from Charlie. "He just doesn't understand how much I really care for him . . . I care deeply about him," Craig admits.

Tom Hornbein, another mountain friend, refers to Charlie as a very dear person, though he was "a curmudgeon in his former life." Hornbein expresses some sadness, however, in that he sees a man who has accomplished so much in his life but whose extreme self-deprecation has deprived him of some of the pleasures of his contributions: "Charlie is a humble man, sometimes too humble." It's true that Charlie was a visionary in many different fields. "He had an uncommon way of turning big dreams into big reality and bringing others along with him," Hornbein says. And it shows no signs of ending: Charlie's boundless curiosity shows no signs of slowing down, even in his nineties. Hornbein sensitively observes that, like many other highly accomplished people, Charlie appears to feel painful regret at not having accomplished enough.

A friendship that has endured since Harvard climbing days is that with Brad Washburn. Charlie's climbing partner from the early 1930s still speaks with him several times a week on the phone. It's often just a minute or two as Washburn, now in his mid-nineties, is checking some date, location, or name. Washburn maintains that Charlie's legacy lies in mountain medicine much more than in mountaineering. A somewhat younger climbing friend, Nick Clinch, thinks it was Charlie's supportive nature that endeared him so deeply to the entire American climbing community—not just a few individuals. He recalls that prior to his Hidden Peak expedition, Charlie offered him unqualified support and encouragement. In return, Clinch felt the same responsibility to climbers who came after him. And so the legacy continued throughout the next generations of climbers. Clinch too has felt Charlie's curmudgeonly nature, but he is convinced that, at heart, Charlie is a kind man whose friendship Clinch values deeply.

Mell Schoening, Pete Schoening's widow, knows well the quality and strength of the bond of friendship that formed within the K2 group. "It's turned into a kind of love, almost into a family situation," she explains, "the kind of friendship more closely associated with wartime experiences." She is convinced that the brotherhood of that group contains important messages that need to be shared: messages about compatibility, shared values, leadership. She remembers a breakfast gathering many years after the expedition: her husband, Pete, and Charlie were standing in a circle of Explorer Scouts. The group of teenagers was agog, listening to their stories and happy to learn—and Pete and Charlie were even happier to share. It's one of her favorite memories of the two of them.

The team's obvious joy in one another was noted by many. Jim Moss recalls with great nostalgia a weekend when he was responsible for shepherding the remaining members of the 1953 K2 team around Telluride. "Every morning I would wake up hearing them in the kitchen laughing . . . I don't know what they were talking about but I kept hearing these great deep laughs coming from all three of them . . . I would lay in bed envious after all those years, still relishing and enjoying each other's company . . . Mountaineering books are full of the fights between climbers. Events are staged to get old climbers back together. To see those life-long friends having such a great time together fifty years later with not one ounce of acrimony was amazing. To hang around those guys was inspirational . . . Charlie . . . his accomplishments are nothing compared to the greatness of his soul."

((((

For much of his later life, when Charlie wasn't traveling the world, presenting his creative work, accepting accolades, and connecting with his beloved mountaineering fraternity, he was at Burlington or Honnedaga with Dorcas. Their children were gone, building their own lives, both professionally and personally. Grandchildren began to appear and the extended family became richer each year. Charlie and Dorcas cherished their time, even teaching some classes together at the university. But just as Dorcas began to relax and enjoy her years with Charlie, tragedy hit.

She broke her hip while at Honnedaga, which presented a logistical challenge in transporting her to proper medical attention. They packed her down to the dock, onto the boat, into the car, and back to Burlington, all without morphine. Fortified only with aspirin, she somehow survived the journey back to Burlington, where her hip was pinned by their doctor, Pat Mahoney. But Dorcas refused to participate in the recommended physiotherapy, and so her recovery was slow. Then a couple of years later she was about to rise from her living room chair when she cried out in pain. She had fractured the other hip. Again, a bout with surgery, and very little physiotherapy. Now she was too weak to travel to Honnedaga, but rather spent her time in the garden, although it was a painful effort. It broke Charlie's heart to see her, sitting down on the ground with their golden retriever, Pooh Bear, beside her, inching along as she weeded in her rose garden. But the garden was her passion, and she wouldn't give it up.

Dorcas's last two years were very difficult. She had been a smoker most of her adult life, and despite Charlie's pressure to quit, hadn't done so until about five years before her death. Or so Charlie thought. He learned later that she used to sneak one or two a day, up until the end. As her breathing became more difficult, it became a trial for her to even ascend the stairs. Then, on a plane journey back to Burlington, she caught a cold and quickly degenerated. Charlie tried in vain to obtain immediate attention from her medical caregivers. Their delayed response made her last days very difficult, although the end result would most certainly have been the same.

Charlie's beloved wife and lifelong partner, Dorcas, died in 1999. It was the low point of his life. His friends observed that Charlie was stunned, and they saw him nearly die of shock. He began sending alarming messages to friends that life was not worth living, then went into an obsessive writing mode, then back to despair. His life became fragmented and he was no longer able to keep up with his business affairs. "I felt sorry for myself; I sat; I moped." Thoughtful friends brought him food and talked to him, but he couldn't regain his equilibrium. He had relied on Dorcas as his sounding board for so long that he felt unhinged. He badly missed her good judgment. Then he spiraled into a deep depression. Nearly suicidal, he felt her presence everywhere in the house: sitting down to the dinner table, wandering in the garden, making a cup of coffee. It didn't matter which room Charlie entered, it was filled with memories of Dorcas: photographs, books, dishes, and clothing. His only comfort came from having outlived her, knowing that she had never experienced these soul-deadening days and nights.

After Dorcas's death, Penny, Robin, and David took care of most of her personal belongings. After some time, Charlie approached her desk. But it turned out he wasn't ready to deal with its contents, so it remained closed for three long years. On his own desk was a photo of her as a young woman in her starched, white uniform, which he gazed at dozens of times a day. Finally he summoned the strength to go through the contents of her desk, and when he read her book of poetry, once again, it was almost too much to bear. That book—a collection of her favorite poems—eventually became the most prized souvenir of her life, and a source of great comfort for Charlie. Not only for Charlie, for she had painstakingly hand-written copies of her book of poetry for each of her children. Her choices of verse beautifully revealed her mind, her sentimentality, and her sensitivity. Finally, Charlie took a long hard look at her death, as well as the possibility of his own, and decided what it was that he wanted to do with the rest of his life. He vowed to be more open with people, to be less critical of himself and others, to use his life experience to mentor those who could gain from his knowledge. It was a great life transition for Charlie.

Mell Schoening recalled that Charlie's grief was palpable. It was a pain that she too would feel within a few short years when her husband and Charlie's climbing partner, Pete Schoening, died in 2004. But she also found Charlie to be a much more approachable person after Dorcas died. She sensed that Charlie was "letting his light shine" more than he had before. That may have been partly due to Dorcas's rather intimidating intensity as the perfect homemaker, but it was undoubtedly the two of them together that made such an impression on Mell. She felt more comfortable speaking with Charlie now, and felt that he was less formal and judgmental. His children too noticed a change. Robin had frequently referred to his father as "curmudgeonly" in earlier days, and noted that there was a certain softening—a welcome one. Tom Hornbein also noticed a softening in Charlie, and he felt it was because Charlie had finally accepted the knowledge that he actually helped people. But though he may have been softening, there was still a certain formality between Charlie and his children. Despite Charlie's obvious love and pride in them, there remained a certain distance—all those years of travel, adventure, research, turmoil, strife, and plain hard work had taken their toll in the closest and dearest of all places—his family. Given Charlie's talents and ambition, it would have proven almost impossible for him to maintain the high level of performance in all his pursuits and to be a hands-on father as well.

Shortly after Dorcas died, Charlie's backyard neighbor, Anne-Marie Littenberg, came over for a visit and was deeply touched when Charlie presented her with freshly made popovers, one of Dorcas's favorite recipes. Littenberg remembered the day: "It was snowing outside, the air was full of snow, the fire was crackling and we ate those popovers together . . . it is one of my most tender memories of Charlie." Then spring came, and Charlie sensed the floral awakening in his amazingly beautiful property, even though he couldn't properly see those young bulbs and buds. Charlie loved to show people his gardens, and had often done so at the famous Houston May Bowl parties. Now, two years after Dorcas's death, Charlie bravely decided to go ahead with the May Bowl. Littenberg offered to help. As they planned the event over their common fence, Littenberg asked him about a book she had been reading. He pointed out that he hadn't read it, and likely wouldn't since his eyesight had degenerated too badly.

"Well, I'll read it to you if you like," she said.

"No, that would be too much."

"My offer is serious, and besides, I think it would be fun," she insisted.

"Okay, let's do it," he rather quickly acquiesced. They became a book club of two. Since then, Littenberg has been reading to Charlie four or five days a week, sometimes choosing the books and sometimes allowing him to do so. Their first was David McCullough's biography of John Adams. They went on to read one of Dorcas's favorites, the entire *Raj Quartet,* then on to *Arrowsmith*, and a number of Civil War novels. Charlie was learning that it was okay to respond positively to kindness, that softness was an admirable trait, and that reaching out had its rewards. It became clear to him that there were new friendships, experiences and pleasures to enjoy. One of the more unusual of these came through another neighbor, Page McConnell, keyboard player for the wildly popular band Phish.

After a thorny first meeting at which Charlie bluntly stated he didn't want some "porno rock star" moving in next door, McConnell somehow passed an ill-defined test and they began meeting each Friday for lunch and conversation. Their discussions were wide-ranging: politics, spirituality, investments, and life. Charlie confided to McConnell that, at one of his lowest points, he had enlisted the help of a therapist. It was apparently not a great success, for the therapist concluded that Charlie was a "cold bastard" and gave up on him. One Friday McConnell described his early days working as a cab driver in Burlington. Charlie was envious, saying "I never got to do that. I never had a job like that . . . how great for you." Somewhat surprised, McConnell sensed it was Charlie feeling the guilt of privilege.

McConnell was rehearsing for one of Phish's large outdoor concerts in Saratoga and thought it might be fun for Charlie—now 91—to attend. Charlie said yes, and was accorded the full VIP treatment. With an audience of more than 50,000, Charlie was driven past hundreds of parked cars, past the VIP parking spots, right up to the stage door. They were ushered inside for a small dinner with the band, and then up onto the stage, where a few seats had been provided. Charlie was too excited to sit. At one point in his performance, McConnell glanced over to see a wash of color panning over the stage—and Charlie standing and waving his arms with a huge grin on his face. Their friendship has deepened, despite their differences. To McConnell's surprise: "He's one of my closest friends. I never expected to have a friend like Charlie. It just happened."

Charlie enjoyed his conversations with McConnell immensely, but wanting to feel useful, he called the King Street Youth Center and offered up his services as a mentor. Charlie was just what they needed, and someone arrived within an hour to set up a mentoring relationship with a few of the troubled teens under the auspices of the center. Every week since then, a small group of teenagers has come by his house to sit and talk. Charlie doesn't have an agenda—he just asks them questions about important human issues and they talk. He was a bit concerned at first that all they would want to talk about was sex, but his worries were unfounded. They sometimes complain that he only asks questions, but he's convinced his questions provoke them to find their own answers. It must be working; after their two-year program, the first group of teenagers was scheduled to move on, making room for new recruits, but they refused, suggesting instead that Charlie could certainly add new people if he wished, but he must maintain his special time for them.

Long after his formal association with learning institutions ended, Charlie continues educating a group of medical students at his home. It began with a student Charlie recruited to assist him with some of his administrative chores. She helped him, and they became friends in the process. In second-year medical school at the time, and sensing his vast knowledge and experience, she suggested bringing her classmates over to chat with Charlie. They could bring bag lunches and discuss medical topics together. He agreed, and eventually the bag lunches progressed to supper. The tradition continues every two or three weeks, and Charlie maintains that he learns as much as they do. "They bring food," Charlie gleefully adds. It is undoubtedly more than food: Rob Roach believes that "Charlie holds students next to children in value."

These dinner parties fill the rambling Burlington house that Charlie calls home. Conversations take over the spacious dining room, fill various corners of the living room, and spill out into the screened porches. Charlie moves from one group to the next, reveling in the exchange of ideas and unashamedly basking in the attention. Asked if it's being around young people that keeps him so young, he jokes, "Oh no, I rub myself down every night—face cream, wrinkle remover, hair dye." He adds that he has never figured out how to mentor, nor does he even know what mentoring is. He just does it, admitting that his very good teachers in medical school may have influenced him.

Sometimes the dinner parties lead to more radical behavior by Charlie. In recent years, particularly when the topic turns to politics, Charlie has found himself goaded and encouraged by his young students to get out and express his views publicly. He happily does so, sometimes on the top of a soapbox down in the city park, lecturing all who will listen. Always a critic of govern-ment, whether regional or federal, he has become more outspoken as he has grown older, writing letters to various newspapers and his elected represen-tatives and pressuring local politicians to initiate environmentally friendly bylaws in Burlington. Charlie is particularly critical of the Bush ideology; in addition to his local speechifying, he has leveraged his considerable network of influential friends to effect change in that flawed administration.

His thesis is consistent. He's convinced that the United States is obsessed with greed—lust for money and power that is destroying the country. He cites medicine as the perfect example, particularly the pharmaceutical com-panies, whom he refers to as "rip-off artists" and "mafia." But he doesn't rest with the pharmaceutical companies; he points out the prevailing fear of litigation that doctors and hospitals must deal with on a daily basis, forcing them to conduct expensive and useless tests in order to protect themselves. And it is with great shame that he points out the 45 to 50 million Americans who live in fear because they have no health insurance. "It's frightening. It's shocking. It's a national disgrace," he avers. As for medicine, he's convinced that the vocation is no longer an art, but a business. Upon reflection, he makes the same observation about climbing.

Charlie's November 16, 2005 letter to the *Burlington Free Press* demon-strated his passion and concerns. He pointed out the fallacy that Americans believe they are the richest country in the world, yet they live with a debt that exceeds 7 trillion dollars. He rued the war in Iraq, stating that it should never have been started, blaming it on the economic connections to "huge corpora-tions favored by the White House." He pointed out the White House's refusal to deal with the "overwhelming evidence of global warming that our chil-dren and grandchildren will suffer the consequences." He was convinced that the United States has alienated much of the Muslim world by the president's words and actions and he begged for more tolerance and compassion—and less arrogance. He ended his letter with, "I believe it is a moral obligation for each of us to speak out, no matter what we believe, and not keep silent." Shortly before his 93rd birthday, Charlie was once again out in the park on his soapbox, lecturing all who would listen on the folly of the Middle East aggres-sion in Lebanon. One could never accuse Charlie of not speaking his mind.

(((

Charlie sits in his favorite chair, gazing contentedly across the expanse of Lake Champlain, tracking the subtle shifts in light. He has more time now:

to reflect, to consider, to savor the memories that flutter around him like the falling autumn leaves outside his window. Some memories are crystal clear, filling him with joy as he reexamines each detail. Others are equally sharp but leave him shameful, mournful, and full of regret. He allows himself no latitude, forcing himself to review, relive, and face the moral consequences of each of those memories. He refuses to ignore his own blemishes but rather skims over his attributes. He is wistful. Tears well up. The next memory causes him to flush with frustration; then his face breaks wide open with that inimitable Houston laugh as some long-gone, hilarious event forces itself to the surface.

There are so many experiences and emotions, some of them ugly and painful: outbursts of temper, personality conflicts, and errors in judgment. He sees patterns in his life—patterns of disappointments brought on by shortcomings in his own personality. He always wanted to go in his own direction—to lead—to "march to a different drummer." Charlie wanted to be that drummer—to lead others in his parade. Sometimes it worked—other times not.

He obsesses over the privileged childhood he enjoyed and berates himself for having done "so little with so much." He deeply regrets the things he ought to have done, wanted to do, and could have. "Failures of omission are the worst," states Charlie. He regrets that his children had to overcome a family of notoriety. Surely it can't have been easy for them, competing for his attention with so many other pressures. He regrets that he didn't give Dorcas more freedom to express herself and that he rarely said how much he appreciated her. Most profoundly, he regrets not having given enough time, attention, thought, and love to the family he treasures above all: "My family—particularly my wife—has been the greatest influence in my life, greater than the mountains, greater than medicine, and without them there would be nothing." He treasures these hours of reflection, difficult though they may be, convinced that the past is his mirror for the future. His personal meditations refine his soul.

As he sits in that favorite chair, he considers the future, and how he would like to be remembered. The phone rings. It's a friend who wishes to read him a letter she thinks will be meaningful for Charlie. The letter was written by a young British Columbia climber, Stephen Canning, a man Charlie never met. The letter was discovered on Canning's computer after he was killed in a climbing accident on Mount Logan in 2004 at the age of twenty-two. Canning's words are simple, yet profound:

> *When I die I want people to say that I inspired them. I don't care so much that they say I was a good man or a kind man or a happy man or a great man. I want them to say that they lived their life a little bit differently because of me. That they saw the world filled with a bit more adventure. That they were a little bit less afraid to do something that they truly wanted . . . If even one person stands up at my funeral and says that I inspired them that will be enough. The world will know I died happily . . . Once you've accepted death your passing should not be tragic; it should be an inevitable real-ity. It's the final chapter which was written before the first. To live without fear of death makes you capable of great things. You worry less about what people think of you. You worry less about money. You worry less about failure. You are able to put yourself more fully into everything you do. This is the inspiration that I want to have given people. To let them live with a bit less fear.*"[33]

With the peace and maturity that now grace Charlie's life, this young man's words resonate for him. Charlie accepts that he no longer needs to worry what people think of him, or about the possibility of failure. He can finally acknowledge that his life has indeed influenced people—in ways that were positive, and in ways that caused them to live their lives more fully and with less fear.

It's winter now. The ground is frozen and covered with a blanket of soft, light snow. The air is sharp and the regal white pines surrounding the house are snapping in the sub-zero temperatures. The sky is a hard, cold blue. Lake Champlain is nearly frozen over. In the distance, vapor rises off the lake, but Charlie can't see it. He can't see any of it. In 2002 Charlie's eyesight began to fail, and gradually the macular degeneration became worse, with peri-ods of sudden deterioration. He is now nearly blind. But he feels the cold through the window. He imagines the colors, the vapor, and he can feel the wan strength of the rising sun. These mornings, gazing out over the lake, feeling its expansive beauty rather than seeing it, Charlie is flooded with memories. And his memory bank is rich: the quiet moments before dinner with Dorcas, the intensity of successfully treating a patient, the initial steps of his firstborn child. There was the thrill of Operation Everest, the camaraderie of HAPS, the excitement of high-altitude research. There was that life-defining moment high on K2 when Art Gilkey crawled out of his tent and fainted, and Charlie alone understood the likely consequences for all of them. There was the epic retreat off the mountain when he fully comprehended the power of the brotherhood of the rope.

Gazing out across the frozen lake, tears well up in Charlie's unseeing eyes. As he confronts the death that he knows can't be far off, he is not afraid. He savors a life that has been full of love and adventure and of challenges met. His tears are not of fear, sadness, anger or regret. They are tears that spring from a deep well of contentment—a life intensely lived.

NOTES

1 Ata-Ullah, Mohammad, *Citizen of Two Worlds*, p. 258.

2 Tilman, H. W., "The Ascent of Nanda Devi." In *The Seven Mountain-Travel Books*, p. 267.

3 The next expedition to attempt Nanda Devi turned out to be a clandestine CIA project in the 1960s led by Barry Bishop. Apparently the CIA had been trying to plant nuclear-powered devices on the mountain when an avalanche had carried one of the devices into the Rishi River. Logically this radioactive device could potentially have been flushed down the Rishi into the holy Ganges. The CIA expedition remained a secret until Morarji Desai's election in 1977, causing huge embarrassment for the Americans, and for Desai. Charlie was surprised to discover that a number of his previous climbing companions were involved.

The next expedition, in 1976, was successful in the traditional sense, but turned tragic when Willi Unsoeld's daughter, Nanda Devi, died. Co-leader Ad Carter left the expedition early, apparently to care for his ailing wife in Delhi. This confused and disappointed Charlie, who insisted that Carter should have left before the expedition got underway, not partway through when his strong leadership was sorely needed.

4 Bates, Robert and Charles Houston, *Five Miles High*, p. 42.

5 In her book, *On Top of the World: My Adventures With My Mountain-Climbing Husband*, Patricia Petzoldt tells a different version of the story. According to her, Mrs. Barker struggled with Petzoldt for control of the loaded shotgun. Dr.

Barker tried to calm his wife down, and Petzoldt wrestled the gun away from her, throwing it out the window and storming out. It was Dr. Barker, Patricia Petzoldt alleges, who knocked down the ashram leader and killed him.

6 According to Betsy Cowles in her "circular letters" back home, she and the senior Houstons were the seventy-fifth, seventy-sixth, and seventy-seventh Americans to visit Kathmandu. Charlie suspects there were many more who had visited the city but who had merely not signed the embassy register. He estimates there could have been as many as 400 Americans in Kathmandu since the doors to Nepal opened in 1950.

7 Robertson, Janet, *Betsy Cowles Partridge: Mountaineer*, p. 107.

8 Tilman, H. W., *The Seven Mountain-Travel Books: Nepal Himalaya*, p. 868.

9 Madge, Tim, *The Last Hero: Bill Tilman: A Biography of the Explorer*, London: Hodder & Stoughton, 1995, p. 124. There may have been more to the story, as Betsy Cowles apparently discussed with Charlie and Dorcas the possibility of marrying Tilman. She ultimately decided that it wouldn't work.

10 Tilman, H. W., *The Seven Mountain-Travel Books: Nepal Himalaya*, p. 886.

11 Houston, Charles S., "Through Nepal to the South Side of Everest. " *Appalachian Mountain Club Newsletter,* p. 505.

12 The report, called the Groth Report, expressed some curious cultural observations: "Confidentially, I believe that one of the primary factors precipitating the dissension which finally arose was the inescapable fact that, although on paper and by law, Wiessner is an American citizen, he is still in many respects largely German in his outlook and actions . . . like every German, he is very forceful in giving commands and totally unaware that the abrupt, blunt manner in which the order may have been given might have wounded the feelings of his associates. . . . "

13 Bates, Bob, *Phillips Exeter Bulletin*, December, 1953.

14 Bates, Bob, *American Alpine Journal*, 1954.

15 Ata-Ullah, Mohammad, *Citizen of Two Worlds*, p. 226.

16 Ata-Ullah, Mohammad, *Citizen of Two Worlds*, p. 235.

17 Schoening, Pete, *K2 1953*, p. 113.

18 Ata-Ullah, Mohammad, *Citizen of Two Worlds*, p. 256.

19 Schoening, Pete, *K2 1953*, p. 148.

20 Schoening, Pete, *K2 1953*, p. 154.

21 McDonald, Bernadette and Amatt, John, *Voices From the Summit*, Tom Hornbein essay, p. 184.

22 Schoening, Pete, *K2 1953*, p. 162.

23 Bates, Bob, *Exeter Bulletin* L, no. 1 (December 1953).

24 Bates, Bob and Charles Houston, *K2: The Savage Mountain*, p. xviii.

25 Bates, Bob and Charles Houston, *K2: The Savage Mountain*, p. 157.

26 Bates, Robert and Charles Houston, *K2: The Savage Mountain*.

27 McNamara was president of Ford Motors at the time.

28 *Aspen Times*, January 8, 1959.

29 Charlie is convinced he would have become head of UNICEF, but believes they wanted a woman at the time.

30 A symptom of AMS (Acute Mountain Sickness).

31 *Summit Magazine*, April 1972.

32 Houston, Charles, *The New York Times*, August 4, 1954.

33 Printed with permission by Helen and Doug Canning.

BIBLIOGRAPHY

Banff Centre Mountain Culture Archives

Charles Houston, "Himalayan Climbing—An Historical Perspective." Lecture at The Banff Mountain Film Festival, 2000.

Charles Houston, Archival Recordings from The Banff Mountain Film Festival, 2000–2004.

Charles Houston and John Roskelley, 2004 Rice Studio Interview with Dr. Charles Houston and John Roskelley at The Banff Mountain Film Festival, 2004.

Charles Houston, "K2: A Look Back with Dr. Charles Houston." Lecture at The Banff Mountain Film Festival, 2004.

Private Papers of Dr. Charles Houston

"Fifty Years of Going Higher." Delivered as a lecture at The Banff Mountain Film Festival, 2002.

Drummer, Private journal.

India letters.

Peace Corps letters.

Private journals.

Urine and Jasmine. Transcript of a lecture delivered to a private group.

Other Private Papers

Stephen Canning papers.

Jim Wickwire correspondence and journals.

Video and Audio Recordings

"Salute to Charles Houston." Recordings from the University of Colorado May 27, 2006.

Newspaper and Magazine Articles

Author unknown. Article on Mount Foraker. *The New York Times,* exact date unknown, 1934.

Charles Houston, Letter to the Editor, the *New York Times,* August 4, 1954.

Kevin Fedarko, "The Mountain of Mountains." *Outside,* November, 2003.

General

Ata-Ullah, Mohammad, *Citizen of Two Worlds.* New York: Harper, 1960.

Bates, Robert and Charles Houston, *Five Miles High.* New York: The Lyons Press, 1939.

Bates, Robert and Charles Houston, *K2: The Savage Mountain.* 1953; rpt. Purdys, NY: The Adventure Library, 1994.

Craig, Robert W., *Storm & Sorrow in the High Pamirs.* London: Victor Gollancz Ltd., 1981.

Houston, Charles, *Going Higher.* Seattle: The Mountaineers Books, 1998.

Kaufman, Andrew J. and William L. Putnam, *K2: The 1939 Tragedy—The Full Story of the Ill-fated Wiessner Expedition.* London: Diadem Books, 1992.

Madge, Tim, *The Last Hero: Bill Tilman: A Biography of the Explorer.* London: Hodder & Stoughton, 1995.

McDonald, Bernadette and John Amatt, *Voices from the Summit.* Washington, DC: Adventure Press, National Geographic, 2000.

Montovani, Roberto and Kurt Diemberger, *K2. Una sfida ai confini del cielo.* Vercelli, Italy: Edizioni White Star, 1995.

Neale, Jonathan, *Tigers of the Snow.* New York: Thomas Dunne Books, 2002.

Petzoldt, Patricia, *On Top of the World: My Adventures with my Mountain-Climbing Husband.* London: Collins, 1954.

Reeves, John T. and Robert F. Grover, *Attitudes on Altitude: Pioneers of Medical Research in Colorado's High Mountains.* Boulder: The University Press of Colorado, 2001.

Ringholz, Raye C., *On Belay! The Life of Legendary Mountaineer Paul Petzoldt.* Seattle: The Mountaineers Books, 1997.

Roberts, David, *Escape From Lucania.* New York: Simon & Schuster, 2002.

Roberts, David, *Moments of Doubt.* Seattle: The Mountaineers Books, 1986.

Robertson, Janet, *Betsy Cowles Partridge: Mountaineer.* Boulder: The University Press of Colorado, 1998.

Schoening, Pete, *K2 1953.* Estate of Peter K. Schoening, 2004.

Tilman, Bill, *The Seven Mountain-Travel Books, Nanda Devi* and *Everest.* London: Diadem Books; Seattle: The Mountaineers Books, 1983.

Washburn, Bradford and Lew Freedman, *Bradford Washburn, An Extraordinary Life.* Portland, OR: West Winds Press, 2005.

INDEX

ABOUT THE AUTHOR

Bernadette McDonald is the found-
er and former vice president of the
Mountain Culture Division at The
Banff Centre. She was director of
The Banff Mountain Film Festival
for twenty years, and was founding
director of The Banff Mountain Book
Festival. She is a founding member of the International Alliance for
Mountain Film and was an invited
speaker at the General Assembly of
the United Nations in 2001 to launch
the International Year of Mountains.
In 2006 she was awarded the King

Albert award for her contributions to the global mountain community.

She is the co-editor of *Voices From the Summit: The World's Great Mountaineers on the Future of Climbing*, editor of *Extreme Landscape*, and co-editor of *Whose Water Is It*. She is author of *Ritratti dalle vette, alpinisti fotografati da Craig Rich-ards*, published in Italian in 2003, and of *I'll Call You in Kathmandu: the Eliza-beth Hawley Story*, published by The Mountaineers Books in 2005.

Bernadette is an avid climber, hiker, and skier and travels the world in search of warm rock and deep snow.

THE MOUNTAINEERS, founded in 1906, is a nonprofit outdoor activity and conservation club, whose mission is "to explore, study, preserve, and enjoy the natural beauty of the outdoors. . . . " Based in Seattle, Washington, the club is now the third-largest such organization in the United States, with seven branches throughout Washington State.

The Mountaineers sponsors both classes and year-round outdoor activities in the Pacific Northwest, which include hiking, mountain climbing, ski-touring, snowshoeing, bicycling, camping, kayaking, nature study, sailing, and adventure travel. The club's conservation division supports environmental causes through educational activities, sponsoring legislation, and presenting informational programs.

All club activities are led by skilled, experienced instructors, who are dedicated to promoting safe and responsible enjoyment and preservation of the outdoors.

If you would like to participate in these organized outdoor activities or the club's programs, consider a membership in The Mountaineers. For information and an application, write or call The Mountaineers, Club Headquarters, 300 Third Avenue West, Seattle, WA 98119; 206-284-6310. You can also visit the club's website at www.mountaineers.org or contact The Mountaineers via email at clubmail@mountaineers.org.

The Mountaineers Books, an active, nonprofit publishing program of the club, produces guidebooks, instructional texts, historical works, natural history guides, and works on environmental conservation. All books produced by The Mountaineers Books fulfill the club's mission.

Send or call for our catalog of more than 500 outdoor titles:

The Mountaineers Books
1001 SW Klickitat Way, Suite 201
Seattle, WA 98134
800-553-4453
mbooks@mountaineersbooks.org
www.mountaineersbooks.org

The Mountaineers Books is proud to be a corporate sponsor of Leave No Trace, whose mission is to promote and inspire responsible outdoor recreation through education, research, and partnerships. The Leave No Trace program is focused specifically on human-powered (non-motorized) recreation.

Leave No Trace strives to educate visitors about the nature of their recreational impacts, as well as offer techniques to prevent and minimize such impacts. Leave No Trace is best understood as an educational and ethical program, not as a set of rules and regulations.

For more information, visit www.lnt.org, or call 800-332-4100.

OTHER TITLES YOU MIGHT ENJOY BY
THE MOUNTAINEERS BOOKS

I'll Call You in Kathmandu: The Elizabeth Hawley Story
Bernadette McDonald
An American ex-pat in Kathmandu, the enigmatic Ms. Hawley finds her calling as the official record keeper of Himalayan expeditions.

K2: The Price of Conquest
Lino Lacedelli and Giovanni Cenacchi
Cheated out of the historic first summiting of K2, or just sour grapes? Lacedelli comes clean about what happened to Walter Bonatti more than 50 years ago.

The Villain: A Portrait of Don Whillans
Jim Perrin
Brawling, hard-drinking hellman—Whillan's reputation was as large as the big walls he conquered.

Minus 148°: First Winter Ascent of Mt. McKinley
Art Davidson
Classic tale of dramatic near-death experiences in the harshest of conditions.

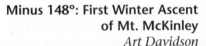

Everest: The West Ridge
Thomas Hornbein
The classic, gripping mountaineering saga of the first ascent of Everest's West Ridge.

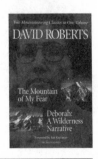

David Roberts: The Mountain of My Fear; Deborah: A Wilderness Narrative
David Roberts
Two of Roberts' most sought-after works collected in one volume.

Mountaineers Books has more than 500 outdoor recreation titles in print.
Receive a free catalog at
www.mountaineersbooks.org

WITH APPRECIATION

Brotherhood of the Rope: The Biography of Charles Houston, the first title in The Mountaineers Books Legend and Lore Series was made possible through the generosity of:

- The Mountaineers Foundation
- Nick Clinch
- Jim and Mary Lou Wickwire
- Tom Hornbein
- Robert Craig
- Robert Maynard

LEGEND AND LORE SERIES

The Mountaineers Books Legend and Lore Series celebrates the lives and preserves the legacies of remarkable individuals whose determination and accomplishments in the mountains reflect an extraordinary spirit of adventure and joy of life.

THE CHARLES S. HOUSTON ENDOWED CHAIR AT THE UNIVERSITY OF COLORADO ALTITUDE RESEARCH CENTER

Scientist, physician, mountaineer, teacher, author and filmmaker, Charlie Houston has devoted much of his life to gathering and disseminating his wisdom about high places and their impact on humans. Charlie's passion is also the mission of the Altitude Research Center at the University of Colorado--to bring together scientists from diverse backgrounds to address how low oxygen states affect the health and well-being of people living, working, and traveling to high altitude as well as those subjected to low oxygen states because of pulmonary or other diseases. A critical piece of this effort is to endow the Charles S. Houston Chair in Altitude Medicine and Physiology at the University of Colorado. For more information about how you can help to achieve this goal, please visit the website *http://www.uchsc.edu /arc/*, or call (303) 724-1670.